Communications and Culture

Communications has been defined as the conveying or exchanging of information and ideas. This wide definition is taken as the starting-point for this series of books, which are not bound by conventional academic divisions. The series aims to document or analyse a broad range of cultural forms and ideas.

It encompasses works from areas as esoteric as linguistics and as exoteric as television. The language of communication may be the written work or the moving picture, the static icon or the living gesture. These means of communicating can at their best blossom into and form an essential part of the other mysterious concept, *culture*.

There is no sharp or intended split in the series between communication and culture. On one definition, culture refers to the organisation of experience shared by members of a community, a process which includes the standards and values for judging or perceiving, for predicting and acting. In this sense, creative communication can make for a better and livelier culture.

The series reaches towards the widest possible audience. Some of the works concern themselves with activities as general as play and games; others offer a narrower focus, such as the ways of understanding the visual image. It is hoped that some moves in the transformation of the artful and the scientific can be achieved, and that both can begin to be understood by a wider and more comprehending community. Some of these books are written by practitioners – broadcasters, journalists and artists; others come from critics, scholars, scientists and historians.

The series has an ancient and laudable though perhaps untenable, aim – an aim new as holography: it aspires to cultures, between the practitioner science and art, between the aca

D1420447

PAUL WALTON

COMMUNICATIONS AND CULTURE

Executive Editors STUART HALL, PAUL WALTON

Published

Tony Bennett and Janet Woollacott   BOND AND BEYOND: THE POLITICAL CAREER OF A POPULAR HERO
Victor Burgin (ed.)   THINKING PHOTOGRAPHY
Victor Burgin   THE END OF ART THEORY: CRITICISM AND POSTMODERNITY
Ian Chambers   URBAN RHYTHMS: POP MUSIC AND POPULAR CULTURE
Erving Goffman   GENDER ADVERTISEMENTS
Stephen Heath   QUESTIONS OF CINEMA
Herbert Marcuse   THE AESTHETIC DIMENSION: TOWARDS A CRITIQUE OF MARXIST AESTHETICS
Anthony Smith   THE POLITICS OF INFORMATION: PROBLEMS OF POLICY IN MODERN MEDIA
John Tulloch and Manuel Alvarado   'DOCTOR WHO': THE UNFOLDING TEXT
Janet Wolff   THE SOCIAL PRODUCTION OF ART

Forthcoming

Jerry Booth and Peter Lewis   RADIO: MEANINGS AND AUDIENCES
Philip Corrigan   CULTURE AND CONTROL
Andrew Davies   OTHER THEATRES: THE DEVELOPMENT OF ALTERNATIVE AND EXPERIMENTAL THEATRE IN BRITAIN
Stuart Hall   REPRODUCING IDEOLOGIES
Dick Hebdige   THE MEANING OF SUBCULTURES
Clarie Johnston   FEMINISM AND CINEMA
John Tagg   THE BURDEN OF REPRODUCTION

Bond and Beyond

The Political Career of a Popular Hero

Tony Bennett
and
Janet Woollacott

M
MACMILLAN
EDUCATION

First published 1987

Published by
MACMILLAN EDUCATION LTD
Houndmills, Basingstoke, Hampshire RG21 2XS
and London
Companies and representatives
throughout the world

Typeset by Wessex Typesetters
(Division of The Eastern Press Ltd)
Frome, Somerset

Printed in Hong Kong

British Library Cataloguing in Publication Data
Bennett, Tony
Bond and beyond: the political career of a
popular hero.—(Communications and culture)
1. Fleming, Ian, *1908–1964*—Characters—
James Bond   2. Bond, James (Fictitious character)
3. Popular culture
I. Title   II. Woollacott, Janet   III. Series
306'.1   PR6056.L4Z/
ISBN 0–333–28620–0 (hardcover)
ISBN 0–333–28621–9 (paperback)

Series Standing Order

If you would like to receive future titles in this series as they are published,
you can make use of our standing order facility. To place a standing order
please contact your bookseller or, in case of difficulty, write to us at the
address below with your name and address and the name of the series.
Please state with which title you wish to begin your standing order. (If you
live outside the United Kingdom we may not have the rights for your area,
in which case we will forward your order to the publisher concerned.)

Customer Services Department, Macmillan Distribution Ltd,
Houndmills, Basingstoke, Hampshire, RG21 2XS, England.

One of the most characteristic attitudes of the popular public towards its literature is this: the writer's name and personality do not matter, but the personality of the protagonist does. When they have entered into the intellectual life of the people, the heroes of popular literature are separated from their 'literary' origin and acquire the validity of historical figures.

ANTONIO GRAMSCI

Contents

Acknowledgements

This book owes a good deal to colleagues at the Open University, particularly those associated with the *Mass Communication and Society* and *Popular Culture* course teams who helped to shape the early stages of this work in many and varied ways. We are particularly grateful to our BBC colleagues, Michael Philps, Victor Lockwood and Noella Smith with whom our first work on the Bond movies began. We are also grateful to the staff and students of those institutions at which draft chapters of this study were presented. Their comments proved invaluable in helping us to see our way more clearly through the problems we were addressing. In particular, we would like to thank Terry Hawkes and Catherine Belsey at University College, Cardiff, Tom Lewis of Iowa University, John Frow at Murdoch University and Noel King at the South Australian College of Advanced Education. Our special thanks, too, to Stuart Hall for his detailed and helpful comments on the manuscript.

We could not have written the book without the help and support of our respective partners, Sue and Tim, whom we thank for their understanding and tolerance – especially over the cost of the telephone calls between Brisbane and New York to co-ordinate the writing of it. We wish we could find it in us to thank the American and Australian postal services for not losing more than 10 per cent of our correspondence, but it would stick in the throat somehow.

However, we are grateful to the School of Humanities at Griffith University for financial assistance in preparing the book, and to Pan Books and Granada Publishing for their permission to reproduce the covers for *Moonraker*, *Diamonds*

are Forever and *Colonel Sun*. Pan Books also assisted us greatly
in supplying detailed figures for the sales of the Bond novels
in Britain. We also owe a very particular debt to Ian
Campbell, whose *Ian Fleming: A Catalogue of a Collection* proved
an invaluable research tool. More than that, had he not very
generously allowed us to consult the rich hoard of Bondiana
he has accumulated over the years, many parts of this book
would not have been possible.

The authors and publishers wish to thank the following who
have kindly given permission for the use of copyright material:
W. H. Allen & Co. for extract from *Sean Connery: His Life and
Films* by Michael Feenay Callan; Jonathan Cape Ltd for
extracts from *The James Bond Dossier* by Kingsley Amis;
Constable Publishers for extract from *Clubland Heroes* by
Richard Usborne; Glidrose Productions Ltd, copyright
holders, for extracts from Ian Fleming's James Bond novels
with permission from Jonathan Cape Ltd for extracts from
*From Russia With Love, Moonraker, Dr No, Thunderball, You Only
Live Twice, On Her Majesty's Secret Service, The Man with the Golden
Gun, Casino Royale, Live and Let Die* and *Goldfinger*; Macmillan
Publishing Company for extracts from *Moonraker, Live and Let
Die, Goldfinger, Dr No* and *From Russia With Love*; New American
Library for extracts from *The Man with the Golden Gun, You Only
Live Twice* and *On Her Majesty's Secret Service*; Viking Penguin
Inc. for extracts from *Thunderball*; and Gildrose Publications
Ltd for extracts from *Casino Royale*; Stephen Heath for extract
from *The Sexual Fix*, Macmillan Press; Indiana University Press
for extracts from *The Role of the Reader* by Umberto Eco; IPC
Magazines Ltd for an extract from 'Glamour Girls in Bondage',
Woman's Own, 30 June 1979; Murray Pollinger and Watkins/
Loomis Agency on behalf of Roald Dahl for '007's Oriental
Eyefuls', *Playboy*, June 1967. Every effort has been made to
trace all the copyright-holders, but if any have been
inadvertently overlooked the publishers will be pleased to make
the necessary arrangement at the first opportunity.

Our thanks, finally, to Eon Productions for confirming our
analysis of the nature of the copyright it holds in the Bond
image. Our request for permission to use some stills from the
Bond films and some publicity posters as illustrations was
refused; their 'corporate attitude' to our project, we were

told, was 'entirely negative'. A starker demonstration of the contradiction between the public nature of the image and its private ownership could hardly be asked for.

TONY BENNETT
JANET WOOLLACOTT

Introduction

The subject of this book is James Bond. However, we are not simply concerned with the Bond novels and the Bond films, although we examine both in some detail. Rather, our interest lies in the figure of Bond, in the diverse and changing forms in which it has been produced and circulated, and in the varying cultural business that has been conducted around, by means of and through this figure during the now considerable slice of post-war history in which it has been culturally active. Our analysis accordingly attempts to go beyond the Bond novels and films to take account of the broader range of texts and coded objects through which the figure of Bond has been put into circulation as a popular hero. In these respects, we shall argue, the figure of Bond constitutes a particular type of cultural phenomenon. Our purpose, in examining the organisation of this phenomenon and the means by which it has been produced, is to convey something of the scope and reach of Bond's popularity as well as to specify and account for the peculiar nature of his appeal as a popular hero.

Thus, whilst this is a book about Bond, it's also about more than that. In order to develop adequate means of approaching 'the Bond phenomenon', and understand its constitution and effects, we have thought it important to 'go beyond Bond' and engage with a number of problems and debates in contemporary cultural theory and analysis. Indeed, it was partly a series of unresolved questions about Bond that prompted us to write the book. Our interest in Bond dates from the mid 1970s since when, in one way or another, we have been engaged in work on various aspects of 'the

Bond phenomenon'. In the context of the Open University
course *Mass Communication and Society*, we were involved,
together with colleagues from the BBC, in producing a series
of television programmes which examined the production
processes and professional ideologies involved in making the
film version of *The Spy Who Loved Me*. Subsequently, through
our association with the Open University course *Popular
Culture*, we extended our interest in Bond, but in a different
direction, by examining Ian Fleming's Bond novels. In the
course of this work, it became clear to us that, apart from
its intrinsic interest and social significance, 'the Bond
phenomenon' was a cultural phenomenon of a rather peculiar
kind. It raised a series of awkward problems which led us to
question some of the customary assumptions and procedures
of cultural analysis and, to a certain extent, to depart from
them.

Our general purpose in writing this book, therefore, was to
identify these problems more clearly, to propose ways of
dealing with them and to explore the implications of such
approaches for adjacent areas of cultural theory and analysis.
We have sought to engage with these issues in a concrete
way – posing and seeking to resolve them in the course of
analysing various aspects of 'the Bond phenomenon' – rather
than employing an abstract critical approach in which
existing theoretical traditions (Marxism, psychoanalysis,
semiotics) are weighed in the balance and found wanting.
Since the theoretical questions we are concerned with are
signposted clearly enough at the appropriate points in the
analysis, there is no need to weigh the reader down with a
lengthy resumé of all those questions here. However, there
are two particular concerns which might usefully be
commented on as they inform the ways in which we approach
other questions and, in many respects, govern the organisation
of the book.

The first concerns the relations between popular fiction
and ideology. The view which once predominated in Marxist
writings on the subject – that works of popular fiction could
be regarded as the mere containers of ideology, conveyer
belts for the reproduction and transmission of dominant
ideology from the 'culture industry' to 'the masses' – is

increasingly recognised as unacceptable. We would suggest that popular fictional forms subject ideological discourses to a work of transformation just as much, although not necessarily in the same way, as do fictional forms which are socially valorised in being classified as 'high culture'. Popular fictional forms are 'relatively autonomous' in relation to ideology in the sense that they subject the ideological discourses which they take as their 'pre-texts' to distinctive forms of reorganisation, 'working' them through the use of formal and narrative devices derived from the repertoire of conventions which constitutes a specific fictional tradition. Such devices involve both a level of determination, and a horizon of possibilities, which is specific to fictional practices. They are not given by nor do they have exact parallels within ideology, conceived as a general category, but are the product of relatively autonomous histories of writing, film-making and so on.

This is not to propose an essentialist distinction between popular fiction and ideology. Formal and narrative devices may migrate across the boundaries between different signifying practices, just as such practices may themselves be reclassified with the result that their social locations and spheres of cultural action are correspondingly modified. In view of this, we would suggest that popular fiction should be regarded as a specific *region* of ideology, and one resting on specifiable institutional supports, which operates in a social space different from that occupied by, say, religious or political ideology. The specificity of popular fiction is better regarded as a particular space – and one that may be variably filled with different kinds of practice at different points in time – than as an assembly of practices which resemble each other in certain necessary and unchanging ways. Provided that the historicality of this space is recognised, and that it is not collapsed back into ideology as a general and undifferentiated category, this is a preferable formulation to those which secure the relative autonomy of popular fiction by proposing that fiction and ideology be regarded as essentially distinct categories.

These are not mere theoretical niceties. The ways in which the relations between popular fiction and ideology are viewed

have significant implications for the forms of political and
critical intervention that may be developed in relation to
both the making and consuming of popular fictions. The
equation of popular fiction with ideology tends to lead to a
politics of simple opposition and to a criticism which is little
more than a constant unmasking of dominant ideologies at
work. In this perspective, works of popular fiction are seen to
be either harmful or valueless, undeserving of shelf-space, a
place on the video rack or serious consideration. Such
approaches fail to take account of the fact that, in order to
become significantly popular, fictional forms must in some
way relate to and connect with popular experience and,
rather than simply imposing dominant ideologies, must
therefore make concessions to the opposing or different values
and ideologies of subordinate social groups. This is far from
suggesting that popular fictional forms give such values and
ideologies a direct or undiluted expression. Nevertheless, we
would argue that the space of popular fiction possesses
an ideological economy which is more complex, more
contradictory and ambivalent, than some orthodox Marxist
approaches imply.

   In approaching the Bond novels and films, we have
accordingly resisted the temptation merely to label them as
sexist, racist and reactionary. Whilst they are all of these
things, and more, they are also more complexly ambiguous
than such unqualified judgements suggest. On the whole, the
history of critical reaction to the Bond forms has been a
history of condemnation: both the novels and the films have
been designated unsavoury and harmful or have been
disparaged as 'mere escapism'. It was thus that the *Daily
Worker* dismissed the film of *Goldfinger* as 'one vast, gigantic
confidence trick to blind the masses to what is going on
underneath'.[1] Unless one subscribes to the view that the
reading, cinema-going and television publics simply enjoy
sexist, racist and reactionary texts, such approaches fail to
explain why the Bond forms have proved so popular,
appealing to readers and viewers of both sexes from across
the entire range of social classes, and at different periods of
times. We know that *From Russia, With Love* was among
President Kennedy's favourite bedtime reading, for example,

and it was widely publicised that Arthur Scargill took time off from the 1983 TUC Conference to see *Octopussy*. Rather than simply condemning the Bond forms, therefore, we have sought to clarify and account for the specific pleasures which the Bond novels and films have offered by examining the ways in which the formal and narrative devices they deploy play with and put into suspense the subject positions produced by the ideological discourses – primarily ones of sex and gender, nation and nationhood and, depending on the period, those of Cold War or détente – on which these texts work.

Of course, it can be argued that this fictional playing with ideologies in the Bond novels and films reinscribes the reader or viewer in the subject positions produced by these ideologies more securely and more deeply than could be accounted for by any approach which construed them as merely passing those ideologies on. But it is also true that the mechanisms through which these ideologies are narrated into and out of fictitious crisis establish, at least temporarily, a disparity between the habituated subject positions produced by the ideologies concerned and the positions occupied by the reader/viewer during the course of the narration. The mechanisms of narrative suspense, in temporarily unclasping the normally closed structure of ideologies, open up a certain cultural space within which contradictory subject positions and identities may be taken up, however provisionally. Indeed, in our view, the reason for the peculiar and sustained popularity of the Bond forms consist in the degree to which they have been able, in opening up this space, to exploit it – not by simply putting the reader or viewer back into the ideological subject positions from which, implicitly, the narratives start, but by moving her/him on to a new set of ideological co-ordinates. The ideological work effected by both the films and the novels, we suggest, is not that of imposing a range of dominant ideologies but that of articulating the relations between a series of ideologies (subordinate as well as dominant), overlapping them on to one another so as to bring about certain movements and reformations of subjectivity – movements whose direction has varied with different moments in Bond's career as a popular hero in response to broader cultural and ideological pressures.

Our second set of interests centres on the problem of developing forms of analysis that are appropriate for the study of a cultural phenomenon – the functioning of the figure of James Bond as a popular hero – that is constituted within a constantly mobile set of inter-textual relations. Many developments in recent years have called into question the value, and even the validity, of those forms of cultural analysis which focus exclusively on the formal properties of texts at the expense of the varying social and ideological relations of reading through which the consumption of those texts is organised. A good deal of recent work has thus concentrated on the study of the audience, theorising both the social and discursive factors which mediate the relations between texts and audiences. Contemporary work on the star system has also provided telling evidence of the part which inter-textual relations play in organising the expectations of readers/viewers. We have sought to support and develop work of this kind in identifying and working through the theoretical problems involved in analysing the relations between a set of texts – the 'texts of Bond' – that are grouped together under the name of the hero figure which they jointly construct and circulate. Rather than using the term loosely, we have sought to theorise the concept of 'popular hero'. Since the conditions of existence of popular heroes are inter-textual – they exist as signifiers produced in the circulations and exchanges between those texts which together contribute to the expanded reproduction of the figure of the hero – we would suggest that it is impossible to analyse any particular text caught up in these processes without, at the same time, considering its relations to other texts of a similar nature. More importantly, this also necessitates taking account of the shifting cultural and ideological currency of the figure of the popular hero which floats between and connects such texts into related sets. In this respect, we argue, the case of Bond throws into high relief the radical insufficiency of those forms of cultural analysis which, in purporting to study texts 'in themselves', do radical violence to the real nature of the social existence and functioning of texts in pretending that 'the text itself' can be granted an existence, as a hypostatised entity, separated out from the always variable systems of inter-textual relations which supply the real conditions of its signifying functioning. In this way, our aim is to demonstrate, in a practical way rather than just theoretically, that 'the text itself' is an inconceivable object.

While these are not the only issues which concern us, they are the ones to which we repeatedly return throughout the analysis and which influence the ways we broach the more particular topics under discussion in each chapter. Indeed, the plan of the book can be briefly stated in terms of the order in which these concerns are developed and interwoven with more localised issues and debates.

Our study falls into four main parts. In the first two chapters, our concern is to specify the nature of 'the Bond phenomenon' and to identify the distinctive problems involved in its analysis. Chapter 1 reviews the various indices of Bond's popularity and argues the respects in which Bond should be regarded as a popular hero rather than merely the principal character within a set of related fictions. Chapter 2 then examines the various moments of Bond's career as a popular hero from the late 1950s to the present, outlines the main similarities and differences within and between the novels and the films, and, in a general way, shows how the cultural and ideological currency of the figure of Bond has been changed and adapted to changing circumstances. Our argument here is that the figure of Bond, in serving to condense and articulate a wide range of contemporary cultural and ideological preoccupations, has done so in different mixes and permutations at different points in time.

In Chapters 3 and 4, our attention focuses more specifically on the Bond novels, but in different ways. Chapter 3 examines the conditions of existence of Bond as a popular hero in closer detail by reviewing the organisation of the system of inter-textual relations whereby texts which, in other respects, are exceedingly heterogeneous are grouped together for consumption as 'texts of Bond' by virtue of the figure of Bond which they share and jointly construct. It further argues that conventional procedures of textual analysis – according to which a text is conceived as the source of a specifiable range of meanings or effects – make it difficult to deal with a cultural phenomenon of this type. In their place, it suggests methods of analysis appropriate to the view of texts as sites around which a constantly varying and always many faceted range of cultural and ideological transactions are conducted. In the light of these perspectives, Chapter 4 proceeds to discuss the Bond novels in greater detail, reading them in the light of the ways in which their consumption has been socially organised via their relations to the other 'texts of Bond' and via the broader functioning of Bond as a popular hero.

The following three chapters are concerned primarily with the Bond films but also with the shifting inter-textual sets established by the films in terms of their production and readership. Chapter 5 focuses on the changes and differences between the novel and the film of *Goldfinger*. Taking *Goldfinger* as a key Bond film, which saw the establishment of the Bond films as a distinctive sub-genre, the chapter examines the differences between the two texts of *Goldfinger* in terms of formal narrative devices, shifts in plot and character and the sets of inter-textual relations through which the two texts were read. In terms of the process of adaptation of novel into film, the chapter argues that it is mistaken to conceive the respects in which the film differs from the novel as either a lack of fidelity or failure – or, indeed, improvement. Rather, it is important to recognise that the novel is only one of the source materials for the film, that the film works over an ideological terrain beyond the novel and that there are, in any case, distinct differences between the formal techniques of writing and film-making and the associated processes whereby ideologies are worked into fictions.

Chapter 6 takes up some of the same themes in relation to the conditions of production of a later Bond film, *The Spy Who Loved Me*. This chapter examines the distinctive production processes of a Bond film, the occupational ideologies of a Bond production team and the ideological projects with which the members of this team were involved. Theoretically, it also takes issue with the use of orthodox Marxist ideas of determination in studying the production processes of films and suggests that the notion of 'conditions of production' provides a more workable framework for examining the relationship between film texts and film-makers. In this chapter, we argue that the analysis of the process and conditions of production of texts is a necessary and often undervalued part of our understanding of specific transformations of ideologies into fictions. In Chapter 7, we examine the textual strategies of the Bond films, and particularly the ways in which they offer different routes of identification and different moments of pleasure for viewers in their representations of Bond, the villains, 'the Bond girls' and the relations between them. In doing so, we also touch on the vexed question of the ideological implications of the pleasures of 'the male look' in the Bond films.

In the two concluding chapters, we return to the wider aspects of 'the Bond phenomenon', broadening and extending our opening remarks on this subject in the light of the more detailed arguments of the intervening chapters. Chapter 8 thus examines the representations of Bond and 'the Bond girl' in a wide array of texts – fanzines, men's and women's magazines, film publicity posters – which, in working alongside the novels and the films, have also actively cued their consumption in specific ways. We also examine the various attempts that have been made to represent the Bond films and novels, especially the latter, as works of serious literary, cultural, moral or aesthetic value. In doing so, we argue the respects in which this admittedly somewhat marginal aspect of 'the Bond phenomenon' (but a part of it none the less) calls into question both essentialist views of 'the text' and essentialist constructions of the relations between high and popular culture. Chapter 9 draws various strands of the argument together in reviewing the complex and ambivalent role which Bond has played in British culture since the 1950s. The final chapter also offers a reprise on the more general theoretical concerns developed in the course of the book.

Finally, a word or two about the different levels at which the book might be read and used. First, at the level of Bond: while there has been no shortage of commentaries on either the Bond novels or the Bond films, there are no studies which address 'the Bond phenomenon' as a whole – at least, not as it has been developed since the early 1960s – and we hope that, in this respect, the book will perform a useful service and be found interesting and informative in terms of what it has to say about Bond. At the theoretical level, the more general value of our study, if it has any, consists in the degree to which the approaches it suggests may prove to be useful in other, related areas of inquiry. We have treated 'the Bond phenomenon' as a 'limit case' in the sense of calling into question some of the stock-in-trade methods of cultural analysis. But it is not an isolated case. The work of John Tulloch and Manuel Alvarado, for example, suggests many similarities, if also important differences, between the figures of James Bond and Doctor Who.[2] Nor are the lessons to be drawn from it entirely negative; indeed, the experience has been productive in the sense of generating new problems. It is not for us to say whether these problems have been resolved satisfactorily; we shall be well pleased, however, if they have been stated clearly enough to interest others in contributing to their further exploration.

Chapter 1

The Bond Phenomenon

It is now more than thirty years since James Bond made his initial appearance in Ian Fleming's *Casino Royale*, first published in 1953. Yet his popularity seems undiminished. Indeed, the currency of Bond received a remarkable fillip in 1983 when the much-heralded 'battle of the Bonds' at last arrived with the release of *Octopussy*, in which Roger Moore played Bond for the sixth time, and *Never Say Never Again*, in which Sean Connery returned to the role for the first time since *Diamonds are Forever* (1971). The critics responded to Connery's return with rapturous yelps of delight. 'Sean Connery is back and greater than ever,' Rex Read enthused in *The New York Post*, whilst Joel Siegal, of ABC's *Good Morning America*, reported: 'Bond is wonderful. For Bond fans I was up there cheering.' The same year also saw a revival in Bond's literary fortunes with the publication of John Gardner's *License Renewed*, three months on the *New York Times* best seller list. 'Literature's most celebrated spy,' according to *Time*, 'still retains his license to kill.'

Bond is somewhat more than 'literature's most popular spy', however. He is arguably the most popular – in the sense of widely known – figure of the post-war period, if not of this century. Certainly, it is difficult to think of a similar contemporary character who has been so consistently popular in quite the same way or to quite the same degree over an equivalent period. Nor have the publishing apparatuses with a vested interest in Bond's success been slow to stress his exceptional qualities. Pan Books, who published the paperback editions of the Bond novels in Britain from 1955 to 1977, claimed that, in Bond, Fleming had created 'a fictional

11

character unrivalled in modern publishing history', or, in another formulation, 'the most famous secret agent ever'. Similarly, the *Daily Express*, when launching its strip-cartoon of Bond in 1957, introduced him as 'the sardonic secret agent who stormed into popularity as THE post-war fiction hero'.[1] Glidrose Productions, the company Fleming established in 1964 to handle his Bond interests made perhaps the most extravagant claims of all in the billing it gave Bond in a contemporary fanzine:

007 JAMES BOND
HM SECRET SERVICE AGENT
and undoubtedly the most famous of them all.

Born for dangerous adventures, bred to take hardship, pain and fearful threats with cold courage, trained till his six senses respond instantly to the menace of a situation, educated to be a gentleman – but one who can mix it with the best and the worst of them – he is the true hero of our day and age.[2]

Nor can such claims be written off as the customary hyperbole of publicity writers. If anything, the objective indices of the scope and degree of Bond's popularity are even more impressive. United Artists estimated that, by 1977, the Bond film had been shown to a worldwide cinema audience of 1000 million, since when – counting *Octopussy* and *Never Say Never Again* – there have been five more Bond films.[3] To this there must be added the substantial television audience both in Britain, where ITV secured the rights to the Bond films in 1975, and in America where ABC paid the dollar equivalent of £7 million for the right to transmit each of the first seven Bond films three times between 1972 and 1978.[4] The statistics regarding novel sales have been equally exceptional. By 1977, paperback sales on the British market totalled 27 863 500. Sales of this magnitude were entirely unprecedented. Their significance, in publishing terms, can perhaps best be gleaned from the fact that the Bond novels accounted for ten of the first eighteen titles in paperback to sell over a million copies in Britain.

Bond as a popular hero

Remarkable though they are, such figures do not adequately convey either the scale or the reach of Bond's popularity. Nor do they quite capture those characteristics which have most clearly distinguished the specific nature of the position that Bond has occupied within contemporary popular culture. Bond is and, from as early as the late 1950s, always has been more than just the central protagonist in a number of novels and the films derived from them. Rather, the nature of his existence has been that of a popular hero, a term which is often used quite loosely although in fact it refers to a cultural phenomenon of a quite specific type with quite specific – and complex – conditions of existence. The most essential quality of Bond's status as a popular hero was clearly illustrated in the programme shown by ITV in May 1983 to celebrate the twenty-first anniversary of Bond's first screen appearance in *Dr No* (1962). The programme consisted of clips from the Bond films interspersed with the views and estimations of Bond held by a series of famous personalities from the worlds of entertainment, sport and politics – James Garner, Henry Cooper, James Stewart, Jill St John and President Reagan, for example. Without exception, all of those interviewed spoke of Bond as a real person. Not seriously, of course – to *genuinely* mistake Bond for a real person would be a category mistake, a sign of dementia. Rather, the point is that, albeit tongue-in-cheek and knowingly, they all entered into the imaginary game, constructed by the programme, of treating Bond *as if* he were a real person with a real history. President Reagan thus entertained a contrary proposition, but only to dismiss it, eroding the boundaries between real life and fiction by projecting a similarity between his own career and Bond's: 'Of course, some critics might say that Bond is nothing more than an actor in the movies. But then we've all got to start somewhere.'

It is then, in being granted a quasi-real status that a popular hero (or heroine) constitutes a cultural phenomenon of a particular type, quite distinct from the hero (or heroine) whose existence is contained within and limited to a particular

and narrowly circumscribed set of texts. Hercule Poirot and
Philip Marlowe, for example, have no significantly developed
existence other than as characters in the novels of Agatha
Christie and Raymond Chandler and the films and television
adaptations based on them; one needs either to have read or
seen these to know who these characters are and the cultural
values they stand for. Whereas popular heroes also usually
have their origins in a particular work or body of fiction, they
break free from the originating textual conditions of their
existence to achieve a semi-independent existence, functioning
as an established point of cultural reference that is capable of
working – of producing meanings – even for those who are
not directly familiar with the original texts in which they first
made their appearance. Robinson Crusoe and Sherlock
Holmes, for example, although initially merely fictional
characters – Crusoe in a novel by Daniel Defoe and Holmes
in Sir Arthur Conan Doyle's short stories – have since
acquired a cultural life that is all their own. These figures are
lodged in the memory bank of our culture. Functioning as
focal points of cultural reference, they condense and connect,
serve as shorthand expressions for, a number of deeply
implanted cultural and ideological concerns. The figure of
Crusoe has thus, in different ways within different cultural
contexts, functioned as the very image of economic man; he
has served as a convenient point of reference for the vices
and virtues of a colonising capitalism, or has personified
romantic conceptions of the condition of 'natural man' or of
the 'dignity of labour'.[5] In a similar way, Sherlock Holmes
has functioned as a model for a certain type of scientific
rationalism and has been treated, institutionally, as if he
were a real person. When Conan Doyle killed Holmes off in
The Final Solution, some London businessmen took to wearing
mourning bands while, in 1954, the BBC broadcasted a
special programme in honour of Holmes' hundredth birthday,
featuring interviews with his old school friends, teachers,
etc.[6]

The figure of Bond has assumed a similar significance
within our culture, particularly since the early 1960s. Apart
from being the period which witnessed the first cycle of Bond
films – those starring Sean Connery – the early 1960s saw

Bond take off into a semi-independent existence as a figure used widely in advertising and commodity design. Spilling over from the world of fiction into everyday life, Bond's cultural presence, in this period, was overwhelming, impossible to avoid. Although it has never since quite achieved a similar degree of centrality, the figure of Bond has remained a known component of the cultural landscape, a household word. So much so that it is more or less impossible, in contemporary Britain – or, for that matter, France, Italy, Germany, America or Japan – not to know who Bond is or, in a vague way, what he stands for whether or not one has read any of the novels or seen any of the films in which he functions as the central protagonist. When the Blunt affair was likened to the world of James Bond everyone knew what was meant; the reference needed no further elaboration.

The question we shall be centrally concerned with in this study is, quite simply: why? Why has James Bond been so massively and enduringly popular? Why has he assumed a position of such central and co-ordinating significance within contemporary popular culture? These are not new questions, of course; nor has there been a shortage of attempts to answer them. There are, however, different ways in which such questions may be put and, accordingly, different ways in which they might be answered. Most existing accounts concentrate on either the novels or the films and the specific types of pleasures associated with them.

Attempts to explain the appeal of the novels have thus usually been couched in terms of the scope they offer for the gratification of repressed desires or for the realisation, by proxy, of otherwise unattainable pleasures. Hugh Gaitskell summarised this line of argument nicely. 'The combination of sex, violence, alcohol and – at intervals – good food and nice clothes,' he wrote in a letter to Ian Fleming, 'is, to one who lives such a circumscribed a life as I do, irresistible.'[7] According to one critic, Fleming's literary technique – he calls it 'the technique of erotic distraction' – maximises such gratifications by gratuitously incorporating 'sensual titillation into the very texture of the stories'.[8] There is clearly much to recommend this line of argument. The dominant structure of identification in the novels does encourage the (male) reader to participate vicariously in Bond's adventures, his sexual exploits and his vodka martinis (shaken, not stirred) and thus to experience imaginarily the enjoyment of food, drink and sex as well as the troubling excitation of narrative suspense as Bond confronts pain, surmounts it or is released from it in the course of his contest with the villain. As Kingsley Amis, remarked: 'We don't want to have Bond to dinner or go golfing with or talk to Bond. We want to be Bond'; the novels support the (male) reader's fantasy projection that 'under this fiendishly clever bank-clerk . . . lurks intrepid, ruthless 0099'.[9]

Similarly, with regard to the films, it has been argued that their popularity can be attributed, variously, to their developed and highly distinctive use of technological gadgetry; to their sheer visual spectacle, particularly the destruction of expensive sets and scenery; or to the opportunity they afford for escapism into a universe governed by the laws of fantasy. It is also clear that their success can be attributed, at least to some degree, to the considerable commercial acumen with which they have been produced and marketed. Cubby Broccoli and Harry Saltzman, producers of the first Bond films, pioneered a new method of film distribution by releasing a large number of prints of each Bond film within the first two weeks of its première: 1100 prints in the case of *Goldfinger*, for instance. This both reduced the interest payments due on the capital invested in the films by accelerating the rate of return through box-office receipts and maximised the effectiveness of the pre-release publicity campaigns. The way in which the basic Bond formula has been manipulated to enable the films to take up – often at the level of parody – the themes of other box-office trend-setters may also help to account for their sustained popularity. *The Spy Who Loved Me*, for example, achieved much of its specific appeal by virtue of the ways in which it played on and inverted the tensions induced in the audience by the, at the time, massively popular film *Jaws* – as when the character Jaws, tipped into a shark tank, reverses audience expectations in proceeding, with evident relish, to sink his teeth into the flank of the hapless shark. *The Spy* is replete with such allusions to other films. The theme from *Laurence of Arabia* is thus played in the scenes in which Bond is in the Egyptian desert, and there is a parodied version of the scene in which Laurence and his companion finally find the Nile after a harrowing journey.

Such cultural/marketing strategies are not, of course, unique to the Bond films. Tulloch and Alvarado show in some detail how the *Doctor Who* programme format has been continuously adjusted to exploit currently popular generic tendencies in order, in the words of one of the series' producers, to grab a new audience 'on the wing, as it were, by tapping into various popular areas'.[10] However, this practice is somewhat more typical in television, where the long-running series format both lends itself to and requires such strategic generic readjustments, than in the cinema where the Bond films are somewhat exceptional in forming a thematically linked corpus of texts produced, over a quarter of a century, by the same production team.

A sign of the times

Clearly, such considerations are important. As we shall argue later, the conditions of production of the Bond films have had a crucial bearing on the specific qualities which distinguish Bond's position in the pantheon of contemporary popular heroes. However, they do not – either individually, or taken as a whole – adequately account for Bond's peculiar status as a popular hero, a figure lodged in the popular consciousness. In order to do so, it is necessary to consider not merely the novels and the films taken separately; nor is it sufficient to consider them solely in their relations to one another. The analysis must also encompass and take account of the vast range of other texts – advertisements, fanzine articles on Bond, interviews with Sean Connery, Roger Moore and Ian Fleming, features on 'the Bond girls' in men's magazines, spoofs and parodies – in which the figure of Bond, severed, to a degree, from the films and novels, has been constructed and put into broader distribution. It is within the circulations and exchanges between such texts and the films and novels that the figure of Bond has achieved the wider popular currency we have described. A currency, moreover, which has been mobile and changing in the respect that, as the relations between these texts have changed, so the figure of Bond has functioned as the bearer of different meanings at different points in time, in different contexts and for different audiences.

Our purpose in this study is to chart the varying currency of Bond's popularity – in part, internationally, but particularly in Britain – and to understand the reasons for it by considering the operation of all the 'texts of Bond' in the light of their changing relations to one another, and to contemporary cultural tendencies and preoccupations more generally, within the different moments of Bond's career as a popular hero. In brief, our contention will be that Bond's popularity has consisted in his ability to co-ordinate – that is, to connect and serve as a condensed expression for – a series of ideological and cultural concerns that have been enduringly important in Britain since the late 1950s. The primary ideological and cultural co-ordinates within which the figure of Bond has functioned have been, first, representations of the relations between West and East or, more generally, between capitalist and communist economic and political systems; secondly, representations of the relations between the sexes, particularly with regard to the construction of images of masculinity and femininity; and, thirdly, representations of nation and nationhood. Throughout his career as a popular hero, Bond has been active in each of these areas of ideological and cultural concern, acting as a sounding board in relation to which – by taking up and echoing other cultural tendencies – specific ideological positions have been constructed. Perhaps more important, the figure of Bond has been active within the *relations between* these different areas of ideological and cultural concern. It has furnished a point of reference in relation to which images of capitalism versus communism, of sexuality and of nationhood have been overlapped on to one another, orchestrated into particular complex unities which have exercised a powerful influence in both organising and giving voice and expression to popular responses to a series of deeply interacting historical changes.

However, the precise way in which the figure of Bond has articulated – that is, connected and expressed – these concerns has varied during different moments of his career as a popular hero. The ideological and cultural elements out of which the figure of Bond has been woven may have been constant, but these have been combined in different mixes and shifting permutations. If Bond has functioned as a 'sign of the times', it has been as a *moving sign of the times*, as a figure capable of taking up and articulating quite different and even contradictory cultural and ideological values, sometimes turning its back on the meanings and cultural possibilities it had earlier embodied to enunciate new ones.

In what follows then, we shall locate our analysis of the Bond novels and films in the wider context of the 'Bond phenomenon', a phenomenon that is constituted in the relations between the novels and films and the other 'texts of Bond' we have mentioned, texts which are constituted into an interacting set precisely by the functioning of the figure of Bond as the signifier which floats between and connects them. This, in turn, will entail approaching the novels and films in a rather different way than is customary. We shall be less concerned with these as separated entities, to be studied and understood on their own terms, than we shall be to analyse the changing orders of meaning on to which they have been grafted during different moments of the Bond phenomenon. Our concern is not with the novels and films 'in themselves' but with the mobile and shifting nature of the cultural and ideological business that has been conducted around, by means of, and through them as a consequence of the ways in which transformations in the wider functioning of the figure of Bond – in fanzines, magazine articles, advertisements and the like – have subtly altered the horizons of meaning within which the novels and films have been activated for consumption.

Another and more simple way of putting this is to say that there is more than one James Bond in the sense that, as a 'sign of the times', the figure of Bond has not always stood for the same values or represented a constant position in relation to the ideological concerns we have enumerated. Indeed, it has been the very *malleability* of Bond in this

respect, his ability to be changed and adapted with the
times, that has constituted the basis of his continuing – but,
at the same time, always modified – popularity. The
appearance of an uninterruptedly popular career masks the
fact that, ultimately, it is not the popularity of *Bond* that has
to be accounted for so much as the popularity of *different
Bonds*, popular in different ways and for different reasons at
different points in time. This is not to suggest that Bond can
mean anything to anybody but, rather, that his coherence as
a figure consists in the way in which he has functioned as a
shifting focal point for the articulation of historically specific
ideological concerns.

It will be useful therefore, before considering any of the
'texts of Bond' in any detail, to review the various moments
of Bond's popularity so as to establish, in a general way, the
different ideological tunes to which the figure of Bond, in
being modified and transformed, has been made to sing. It
is, in some respects, a depressing history. David Cannadine
has observed that when *Casino Royale* was first published in
1953, the coronation celebrations provided a 'retrospectively
unconvincing reaffirmation of Britain's continued world
power status'. He went on to remark that the last of Fleming's
novels, *The Man with the Golden Gun*, appeared in 1965, the
year of Churchill's funeral, 'self-consciously recognized as the
requiem for Britain as a great power'.[11] So far as his role in
British popular culture has been concerned Bond's role in
organising and co-ordinating popular responses to the
changing fate of the nation – the shifting self-conceptions,
imaginary pasts and possible futures that have been
constructed for it – has been perhaps the most vital of the
diverse functions he has fulfilled. To reflect on Bond in the
current political climate, when great power illusions have
been kicked into a macabre half-life again in the aftermath of
the Falklands Crisis and when the seemingly endless series of
royal celebrations make the coronation look like a shabby
dress rehearsal for today's continuously unfolding royal
pageant, throws into high relief the degree to which the
national clock is being remorselessly pushed back into the
past. It is therefore worth recalling that in the 1960s, when
Bond's popularity was at its peak, he functioned above all as

a hero of modernisation. Representing a break with the constraints of dodoism and tradition, he embodied a prospect for Britain which, whilst hardly without its contradictions, appears in retrospect positively millenarian.

Chapter 2

The Moments of Bond

Ian Fleming always maintained that he wrote *Casino Royale* in order to take his mind off his impending marriage, as an amusing diversion rather than a determined attempt to become a best-selling writer. Similarly, when, towards the end of his life, Fleming tried to categorise his work, he argued that 'while thrillers may not be literature with a capital L, it is possible to write what I can best describe as "Thrillers designed to be read as literature",' and cited, as his models in this respect, Raymond Chandler, Dashiell Hammett, Eric Ambler and Graham Greene.[1] Although it is clear Fleming always kept a weather-eye on the market for popular fiction, this does not seem to have been the market he had primarily in view when he first started writing. Indeed, he was somewhat surprised when it became clear that the Bond novels appealed to a wider readership than he had anticipated. In a letter to CBS in 1957, he wrote:

> In hard covers my books are written for and appeal principally to an 'A' readership but they have all been reprinted in paperbacks both in England and America and it appears that the 'B' and 'C' classes find them equally readable, although one might have thought that the sophistication of the background and detail would be outside their experience and in part incomprehensible.[2]

That Jonathan Cape, Fleming's publishers, envisaged a similar readership is evident from the jacket designs they commissioned. Such designs constitute one of the primary means whereby literary texts are inserted into available aesthetic and marketing categories; they aim both to solicit a particular readership and, in establishing a set of inter-textual associations, to locate reading within a particular cultural framework. The jacket designs for the first hardback editions of the early Bond novels thus typically consisted of a collection of objects associated with either espionage or luxurious living, or both, and connoted the category of superior quality, 'literary' spy fiction. Furthermore, the evidence from the reviews in the literary weeklies and monthlies of the period suggests that this is precisely how they were initially regarded and read by their intended public. Such reviews both addressed and sought to produce a 'knowing reader' who, in being familiar with or informed, by the reviewer, of the series of literary and mythic allusions deployed in the novels would be able to read and appreciate them as flirtatious, culturally knowing parodies of the spy-thriller genre. They thus functioned as 'critical legitimators', making the Bond novels permissibly readable in discounting their evident chauvinism, racism and sexism. The 'knowing reader', aware that Fleming was writing tongue-in-cheek, would not, it was implied, be adversely affected by these aspects of the novels to the degree that he/she (but mainly he) would appreciate their purely formal role in parodying, by means of excess, the earlier imperialist spy-thrillers of such writers as John Buchan and Cyril McNeile.

Installed ambiguously between the aesthetic and marketing categories of 'literature' and 'popular fiction', the Bond novels thus initially reached only a limited readership, largely restricted to the metropolitan literary intelligentsia. Even so, they sold quite well. The first imprint of *Casino Royale* (4750 copies), published in April 1953, had sold out by May of the same year and the title sold more than 8000 copies on its second imprint in 1954. *Live and Let Die*, published in 1954, sold more than 9000 copies in its first year of publication. Conceived as 'literary' sales, of course, such figures were more than respectable, but they were relatively small beer in relation to the market for popular fiction. Nor, initially, did the novels make much headway outside Britain. *Casino Royale* was turned down by three publishers in America on the grounds that it was too British for the American market and, when it was eventually published there by Macmillan, sold less than 4000 copies.[3] However, there were signs of interest in Bond from American television. CBS paid Fleming $1000 for the right to produce an hour long television adaptation of *Casino Royale* and, later (1956–7), Fleming was asked to write a script for NBC. (In the event, this was not used, although it subsequently formed the basis for the plot of *Dr No*). There were also signs of an awakening interest in the film industry when, in 1954, Sir Alexander Korda asked to see an advance copy of *Live and Let Die*. However, it is only in retrospect that these overtures seem portentous of greater things to come. By 1955, when Fleming had added a third title – *Moonraker* – to the list, the novels had been printed only in hardback editions, none had sold more than 12000 copies in Britain and Fleming's total earnings from sales were less than £2000. According to Pearson, Fleming's biographer, Fleming had decided, by mid 1955, that his financial return from the Bond novels no longer justified the time and effort he put into them. He accordingly conceived *From Russia, With Love* as his last Bond novel, determining to kill his hero off on the last page.

A political hero for the middle classes

The first turning point in both the degree and social reach of Bond's popularity came in 1957. Pan had published a paperback edition of *Casino Royale* in 1955, adding *Moonraker* in 1956, pushing the British sales for the Bond novels in those years up to 41000 and 58000 respectively (see Table 1). It was 1957, however, that witnessed the first stage in the transformation of Bond from a character within a set of fictional texts into a household name. This was chiefly attributable to the serialisation of *From Russia, With Love* in the *Daily Express* and, later in the same year, to the *Daily Express*'s publication of a daily strip-cartoon of Bond. The *Daily Express* also subsequently organised a competition in which readers were asked to choose, from a specified range, the actor they felt best suited to play the part of Bond on the screen. The effects of the *Daily Express*'s promotion of Bond on the sales of the Bond novels are easily discernible. Sales in Britain rose from 58000 in 1956 to 72000 in 1957, 105000 in 1958 and 237000 in 1959. This, then, was the first moment in the history of Bond as a popular hero, but a moment still characterised by a limited and socially restricted popular appeal. Although no detailed research has been done that would establish the point conclusively, it is reasonable to assume an approximate fit between the readership of the Bond novels and that of the *Daily Express* and similar papers; that is, a predominately lower middle class readership. It is, accordingly, in relation to the concerns of this class that the functioning of the figure of Bond in this period must be assessed.

Unsurprisingly, perhaps, the network of cultural and ideological concerns Bond served to condense and articulate in the late 1950s centred most closely on the relations between East and West, relations which had become particularly tense as a consequence of Russia's invasion of Hungary in 1956. Bond, that is to say, functioned first and foremost, although not exclusively, as a Cold War hero, an exemplary representative of the virtues of Western capitalism triumphing over the evils of Eastern communism. Except for *Diamonds are Forever*, the villain in all the novels Fleming wrote in the 1950s is either directly in the service of the Soviet Union – Le Chiffre in *Casino Royale*, and Red Grant in *From Russia, With Love* for example – or indirectly in its employ, as is the case with Dr No. In all cases, the villain's conspiracy constitutes a threat to the peace and security of the 'Free World', usually as represented by Britain or the United States. In frustrating the villain's conspiracy, Bond effects an ideologically loaded imaginary resolution of the real historical contradictions of the period, a resolution in which all the values associated with Bond and, thereby, the West – notably, freedom and individualism – gain ascendancy over those associated with the villain and, thereby, communist Russia, such as totalitarianism and bureaucratic rigidity.

This is not to suggest that these aspects of the relations between Bond and the villain constitute the only source of narrative tension in the novels of this period. But these were the aspects of the novels that were most clearly and explicitly

TABLE 1

Fleming's Bond novels: British paperback sales, 1955–77
Column figures: in thousands (details supplied by Pan Books Ltd)

Title	1955	1956	1957	1958	1959	1960	1961	1962	1963	1964	1965
Casino Royale (April 1955)*	41	15	15	22	35	40	81	145	399	593	472
Moonraker (October 1956)		43	7		60	48	87	136	439	604	474
Live and Let Die (October 1957)			50	15	40	35	82	137	447	618	476
Diamonds are Forever (February 1958)				68	22	45	92	142	426	592	471
From Russia With Love (April 1959)					80	40	82	145	642	600	457
Dr No (February 1960)						115	85	232	437	530	476
Goldfinger (May 1961)							161	152	429	964	564
For Your Eyes Only (May 1962)								226	441	615	480
Thunderball (May 1963)									808	617	809
On Her Majesty's Secret Service (Sept. 1964)										125	1794
You Only Live Twice (July 1965)											309
The Man With The Golden Gun (July 1966)											
The Spy Who Loved Me (May 1967)											
Octopussy (July 1967)											
Annual Total	41	58	72	105	237	323	670	1315	4468	5858	6782

O/P = Out of Print
* Dates denote first publication in paperback

1966	1967	1968	1969	1970	1971	1972	1973	1974	1975	1976	1977	Total by title
158	177	9	20	20	15	16	30	7	13	19	29	2371
158	47	16	14	21	14	31	25	17	20	11	10	2282
159	51	8	24	22	10	O/P	240	14	22	16	1	2467
146	43	24	15	14	77	72	15	26	22	13	8	2333
149	42	20	7	33	9	33	30	17	9	14	5	2414
134	36	19	9	15	15	31	30	3	20	12	8	2207
111	35	12	10	17	O/P	41	26	14	19	13	14	2582
152	49	2	28	22	8	32	16	20	22	12	13	2138
201	26	17	21	15	10	44	21	11	8	13	14	2635
16	39	30	117	20	20	13	25	23	24	12	9	2267
908	178	15	9	18	5	44	23	19	23	12	16	1579
273	485	68	48	48	4	44	24	16	131	11	16	1168
	517	57	33	57	61	21	19	20	22	0.5	O/P	807.5
	79	362	34	40	10	17	26	16	10	6	13	613
2565	1804	659	389	362	258	439	550	223	365	164.5	156	Overall Total 27863.5

foregrounded in the broader functioning of the figure of
Bond. It is no accident, for example, that the *Daily Express*
should have chosen *From Russia With Love* to introduce Bond
to a broader public since, of all Fleming's novels, this is the
one in which Cold War tensions are most massively present,
saturating the narrative from beginning to end. Moreover,
this is the only one of Fleming's novels bearing an author's
preface in which Fleming sought to locate reading within a
horizon of realist expectations, to instruct the reader that the
novel was not entirely fictional:

> Not that it matters, but a great deal of the background to
> this story is accurate.
> SMERSH, a contraction of Smiert Spionam – Death to
> Spies – exists and remains today the most secret department
> of the Soviet government. At the beginning of 1956, when
> this book was written, the strength of SMERSH at
> home and abroad was about 40000 and General
> Grubozaboyschikov was its chief. My description of his
> appearance is correct.
> Today the headquarters of SMERSH are where, in
> Chapter 4, I have placed them – at No. 13 Sretenka
> Ulitsa, Moscow. The Conference Room is faithfully
> described and the Intelligence chiefs who meet around the
> table are real officials who are frequently summoned to
> that room for purposes similar to those I have recounted.

However, Bond also functioned, in this period, as a site for
the elaboration – or, more accurately, re-elaboration – of a
mythic conception of nationhood. Again, it is no accident
that Bond's fame began to spread, to any significant degree,
in 1957. In the aftermath of the national humiliation of the
Suez fiasco, Bond constituted a figure around which,
imaginarily, the real trials and vicissitudes of history could
be halted and put into reverse. As, above all, a pre-eminently
English hero, single-handedly saving the Western World from
threatening catastrophe, Bond embodied the imaginary
possibility that England might once again be placed at the
centre of world affairs during a period when its world-power
status was visibly and rapidly declining. An imaginary outlet

for a historically blocked jingoism, Bond thus furnished a point of cultural reference in relation to which a chauvinism well and truly on its uppers could be reconstituted and symbolically refurbished. At the same time, of course, Bond's appeal consisted partly in the ways in which the organisation of the novels enabled questions of nation to be transposed on to those of sexuality.

In short, during the first phase of his career as a popular hero, the way in which the figure of Bond was constructed and made to stand in relation to the ideological preoccupations of the period enabled Bond to function primarily as a political and sexual hero for the lower middle classes. Yet, paradoxically, it was also during this period that Bond first became a subject for 'public concern' as evidenced by the development of a 'moralising criticism' concerned, as is ever the case, with the effects the Bond novels might have on 'other people'. Rather than, as had earlier been the case, aiming to produce a 'knowing reader' innoculated against the potentially adverse effects of the Bond novels, the purpose of this moralising criticism was to protect the 'untutored reader' from undue harm. Paul Johnson's attack on the 'sex, sadism and snobbery' of the Bond novels in the *New Statesman* is probably the most famous critical reaction of this type.[4] However, an article by B. Bergonzi in *The Twentieth Century* accusing Fleming of gratuitous sex and violence and of falling short of the moral and literary standards set by John Buchan and Raymond Chandler also proved influential.[5]

A hero of modernisation

Although a significant cultural presence by the end of the 1950s, the social basis of Bond's popular appeal remained limited. Moreover, he was virtually unknown outside Britain. The cycle of Bond films released in the early 1960s – starting, with *Dr No*, in 1962 – both significantly broadened the social basis of Bond's popular appeal in Britain and extended the horizons of his popularity internationally. At the same time, together with other constructions of Bond characteristic of the period, they contributed to the transformation of the figure of Bond – not, however, a total transformation so much as an ideological remodelling. The various ideological and cultural elements out of which the figure of Bond had earlier been constructed were, so to speak, dismantled and separated from one another in order to be reassembled in a new configuration which pointed, ideologically and culturally, in a number of new and different directions.

By comparison with the Bond novels, the Bond films were instantly and have remained quite spectacularly successful in terms of box office receipts, their rate of profitability and, as we have seen, the size and composition of the audience they have reached. This was achieved, at least initially, without much assistance from the financial backers of *Dr No* who did not expect the film to be more than an average earner. Accordingly, very little was spent promoting the film in America; indeed, it was premièred in the mid-West rather than New York. *Dr No* also had to make its way in the market place against what were, initially, either lukewarm or, at worst, savagely hostile critical reactions, such as that of Ian Cameron: '*Dr No*: no, no. Too inept to be as pernicious as it might have been. Costly gloss flawed by an insidious economy on girls. Superannuated Rank starlet tries to act sexy. Grotesque.'[6]

The figures tell a different story. By 1976, *Dr No* had earned global profits in excess of $22 million. *From Russia, With Love* grossed takings of $460 000 during the first week of its release in New York in 1963. *Goldfinger* became the fastest money-maker in the history of cinema, grossing $10 374 807 in fourteen weeks of its release in the USA and Canada in 1964. *Thunderball*, released in 1965, had grossed takings of $45 million by 1971 and, in the same year, *Diamonds are Forever* earned $15.6 million during the first twelve days of its release. And, of course, in the film industry, nothing succeeds like success. Cubby Broccoli and Harry Saltzman, co-producers of the early Bond films, had some difficulty in capitalising the production of *Dr No*. In the end, they had to settle for a production budget of $950 000 and for only a little more than $1 million in financing *From Russia, With Love*. *Thunderball*, by contrast, cost $6.6 million; *On Her Majesty's Secret Service*, $8 million; *Diamonds are Forever*, $7.2 million whilst *The Spy Who Loved Me* was budgeted at $13 million.

Nor can the cultural impact of the films be measured solely in terms of their own commercial success. They totally transformed the market for the novels, too, as an exemplary tale by Harry Saltzman testifies: 'The *Dr No* book had sold virtually nothing when we made the film. Then I went to Pan and suggested they print an extra 500000 copies. They laughed at me. And, do you know, in the next seven months, they sold one and a half million copies.'[7]

The more general pattern of the influence of the films on paperback sales in Britain is clearly discernible. As might be expected, Table 1 shows a close connection between the release dates of particular films and the peak point in the sales graph for the individual novels on which those films were based. The release of *From Russia, With Love* in 1963 saw the British sales for that title peak at 642000 in the same year; the release of *Goldfinger* in 1964 pushed the sales for that title up to their peak of 964000, and so on. However, the relationship is not entirely that of a one-to-one correlation. The peak of the sales graph for *Live and Let Die* – 618000 – is reached in 1964, for example, and whilst the release of the film of that title in 1973 lifted sales from their previously flagging level of 10000 to 20000 annually to 240000, this was well below their earlier peak and, just as important, this level of sales was not sustained for any appreciable period (only 14000 copies were sold in 1974). The story is much the same for *Diamonds are Forever* with sales peaking at 592000 in 1964, falling to around 15000 annually in the late 1960s to rise to 77000 on the release of the film in 1971, and maintaining that level for a couple of years before falling back to the sales levels of the late 1960s.

Indeed, it can be seen from Table 1 that the peak point in the sales graph for *each* title occurs sometime in the period between 1963 and 1966. Equally important, the table shows a marked lift in the sales for *all* the Bond novels over the period 1962 (1315000) to 1967 (1804000), a lift that was especially pronounced in 1963, 1964 and 1965 with sales in those years of 4468000, 5858000 and 6782000 respectively. It was precisely during this period that the first cycle of Bond films – those starring Sean Connery before his replacement in the part by George Lazenby – appeared. Released on more or less an annual basis – *Dr No* in 1962, *From Russia, With Love* in 1963, *Goldfinger* in 1964, *Thunderball* in 1965 and *You Only Live Twice* in 1967 – it is clear that the effect of the films in this period was to revivify the market for the Bond novels *as a whole*. It was as an *integrated set*, rather than as individual titles, that the Bond novels sold over this period. Subsequently, by contrast, the release of new Bond films has resulted in increased sales only for the individual titles from which they were derived. For example, in 1973, sales increased only for *Live and Let Die*; the sales for most of the other Bond novels actually fell significantly from their 1972 level.

Apart from themselves directly recruiting an international audience, the films had similar effects on the sales of the Bond novels in other countries. In France, Bond was virtually unknown until the release of *Dr No*. Two of the novels had been published in translation but sales had proved so sluggish that the publishers, Plon, had decided against issuing any of the remaining titles. In 1964, however, 480000 copies of the Bond novels were sold in France; *France Soir* serialised *Dr No*; *Elle* made Bond its male hero for the summer season and, in 1965, sales of the novels were topping the 2 million mark. Similarly, in Italy, where the novels had been published in translation since 1958, the release of *Dr No* occasioned such a spate of Italian films exploiting the 007 trademark that United Artists had to threaten legal action for breach of copyright. In Denmark and Sweden, the *Daily Express* strip-cartoons of Bond were published in comic book form; a strip-cartoon of Bond even appeared in Yugoslavia.[8] Perhaps the most distinctive development in America was the appropriation of Bond by *Playboy* which, in 1963, 1964 and 1965 respectively, serialised *On Her Majesty's Secret Service*, *You Only Live Twice* and *The Man with the Golden Gun*, all within a month or so of their initial publication in hardback editions. At the same time, *Playboy* also instituted, as a regular feature, photo-articles of 'The Girls of James Bond' type as did magazines like *Penthouse* and, in Britain, *Mayfair*. Finally, the early 1960s also witnessed, for the first time, the significantly widespread use of the figure of Bond in advertising and commodity design.[9]

The most significant changes in the cultural and ideological currency of Bond during this period are attributable to the effects of the films, particularly to the way they transformed the plot elements of the novels and subtley modified the characterisation of Bond. However, the use of Bond as a figure in advertising and commodity design tended to work alongside the films, modifying the associations Bond served to orchestrate so as to place him at the centre of a significantly reorganised set of ideological and cultural concerns. Three changes stand to the fore.

First, the figure of Bond was detached from the ideological co-ordinates of the Cold War period and adjusted to the prevailing climate of détente. In part, this change is attributable to Fleming himself. Beginning with *Thunderball* (1961), Fleming abandoned the SMERSH formula of his earlier novels, in which Bond is pitted against a representative of the Soviet Union or a villain in some way in the service of the Soviet Union, and wrote all his subsequent novels, except for *The Man With The Golden Gun* (1965), in the SPECTRE formula. In these novels – *Thunderball, On Her Majesty's Secret Service* (1963) and *You Only Live Twice* (1964) – Bond's mission involves him in a contest with SPECTRE – the Special Executive for Counter-Intelligence, Terror, Revenge and Extortion. Headed by the mad but diabolically clever Ernst Stavro Blofeld, SPECTRE is an international criminal organisation, an assembly of free-lance villains, which seeks to exploit the fragility of the relations between East and West, holding one or the other or sometimes both to ransom, for the purpose of private gain. Typically, the threat which Bond thus averts in these novels is that Blofeld's machinations, in sowing the seeds of misunderstanding between Russia and the West, might result in a global conflagration.

Whilst Fleming thus provided the means by which Bond was attuned to the ideological climate prevailing in the period of détente, the primary impetus for this ideological readjustment came from the requirements of the film industry. *Thunderball* itself was developed from a film script Fleming had written in co-operation with Kevin McClory and Jack Wittingham and thus constituted the first reshaping of Bond undertaken in response to the pressures of the film industry which, as we argue in detail in a later chapter, has consistently, although only in a relative sense, 'de-politicised' Bond in the interests as, Cubby Broccoli put it, of giving the Bond films 'legs worldwide'.[10] Thus, from the very first, Broccoli and Saltzman eschewed the SMERSH formula in favour of the SPECTRE formula, adapting those novels written to the former – even *From Russia, With Love* – so as to adjust them to the latter. That Fleming continued to write to this formula is, of course, attributable to the fact that, after the success of the film of *Dr No*, he wrote with a different public in mind and in anticipation that his novels would ultimately be transformed into films.

Secondly, Bond's functioning in relation to ideologies of nation and nationhood was also significantly modified. This was, in part, a consequence of the ways in which the relations between Bond and M were represented, with Bond being increasingly distinguished from and constructed in opposition to the films' portrayal of M as a fuddy-duddy Establishment figure. More generally, however, it was attributable to the associations established by Bond's incarnation, in this period, in the concrete form of Connery/Bond – the visual signifier through which the figure of Bond was most widely circulated. Whereas, in the late 1950s, Bond had supplied a point of reference in relation to which the clock of the nation had been put imaginarily into reverse, recalling a brighter past, the Bond of the early to mid 1960s functioned as the condensed expression of a new style and image of Englishness around which the clock of the nation was made to run imaginarily ahead of itself, a pointer to a brighter and better future. More particularly, in the context of 'swinging Britain', Bond provided a mythic encapsulation of the then prominent ideological themes of classlessness and modernity, a key cultural marker of the claim that Britain had escaped the blinkered, class-bound perspectives of its traditional ruling élites and was in the process of being thoroughly modernised as a result of the implementation of a new, meritocratic style of cultural and political leadership, middle class and professional rather than aristocratic and amateur.

Finally, and as perhaps the most crucial addition to Bond's signifying currency in this period, the figure of Bond and, closely related, the figure of 'the Bond girl', a new construction, constituted key sites for the elaboration of a (relatively) new set of gender identities. This aspect of Bond was closely related to his functioning as a representative of a modernising Britain. Between them, Bond and 'the Bond girl' embodied a modernisation of sexuality, representatives of norms of masculinity and feminity that were 'swinging free' from the constraints of the past. If Bond thus embodied a male sexuality that was freed from the constraints and hypocrisy of gentlemanly chivalry, a point of departure from the restraint, a-sexuality or repressed sexuality of the traditional English aristocratic hero, 'the Bond girl' – tailored to suit Bond's needs – was likewise represented as the subject of a free and independent sexuality, liberated from the constraints of family, marriage and domesticity. The image of 'the Bond girl' thus constituted a model of adjustment, a condensation of the attributes of femininity appropriate to the requirements of the new norms of male sexuality represented by Bond.

This aspect of Bond's functioning was perhaps most clearly evident in his use in advertising and commodity design, not just in Britain but internationally. Typically, in such contexts, the figure of Bond served as an ideological shorthand for the appropriate image of masculinity in relation to which feminine sexual identities were to be constructed – as in a French lipstick advertised as 'a good Bond for the lips' or an Australian brand of women's lingerie marketed under the slogan 'Become fit for James Bond'.[11] In this respect, to borrow loosely from Lacan, the figure of Bond provided a *point de capiton* within the ideological construction of gender relations and identities.[12] In a period that experienced a considerable cultural redefinition, a flux and fluidity, of gender identities, the figure of Bond furnished a point of anchorage in relation to which the sliding of meaning that had been introduced into the ideological ordering of gender relations, while not halted, was moved on and pinned down to a new set of ideological co-ordinates.

The early to mid 1960s, then, constituted the second significant moment in Bond's career as a popular hero. Indeed, to adopt the hyperbole of Bond's publicity writers, it constitutes *the* moment of Bond. In comparison with both the late 1950s and the periodic resurgence of interest in Bond prompted by the release of each new Bond film in the 1970s and 1980s, the impact of Bond in this period was a peculiarly concentrated one. Except for 1966, the films were released on an annual basis from 1962 to 1967; 22 792 000 copies of the Bond novels were sold in Britain between these years compared with the 1 506 000 copies sold between 1955 and 1961 and the 3 565 500 copies sold between 1968 and 1977; and, in advertising and commodity design, the figure of Bond was omnipresent. Furthermore, the social reach of Bond's popularity had been significantly expanded. No longer a cult figure for the metropolitan intelligentsia or, less exclusively, a political hero for the middle classes, the figure of Bond functioned as a popular icon in ways which cut significantly, if also unevenly and contradictorily, across class, generation, gender and national divisions.

Apart from being the period in which Bond's popularity manifestly peaked, the early 1960s can also be counted as *the* moment of Bond in the sense that his popularity was unrivalled by that of any other cultural figure. Indeed, this was true for the greater part of the 1960s when, in its taken-for-grantedness, the figure of Bond supplied an established point of reference to which a wide range of cultural practices referred themselves in order to establish their own cultural location and identity. Most obviously, Bond functioned as either an explicit or an implied point of reference for the rival spy-thrillers which flooded the bookstalls, the cinema and the television screens, in both Britain and America – the novels of Len Deighton and the films derived from them, *The Man from UNCLE*, *The Avengers* and so on. Each of these either directly negotiated its own specific cultural space and sphere of ideological action within the region of the spy-thriller, or had such a space negotiated for it by the critics, through the construction of relationships of similarity to/difference from

Bond. Len Deighton's hero (anonymous in the novels, portrayed as Harry Palmer in the films) was thus both likened to and distinguished from Bond – like him (a British secret agent), yet also significantly unlike him (a working-class anti-hero).

Nor was the operation of this system of references restricted to the cultural region of the spy-thriller. In the same period, when Jon Pertwee played the title role, the producers of *Doctor Who* adapted the series to a 'science fiction James Bond formula' specifically in order to 'co-opt the success of the "Swinging Sixties" and the world-wide marketing of "liberated" affluence via Carnaby Street and Biba'.[13] The significance of this is not that such comparisons were made (a fairly common occurrence in popular fiction) but that, where they were, it was always Bond who furnished the point of comparison. Other fictional heroes were likened to/distinguished from Bond, rarely the other way round.[14]

Bond as ritual

By the mid 1960s, all the cultural and ideological elements out of which the figure of Bond had been constructed were well and truly in place; Bond's currency was established. The distinguishing characteristic of the third moment in Bond's career as a popular hero – roughly, from the 1970s onwards – consists in its selective and strategic activation of that currency together with the more episodic and ritualistic nature of Bond's popularity.

The point has already been made that, in the 1970s, the Bond films – released every two years rather than annually – had a more discrete impact on novel sales, promoting them only as individual titles rather than as an integrated set. Perhaps more important, the ideological and cultural concerns to which the figure of Bond resonated had become somewhat less vital, assessed in relation to the changing configuration of British popular culture as a whole. The spin-offs from the Bond films and the use of Bond-derived motifs in advertising remained legion, but the markets aimed at had changed significantly. In the 1960s, the Bond image and Bond products were closely associated with constructions of sexuality and nationhood. The dominant sponsored products of the 1970s, by contrast, were technological – such as Rolex watches – whereas most spin-offs were designed for children: Corgi cars, helicopters and rockets; Airfix kits of Moonraker; Action Man type dolls of Bond and Jaws, and so on. As a popular hero, and the more so as the decade progressed, Bond thus markedly descended the age scale. In the 1960s, the audience for the Bond films had consisted, in the main, of adolescents and young adults. By the time *Moonraker* was released in 1979, the audience consisted mainly of parents with pre-adolescent children. At the time of writing, local cinemas book the Bond films for the school holidays alongside or as an alternative to Disney films, while Bond imagery is now used to advertise peanuts and instant whip.

Not only did Bond's popularity become more episodic, an isolated occurrence every two years; it also became more routinised, a more or less institutionalised ritual, especially when, after 1975, the transmission of a Bond film by ITV on Christmas Day established a regular place for Bond in the 'way of life' of the British people. This is not to suggest that Bond was no longer popular but rather that the nature and periodicity of his popularity, the time rhythms to which it conformed, had been significantly reorganised. Bond thus operated as a 'dormant signifier', inactive most of the time but capable of being periodically reactivated, albeit in a fairly ritualised manner, with the release of each new Bond film, only to be put back on ice again pending the publicity build-up to the next film – or the next Christmas.

Paralleling these changes, the range of cultural and ideological concerns Bond served to articulate was subject to a considerable contraction during the 1970s. In effect, it was really only in relation to ideologies of gender and sexuality that the figure of Bond retained any significant degree of ideological potency. While all the films produced in the period continued to use the SPECTRE formula, their relation to that formula became increasingly parodic and self-mocking, instances of a *paraded* fantastic. Similarly, rather than articulating any new image of nation and nationhood, Bond functioned more as a negative site in relation to which earlier conceptions of Englishness – including those represented by Bond in the earlier phases of his career – were parodied and debunked, punctured so as to release laughter, by means of carrying them to excess. The most significant change associated with the films of this period, however, consisted in a shift in the centre of narrative interest, increasingly pronounced as the 1970s progressed, away from the relations between Bond and the villain towards the relations between Bond and 'the Bond girl'. Usually portrayed as 'excessively' independent – a fellow professional who works alongside Bond, threatening to best him in the traditionally masculine preserve of espionage work, as does Anya in *The Spy Who Loved Me* – the destiny of 'the Bond girl' in the films of this period is to meet her come-uppance in her encounter with Bond. The main ideological work thus accomplished in the unfolding of the narrative is that of a 'putting-back-into-place' of women who carry their independence and liberation 'too far' or into 'inappropriate' fields of activity. Of course, similar tensions were worked through in the narratives of the earlier films as well as in the novels, but they were usually subordinated to and worked into the relations between Bond and the villain rather than, as in the films of the late 1970s, the other way round. This shift in narrative organisation clearly constituted a response – in truth, somewhat nervous and uncertain – to the Women's Liberation movement, fictitiously rolling-back the advances of feminism to restore an imaginarily more secure phallocentric conception of gender relations.

Finally, Bond no longer occupied centre-stage within the reorganised system of inter-textual relations which characterised the popular culture of the period. Rather than supplying the centre around which such inter-textual references were co-ordinated, the cultural space within which the figure of Bond operated was incessantly renegotiated by referring it to new tendencies and developments within popular culture, especially the cinema. The films of this period are thus characterised by what can perhaps best be termed a double referential structure. Playing on popular memory by referring to the earlier Bond films and to the more general figure of Bond associated with the 1960s, essentially by means of parody, they also selectively activated the established currency of Bond and, in so doing, reorganised its cultural associations by referring it to more influential genres within the contemporary cinema – to police fiction movies in *The Man with the Golden Gun*, for example, or to science fiction spectaculars in *Moonraker*. It was only by being thus constantly transformed that Bond was kept culturally alive.

The pattern of increasing use of parody and dependence on other popular films was reversed in the 1980s after *Moonraker* (1979). *For Your Eyes Only* (1981) showed a clear attempt to activate some lapsed and inactive parts of the Bond mythology. In terms of production this meant abandoning Christopher Wood, who had scripted *The Spy Who Loved Me* and *Moonraker*, and returning to Richard Maibaum who had scripted many of the earlier Bond films. Textually, *For Your Eyes Only* abandoned comic parody, for the greater part, to concentrate on a 'straight' Bond adventure story organised around the Cold War. Some critics welcomed the absence of parody and the return to a 'human Bond'. Rubin argues that 'the fact that Roger Moore was consistently beaten up and endangered, indicated to critics and public alike that the era of the automoton Bond was ending'.[15] He suggests that the summer of 1981 was a period of 'joyous celebration' for Bond fans because of this. Interestingly and unusually, however, *For Your Eyes Only* makes direct references to the British government of the time. The minister in charge of Bond is represented as in fear of Thatcher ('She'll have our guts for garters.'), while Thatcher herself is the subject of comic parody which the film otherwise largely eschews. In a typical Bondian contradiction, Thatcher's views of the Cold War are incorporated into the plot of the film, but Thatcher is the object of the Bondian sexual joke; to be found, at the end of the film, in the kitchen, that 'rightful place' for womanhood. Thatcher thanks Bond for his services to his country, but as Bond abandons his radio watch for a midnight swim with the current Bond girl, a parrot takes his place uttering the words, 'Give us a kiss, give us a kiss'. Thatcher coyly pats her hair, clearly flattered by the thought.

Both *Octopussy* and *Never Say Never Again*, produced respectively by Broccoli and Kevin McLory and in opposition to one another, relocate Bond in the political concerns of the 1980s where he is reactivated as a Cold War hero, but also takes to spying in the Middle East. In the pre-credit sequences of both *Octopussy* and *Never Say Never Again*, Bond appears to be engaged in a South American caper, clad in *Never Say Never Again* like a member of the SAS, although this proves to be a training exercise. There are other noticeable shifts in emphasis from the Bond of *The Spy* and the 1970s. *Never Say Never Again* boasts a novel villainess for the Bond films, a beautiful and murderous member of SPECTRE who Bond kills in an unusually powerful explosion from a fountain pen, engineered by the unhappy Q who, although suffering like England from cuts and contraction, is still capable of producing violent phallic solutions. The traditional narrative by which Bond puts attractive women back in their place *sexually* but reserves violence and killing for the villain is reworked to deal violently and finally with those women who cannot be conquered sexually.

Although Bond had dealt with major women villains before (Rosa Klebb in *From Russia, With Love* and Irma Bunt in *On Her Majesty's Secret Service*) they had always been characterised by extreme ugliness and sexual deviance or, in the films, had usually played a very minor part in the plot. The most notable exception to this in the novels is the part of Vesper Lynd in *Casino Royale*, a part in which the roles of 'the girl' and villainess are complexly fused. *Never Say Never Again* breaks with both these earlier models. Moreover, the villainess here is to be killed partly because she has attempted to kill Bond and has killed his girl assistant, but also because, as she holds Bond at gunpoint, she demands an acknowledgement that she has conquered him sexually. Bond is supposed to write a note in proof of this. Instead he fires his fountain pen/gun at her. A tiny dart hits her and there is a reaction shot of her incredulous laughter at Bond's response before the resounding explosion. Both the image of the villainess (aggressive, dark, sexual, vampish) and her 'punishment' seem to resort to earlier traditions in British and American cinema narratives as does the image of 'the Bond girl' in this case (fair, frightened and clinging).

It is clear, of course, that these developments have been, in part, prompted by the changed political conditions of the 1980s. The increasing centrality of Cold War rhetoric in the discourse of Reaganism and Thatcherism; the return, in the wake of the Falkland's Crisis, of 'the nation', in its most atavistic forms, to the centre of political life; the attempt to roll back feminism and, with it, women to their 'proper place', in the home: these developments have combined to lend to the Bond films a much harder and sharper political edge than they had in the 1970s.

A mobile signifier

To summarise, our purpose in this chapter has been to single out a number of distinct moments in the history of Bond, first as a cult phenomenon for the intelligentsia, and, subsequently, as a popular hero. In doing so, we have sought to indicate the respects in which the figure of Bond has changed between these various moments, the different sets of ideological and cultural concerns that figure has served to co-ordinate and the ways in which the ideological and cultural components of which it has been comprised have been mixed in different combinations at different points in time. It can thus be seen that the figure of Bond has been differently constructed at different moments in the Bond phenomenon. 'James Bond' has been a variable and mobile signifier rather than one that can be fixed as unitary and constant in its signifying functions and effects.

To some extent, of course, such changes are the product of new additions to the 'texts of Bond'. The Bond of the late 1950s was primarily a literary phenomenon whereas, in the 1960s, the figure of Bond was a compound product operating in the relationships between Fleming's novels, the films derived from them, advertisements, commodities, and the like. However, it would be mistaken to regard such additions as simply expanding the 'texts of Bond' without, at the same time, reorganising that set of texts and, accordingly, modifying the signifying function and value of the individual texts within it. We have seen, for example, that a mass readership for the novels was produced by the films. Yet it is unlikely that the films produced that readership without, at the same time, organising it, predisposing readers to read the novels in certain ways, privileging some of their aspects at the expense of others, and so on. It will therefore repay our attention to look more closely at the various 'texts of Bond' and at the ways in which the relations between them have been reclassified and reordered. For such considerations have an important bearing on the ways in which the novels and the films have been interpreted and received – and, thereby, have been actually culturally active – at different moments in Bond's career as a popular hero.

Chapter 3

Reading Bond

It is now possible to specify more precisely the conditions of existence of Bond as a popular hero. In functioning as a moving point of reference within post-war popular culture, the figure of Bond has been constructed and been operative in the relations between a considerable and accumulating set of texts, different in its total size and composition as well as in its internal configuration at different moments in Bond's career as a popular hero. These texts have included the films and novels in which Bond has functioned as the central protagonist, the serialisations of the novels in, for example, the *Daily Express* and *Playboy*, interviews with Sean Connery, Roger Moore and Ian Fleming, photo-features on 'the girls of James Bond' and many more: John Barry's 007 theme music; the impressive list of hit singles derived from the films – Shirley Bassey's *Goldfinger*, for example – and so on. Added to these have been the sedimentations of Bond in the world of objects. Through its use in advertising and commodity design, the figure of Bond has become tangled up in the world of things resulting in a series of coded objects (lipstick, lingerie, Action Man type dolls), functioning like textual meteorites, highly condensed and materialised chunks of meaning.

In short, the conditions of Bond's existence have been *inter-textual*. (We use the hyphenated form to avoid confusion with the concept of *intertextuality* associated with the work of Julia Kristeva. The significance of this distinction will be made clear later in this chapter. In brief, whereas Kristeva's concept of *intertextuality* refers to the system of references to other texts which can be discerned within the internal

44

composition of a specific individual text, we intend the concept of *inter-textuality* to refer to the social organisation of the relations between texts within specific conditions of reading.) The figure of Bond has been produced in the constantly changing relations between a wide range of texts brought into association with one another via the functioning of Bond as the signifier which they have jointly constructed. In turn, it is this figure which, in floating between them, has thereby connected these texts into a related set in spite of their manifold difference in other respects.

Moreover, the composition and organisation of this set of texts has been unusually rich and complex. This is mainly because the figure of Bond has been constructed through the combination of two different systems for the production of popular heroes. The first of these operates by means of the transformation of fictional biographies into quasi-real ones; the second operates via the transformation of 'real biographies' into semi-fictional ones. We have already commented on the first of these processes, whereby Bond has been transformed into a quasi-real person, even to the point of the production of a 'fictional biography',[1] so as to assume a mythic identity within popular consciousness. However, the close association between the figure of Bond and the constructed screen and off-screen identities of Connery and Moore – and, in certain regions of textual distribution, the person of Fleming – bear witness to the reverse process, best exemplified in the star system, whereby 'real lives' become fictionalised and blended with screen images to result in the construction of a mythic figure poised midway between the two: the cases of Marilyn Monroe and John Wayne, for example. Produced in the interaction between these two processes, the figure of Bond has consisted of elements of fiction translated into a mythic identity which has accumulated an added 'reality effect' in subsuming within it elements of 'real lives' transformed into exemplary fragments of the myth.

More follows from this specification of Bond's conditions of existence than at first sight meets the eye. In particular, it has far-reaching implications for the ways in which the various 'texts of Bond' and the relations between them should be analysed. It also raises some awkward questions regarding the principles which customarily govern the ways in which texts are grouped into sets for the purposes of analysis. The most usual means by which this is done is through the application of author-based principles of textual classification. The Bond phenomenon, however, provides an instance of a cultural phenomenon – exceedingly common in popular culture – constituted by the operation of a system of classification which, in being fashioned by the functioning of a popular hero, conforms to a different logic and has different effects. It will be important to take account of these if we are to gain an adequate analytical purchase on the varying cultural and ideological business that has been conducted around, by means of, and through the 'texts of Bond' in the different phases of Bond's career as a popular hero.[2]

The texts of Bond

Michel Foucault has attributed three main effects to the way in which the name of an author typically functions within literary criticism. First, he argues, it serves as a principle of classification. It groups together all the literary texts written by the named person concerned, representing them as an integrated *oeuvre*, and draws other texts written by or bearing the name of that same person – letters, diaries, unpublished manuscripts – into an association with these. In doing so, it organises the relations between these texts in such a way that they can be held to mutually illuminate one another in construing the author as 'a particular source of expression who, in more or less finished form, is manifested equally well, and with similar validity, in a text, in letters, fragments, drafts, and so forth'.[3] Secondly, and as a consequence, the author functions as a principle of explanation in relation to those texts which are circulated under his/her name, accounting for their form and the order of their relations to one another. The grouping of a set of texts under the name of an author articulates the hermeneutic demand for consistency of meaning. At the same time, it supplies the means of meeting that demand in constructing, in the author, an extra-textual point of origin – a life, a set of views, tastes and preferences – in relation to which all the apparent contradictions and inconsistencies within and between the texts concerned can be explained. Finally, Foucault argues, 'the name of an author is a variable that accompanies only some texts to the exclusion of others', contending that in this, its selective use, it functions as a sign of value.[4]

It would, of course, be possible to group the Bond novels written by Fleming into a set of texts whose unity and meaning, together with his other writings, might be held to have their source in Fleming's life, views, tastes and preferences. Indeed, this has been done, several times, albeit in different ways. For example, Pearson – Fleming's biographer and also, incidentally, Bond's – construes the Bond novels as essentially transformations of Fleming's real-life experiences. He thus traces a series of correspondences between the latter and the plot elements of various novels – Fleming's trip to a health clinic and the opening chapters of *Thunderball*, for example. Pearson also construes Bond as essentially an emanation of Fleming: Bond's background is also Fleming's background (public school and the navy); Bond's preferences are also Fleming's preferences (martini, scrambled eggs, Sea Island cotton shirts), and so on. In another vein, David Cannadine, tracing the similarities between Bond's social and political views and those expressed by Fleming in his journalist writings, construes Bond as Fleming's mouthpiece and is thereby able to interpret Fleming's writings as a whole as the expression of a unified authorial world-view.[5]

The figure of Fleming has even been constructed and made to stand in relation to the Bond novels in such a way as to serve as the sign and source of the cultural value of the latter. Anne Boyd has thus interpreted the Bond novels as a mythic cycle comprising a series of ethical trials through which Bond emerges triumphant, and argues that, in this, they bear witness to a unifying moral purpose which justifies their being regarded as a body of work of considerable moral and aesthetic value.[6] Nor has it merely been within the secondary elaborations of critics that the name of Fleming has been attached to the Bond novels in this way. It was, as we have seen, precisely as 'texts of Fleming' that the early

Bond novels were first produced and circulated among the literary intelligentsia. Similarly, *Playboy*, in serialising the Bond novels, sought also to aestheticise them. Each of the serialisations was accompanied by reproductions of oil paintings depicting scenes from the novels; these were specially commissioned for this purpose and were signed by the artist. *Playboy* also sought, through a series of interviews with and articles by him, to establish Fleming as the author of a body of work of implied literary merit.

However, it is clear that, in the culturally preponderant forms of their distribution, it is as 'texts of Bond' rather than as 'texts of Fleming' that the Bond novels written by Fleming have been bought and read. In the actual material and cultural forms through which their reading has been socially organised, they have formed part of a network of inter-textual relations established by the figure of Bond which, in this respect, has functioned as a principle of textual classification which has overridden the operation and cultural purchase of author-based principles of classification. (Interestingly, Cubby Broccoli frequently confuses Bond and Fleming and uses the terms 'in the spirit of Ian Fleming' and 'in the spirit of James Bond' interchangeably.) The same is true of the films. The film of *Dr No* is, first and foremost, in its most culturally active and consequential form, a 'text of Bond'. In relation to this, its grouping, within *auteur* theory, as a part of the *oeuvre* of its director, Terence Young, is culturally secondary – not an impossible classification but one that has been inhibited by the fact that the text has already been made to point, through the inter-textual associations established by Bond, in a different direction.

Yet, although constructed into a unity in relation to the figure of Bond and actively consumed in the light of the associations established by this figure which floats between and connects them, the Bond films and novels are radically hetero-geneous in terms of the originating conditions of their produc-tion, their generic conventions and, of course, their authors/ scriptwriters/directors/producers/leading actors. Although circulated under a variety of names, the relations between these are organised according to a definite order or priority such that the name 'Bond' overwhelms all the other names and the contending principles of classification they putatively embody.

Whilst most of the novels within which Bond functions as the central protagonist thus bear the name of Fleming, not all of them do. There are also several Bond novels which carry the names of other writers: *Colonel Sun* bears the name of Robert Markham and, inside, another name, Kingsley Amis, the 'real writer' behind the pseudonym of Markham; *License Renewed* bears the name of John Gardner; the novelisations of the later films bear the name of Christopher Wood. An added complication is the fact that *The Spy Who Loved Me* was not written solely by Fleming, whilst *Thunderball* was based on a film script he co-wrote with Kevin McClory and Jack Whittingham – names which, as a result of legal action, are now appended to this title, although they were not originally. Yet, in terms of publishing and marketing operations, jacket designs, etc., all these texts are grouped together and circulated under the name of Bond. In all cases, as can be seen from Figures 1 and 2, the name of Bond dwarfs that of the writer, thereby culturally activating them for consumption in a particular way.

There is also a legal aspect to the functioning of the name 'Bond'. Whereas copyright is usually vested in an author, copyright in the Bond novels – all of them, not just those written by Fleming – is held by Glidrose Productions. However, the copyright which Glidrose productions holds is not in the works of Fleming or those of the other writers we have named but in the name of Bond. It is thus in the strict legal sense that Pearson's 'fictional biography' of Bond and the novels of Markham/Amis, Gardner and Wood are presented as 'authorised' versions of Bond. In the case of the Bond novels, the legal power of authorisation has thus passed from the writers to their creation. The former have been eclipsed by the figure of Bond legally just as much as culturally in the sense that it is Bond who functions as the primary legal subject – a name with rights to be protected and claims to be advanced – in relation to the 'texts of Bond'.

This applies to the films, too. With the exception of *Casino Royale*, the film rights to which were bought by Gregory

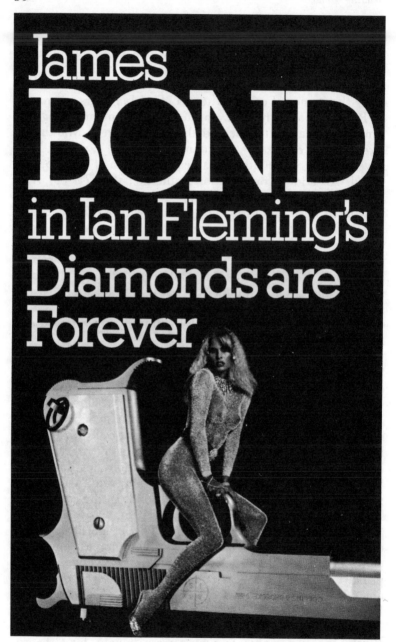

Figure 1

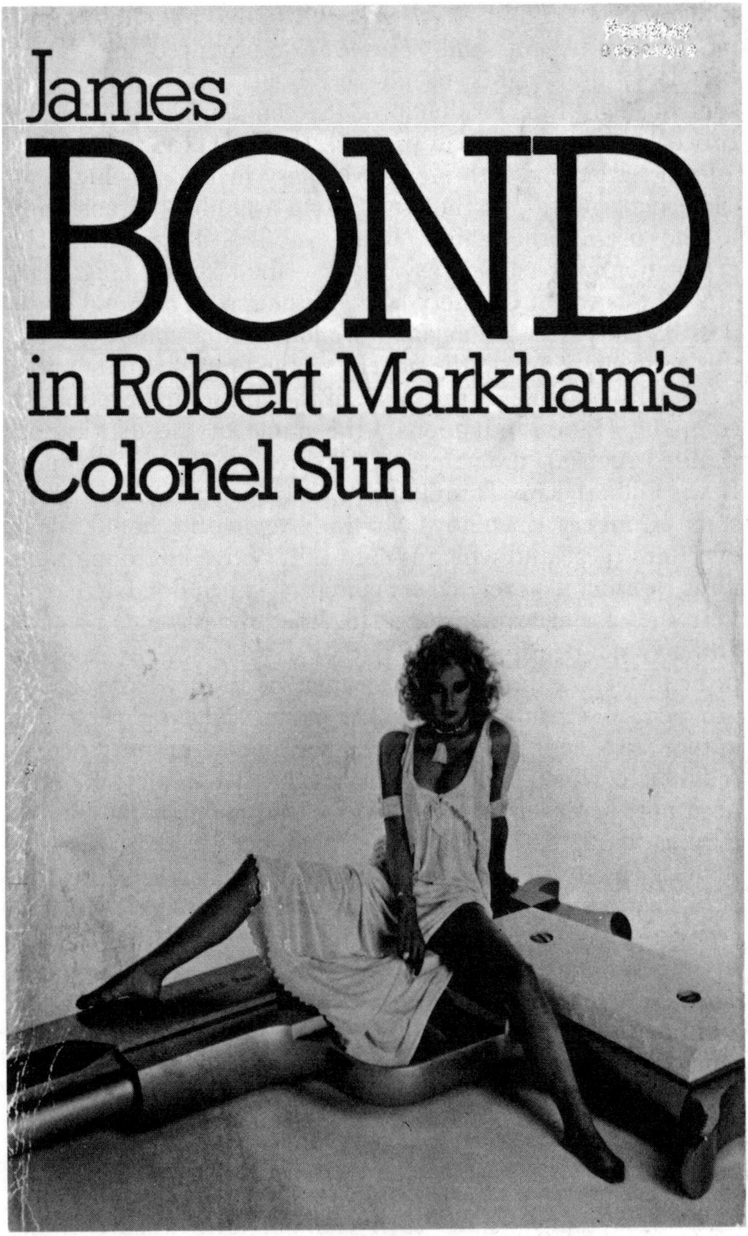

Figure 2

Rafferty in 1955 and which was eventually made into a film by Woody Allen, and *Thunderball*, produced by Kevin McClory, film rights to all the Bond novels have been controlled by Eon Productions, the company established by Broccoli and Saltzman to produce *Dr No*. These rights, after a legal settlement with Kevin McClory in 1965, included an exclusive legal title to the use of Bond as a film character and to the use of the name 'Bond' in film description. The production of *Never Say Never Again* – the last in a long series of attempts to get Connery back on the screen as Bond – was possible only because means were found of circumnavigating this restriction. As do the novels, so the films circulate under a diversity of names – the name of the controlling production company (Eon Productions); the name of the distributors (United Artists); the names of the directors (Terence Young, Lewis Gilbert, Guy Hamilton, Peter Hunt); the names of the stars (Connery, Lazenby, Moore). Again, the name which overrides these and which is culturally active in grouping the films together as a related set is that of James Bond.

In the case of texts grouped together under the name of an author, the death of that author establishes, at least in principle, finite limits to the range of texts which can be grouped together under his/her name. The figure of the author also supplies a (constructed) point of reference in relation to which the texts bearing his/her name may (but need not) be ordered into a definite and unchanging relation to one another. The situation is quite different where a popular hero furnishes the operative principle of textual classification. First, the range of texts which may be thus grouped together is potentially infinitely expansible so long as that popular hero remains a culturally active signifier. This entails that account must be taken of the ways in which additions to that textual set may play into and reorder the relations between the texts which previously comprised that set and, consequently, modify the cultural and ideological business that is conducted around and in relation to those texts. It also entails that account be taken of the ways in which the broader aspects of the functioning of that popular hero may change, since such changes form a part of the social and cultural determinations which influence the way the texts concerned are available to be read.

Consideration of an analogous case may help to place these problems in a broader context. In his discussion of the construction of character within the cinema, Richard Dyer has argued that the 'always-ready signifying nature of star images' may function contradictorily in relation to the other aspects of characterisation (name, speech, action, gesture) at work in a particular film. The foreknowledge of star images which audiences derive from previous films, fanzines, publicity handouts, biographies and the like constitutes a meta-signifying system which may powerfully disorganise or make more complexly polysemic the other sign clusters at work in a particular film. One of the cases Dyer cites is the character Lorelei Lee played by Marilyn Monroe in Howard Hawks' *Gentlemen Prefer Blondes*. There is, he argues, a massive disjunction between Monroe's star-image as the per-sonification of an essentially innocent, narcissistic sexuality and the characterisation of Lorelei as a 'cynical gold-digger' effected by the other aspects of character construction at work in the film. The consequence, he argues, is that 'the character of Monroe as Lorelei becomes contradictory to the point of incoherence'.[7] It needs only to be added that Monroe's star image is constantly being revised for it to be seen that the reference point for viewers watching her films is an unstable one. In a similar way, the figure of Bond has acted as a constantly *destabilising* point of reference, grouping the 'texts of Bond' into a unity but only at the price of constantly modifying the relations between them.

The relations between the 'texts of Bond'

The most obvious and most usual approach to this problem would be to fix Fleming's novels as a static point of reference and to view and analyse all the other 'texts of Bond' as more or less faithful adaptations of these. Such a construction, privileging the moment and the forms of Bond's origin, is impossible to maintain. The 'texts of Bond' have comprised a constantly accumulating and 'mutating' set of texts, 'mutating' in the sense that additions to the set have connected with the pre-existing 'texts of Bond' in such a way as to reorganise kaleidoscopically the relationships, transactions and exchanges between them. None of the texts in which the figure of Bond has been constructed can thus be regarded as privileged in relation to the others in any absolute or permanent sense. Rather, each region of this textual set occupies a privileged position in relation to the others, but in different ways depending on the part it has played in the circulation and expanded reproduction of the figure of Bond.

Fleming's Bond novels are thus undoubtedly privileged in the sense that, historically, they came first and have subsequently functioned as a textual source for the films in supplying their titles and, albeit sometimes loosely, their plot elements. In these respects, the films can be regarded as secondary and derivative in relation to the novels. From the point of view of their role in the construction and expanded circulation of the figure of Bond, however, the films have arguably been privileged in relation to the novels throughout the successive phases of Bond's popularity since the release of *Dr No* in 1962.

As we have seen, for the majority of readers, their acquaintance with the novels was mediated by their prior familiarity with the films, suggesting that the films constitute a determination that must be taken into account in assessing their relationship to and mode of reading the novels. This entails a more complex construction of the relations between the films and the novels than is usually applied in analysing films adapted from some pre-existing fictional source. Normally, such relations are construed as unidirectional. The film concerned is viewed as a creative transformation of its source, the task of analysis being regarded as that of assessing the relationships of similarity and difference between the two as if the fictional source remained an untroubled origin, unaffected and undisturbed by its adaptations. Yet it is clear that the Bond films have exerted a reactive, transformative power on the novels. Influential determinations within the social and ideological relations of reading within which – for the most part and by most people – the novels have been read, they have culturally activated the novels in particular ways, selectively cueing their reading, modifying the exchange between text and reader, inflecting it in new directions by inserting the novels within an expanded inter-textual set.

Consideration of the organisation of the (male) reader's identification with Bond will throw some light on these issues. Arguably, such identification is produced by the organisation of the relations between Bond, the villain, and 'the girl' within the novels. However, the precise nature of the mind's eye image of Bond which animates the reader–hero identification and fills out the figure of Bond in specifying its cultural resonances will vary according to the reader's specific mode of insertion within the inter-textual relations which bear on his/her reading of the novels. O. F. Snelling alludes to these considerations in his *Double O Seven: James Bond: A Report*.[8] Remarking that he came to the Bond novels through an earlier acquaintance with the tradition of the imperialist spy–thriller represented by John Buchan and Cyril McNeile, he relates that his mind's-eye image of Bond was essentially that of the English gentleman–hero derived from this tradition but as portrayed visually in a series of Hollywood films in the 1930s and 1940s. It is likely that identifications of this sort, in which the figure of Bond is made to echo to the tunes of an earlier textual set, predominated during the early stages of Bond's career as a popular hero. Certainly, the established screen identities of most of the actors initially considered for the part of Bond – James Mason, Trevor Howard, David Niven (Fleming's preferred choice), Rex Harrison, Richard Burton and James Stewart – reflected a tendency to assimilate Bond within the tradition of English ruling class heroes. Michael Caine has subsequently reported that he was surprised that Connery got the part: 'I felt sure they'd give it to Rex (Harrison), because he was your living image of upper crust good living.'[9]

The casting of Connery as Bond, however, was clearly an intentional break with such culturally latent patterns of identification. With the requirements of the American market primarily in mind, particularly in view of the more demotic associations of American popular heroes, Broccoli and Saltzman wanted Bond to be portrayed as a 'man of the people', stalking within the Establishment but distinguished from it iconographically in terms of physical appearance (Connery's plebeian ruggedness versus, say, the slender, aristocratic frailty of Niven) and voice (the attraction of Connery's Scottish burr, mid-Atlantic rather than specifically English in its associations). They also wanted the part to be played laconically, but with an underlying aggressiveness, rather than with the pointed cool of the aristocratic hero. Connery seemed to fit the bill. As Broccoli put it: 'He looked like he had balls.'[10]

The point of this is not to measure the difference between Fleming's Bond and his screen portrayal by Connery but concerns the effects of the latter on the way the novels have been read. To account for these, it is necessary to dispute the assumption that Fleming's novels have ever been available to be read in a way that has not been profoundly affected by the reader's specific preorientation to the novels produced by his or her insertion in the orders of inter-textuality which, in different ways for different groups of readers in different circumstances, hover between text and reader, connecting the two within specific horizons of intelligibility. The process of reading is not one in which reader and text meet as abstractions but one in which the inter-textually organised reader meets the inter-textually organised text. The exchange is never a pure one between two unsullied entities, existing separately from one another, but is rather 'muddied' by the cultural debris which attach to both texts and readers in the determinate conditions which regulate the specific forms of their encounter.

Snelling's mind's eye image of Bond, for example, cannot be construed as an 'original' or 'true' response in relation to which the subsequent portrayal of Bond by Connery can be found wanting. Rather, it is an identification produced by the preorientation of a male reader, of a particular age and culture, as a result of his biographically specific (but not untypical) insertion within the sphere of inter-textual relationships. American male readers may – indeed, certainly did – construe the figure of Bond differently as a consequence of seeing him through the prism of hard-boiled detective fiction. Moreover, women readers, as Kingsley Amis has noted, are likely to have filled out Bond's character differently again in view of the greater likelihood of their having a prior acquaintance with romance fiction. We shall explore this claim more fully in a later chapter. Suffice it to note here that, viewed in this perspective, Amis argues that Bond can be construed as a latter-day Byronic hero, 'lonely, melancholy, of fine natural physique which has become in some way ravaged, of similarly fine but ravaged countenance, dark and brooding in expression, of a cold or cynical veneer, above all *enigmatic*, in possession of a sinister secret'.[11]

Whatever, the nature of the reader's earlier, pre-film image of Bond, the screen incarnation of Bond as Connery/Bond is likely to have overridden it *even as evoked in reading the novels themselves*. We have Fleming's word for it that this was true even for him. 'Not quite the idea I had of Bond,' he said of Connery, 'but he would be if I wrote the books over again.'[12] In these and other ways, the films have culturally activated the novels in ways that cannot be undone so as to yield an unfettered access to those texts. The Bond novels now reach us as already humming with the meanings established by the films and, as a consequence, have been hooked into orders of inter-textuality to which, initially, they were not connected.

Again, an analogy may help to make this point clearer. Wolfgang Iser has argued that the filmed version of *Tom Jones* exhibits a greater degree of determinacy than the novel. 'When we imagine Tom Jones, during our reading of the novel,' he writes, 'we have to put together various facets that have been revealed to us at different times – in contrast to the film where we always see him as a whole in every situation.'[13] Without commenting on the general differences between written and film texts which this argument presupposes, it is clear that, for the modern reader, the character of Tom Jones in the novel is always-already filled out by Albert Finney. Moreover, in one way or another, this has always been true: the character of Tom Jones has always been encountered as, to a degree, always-already filled out by the inter-textual associations which inform the reader's practice.

This is not to suggest that the Bond films should be regarded as being privileged in anything other than a relative

sense. For these, too, reach us as already culturally activated –
by the publicity mechanisms through which they are
promoted, for example. Interviews with Connery and Moore
have proved particularly influential in this respect. While
texts of this type have come last, chronologically speaking, in
relation to the other 'texts of Bond', their role, viewed from
another perspective, has been of a primary significance. They
have functioned, in effect, as 'textual shifters', selectively
organising and reorganising the frameworks of ideological
and cultural reference within which both the films and novels
might be read.

Connery's famous *Playboy* interview affords an appropriate
illustration in its construction of Bond/Connery as a composite
figure, a unified subject, to whom there is ascribed a
uniform set of values. And this in spite of the fact that
Connery seeks to reject the equation between himself and
Bond which the interview constructs: 'Let me straighten you
out on this. The problem with interviews of this sort is to get
across the fact, without breaking your arse, that one is *not*
Bond, that one was functioning reasonably well *before* Bond,
and that one is going to function reasonably well *after* Bond.'[14]

However, this is a mere interruption, a refusal of the
invitation to merge the two identities which, in the rest of the
interview, Connery (or is it Bond speaking?) implicitly
accepts. When asked which of Bond's characteristics he most
admires, Connery replies: 'His self-containment, his powers
of decision, his ability to carry on through till the end and to
survive. There's so much social welfare today that people
have forgotten what it is to make their own decisions rather
than leave them to others. So Bond is a welcome change.'[15]

That's Connery speaking about Bond and his 'world of
values'. Here he is speaking about his own values: 'If there is
a malnutrition of any kind in this country – and I think there
is – it's self-inflicted. The only competition you'll find today
is the conflict between those few who try to correct a wrong,
and the majority who hope it will just cure itself in the end.'[16]

Bond/Connery, Connery/Bond: the two are indistinguishable, welded into a single figure which, in condensing
the theme of a self-reliant and competitive individualism,
yokes reading on to a definite set of ideological co-ordinates.

Finally, such subsequent additions to the 'texts of Bond' have reacted back on the 'original' ones in the sense of modifying their very material form. Initially, the covers for the paperback editions of the Bond novels bore a close relation to those of the hardback editions – a collection of objects associated with espionage and, in the case of *Moonraker* for example, the understated luxury and elegance of London's clubland world (see Figure 3). After a brief period in which the paperbacks featured Connery/Bond on their covers, the entire design concept of the covers was radically modified. In depicting one or more exotically but scantily clad women placed astride a large golden gun, the covers of this period clearly cue, as the central concern of the novels, the subordination of women to the regime of the phallus (see Figures 1 and 2). In thereby culturally activating the novels in a specific way, such covers relocated the novels within the new set of ideological co-ordinates established, in the Roger Moore films, by the shift in the centre of narrative interest away from the relations between Bond and the villain towards those between Bond and 'the girl'.

Texts and their readings

It is not possible to analyse a cultural phenomenon constituted in this way merely by studying the various 'texts of Bond' one by one and sequentially. To seek thus to stabilise them as objects of analysis would be to abstract them from the shifting orders of inter-textuality through which their actual functioning has been organised and reorganised. This would be to close off in advance the possibility of understanding the concrete history of their functioning in diverse social and ideological relations of reading. In order to do this, it is necessary to abandon the assumption that texts, in themselves, constitute the place where the business of culture is conducted, or that they can be construed as the sources of meanings or effects which can be deduced from an analysis of their formal properties. In place of this view, so powerfully implanted in our intellectual culture, we shall argue that texts constitute sites around which the pre-eminently social affair of the struggle for the production of meaning is conducted, principally in the form of a series of bids and counter-bids to determine which system of inter-textual co-ordinates should be granted an effective social role in organising reading practices.

The key question to which these considerations point concerns the relations between texts and their readers and the means whereby these might be analysed. Ordinarily, approaches to this question fall within two broad categories. First, there are those approaches concerned to analyse the formal mechanisms by which a text produces a position or positions for reading, organising its own consumption in the implied, model or preferred reader – the terms vary, but the approach is essentially the same – it implicitly posits as a condition of its own intelligibility.[17] Attention here thus focuses on the intra-textual determinations of reading. Within the second approach, attention focuses on the extra-textual determinations of reading, particularly on the situationally determined frameworks of cultural and ideological reference which supply the grids of intelligibility through which different groups of readers read and interpret a given text. David Morley's study of the audience for *Nationwide* constitutes perhaps the most sophisticated application of this approach in its combination of both discursive and situational determinations.[18] Arguing that the ideological discourses which, in a particular context, mediate the relations between text and reader will influence the way a text is perceived and read, Morley gives such varying reading practice a social base in arguing that an individual's location within class, gender, ethnic and national relations will condition the mode of his/her access or exposure to the discourses which thus mediate his/her encounter with a text. The advantages of this approach are considerable in that it enables readings to be patterned into identifiable clusters whose distinguishing characteristics are explained by the operation of both cultural (discursive) and structural (social positionality) factors.

While work of considerable value has been done within both approaches, their inadequacies tend to complement one another inasmuch as both concur in accepting an essentially metaphysical view of texts. It is assumed, within the first

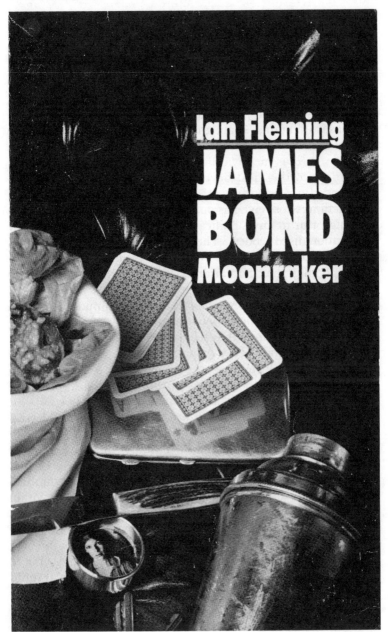

Figure 3

approach, that the intra-textual processes through which reading is organised can be specified independently of the extra-textual determinations which mould and configure the reading practices of empirically diverse groups of readers. This is to suppose that there is an immovable frame separating the intra-textual from the extra-textual.[19] Similarly, while the second approach allows for a variability of reader response, it retains intact the virtual identity of the text in the respect that, when all is said and done, such variations are conceived as merely different responses to 'the same text'. According to the most developed variant of this approach – the encoding/decoding model – the process of textual production is conceived as one in which 'messages' (seemingly existing prior to any signification) are translated into socially conventionalised codes. The text which results from this process is construed as the container of 'fixed codes' which, although they may be variantly decoded, remain unaffected by such different decoding practices.[20]

Moreover, both approaches rest on and support a definite ordering of the relations between the study of texts and the study of readings such that the former always comes first and the latter second. This usually results in a normative approach to the history of reading such that readings which do not conform to the dictates of the 'fixed codes' proposed by the analyst are regarded as selective distortions or miscomprehensions of what are claimed to be objective properties of 'the text itself'. Furthermore, this has the added consequence that, in practice, nothing different actually happens. The supposition that the text must be analysed first and readings afterwards happily means that the empirical history of the diverse patterns of reading produced within different social and ideological relations of reading need not be allowed to complicate or muddy the analytical exchange between analyst and text. Robert Holub has thus commented that Iser's concept of the implied reader makes it possible to analyse the role of the reader without having to take account of the practices of real or empirical readers, thereby foreclosing any analytical 'integration of historical information in anything but a superficial fashion'. Holub's conclusion is a sufficient warning against merely tacking the study of reading on to the already completed textual analysis: 'A historical perspective cannot be attached *ex post facto* in the guise of illustrative material or mere content for the empty structure of a repertoire; it must be integrated into the very conceptual apparatus of the system.'[21]

The failure to do this has meant that most approaches to the problem of reading have amounted to little more than a series of no doubt well intended but none the less, largely gestural nods in the direction of the reader – a question of doing the same old thing, analysing texts, and then saying generously that, of course, interpretations may vary, even to the point of entertaining the prospect of unlimited semiosis. Such open-mindedness does not in itself, however, afford the means whereby the range of meanings that have *actually* been produced in relation to a particular text might be accounted for. The empirical study of reading practices is notoriously difficult, and for eminently practical reasons, particularly when the study of past readings is concerned in that, at the best, the evidence relating to these is usually wholly indirect and, therefore, largely inconclusive. While relying mainly on evidence of this kind, and thus falling short of real flesh and blood readers, we are concerned, at various points in this study, to open up a theoretical space within which the empirical study of reading practices might be located and given a more productive direction than the 'show and tell' orientation which, for the greater part, has characterised this area of work in the past.

It is worth noting, in this respect, that most approaches to the study of reading assume that texts are able to exert an appreciable social and cultural influence only once a meaning has been imputed to them through the operation of a system of interpretation, be it implicit or explicitly formulated. While such concerns are important, the tendency to pose questions relating to the social effectivity of texts solely within the framework of such a hermeneutic model has proved unduly restrictive. Recent work concerned with the functioning of literary texts within educational institutions suggests that the part they play in forming human aptitudes and capacities is not reducible to an analysis of their received meanings. In other words, the position of the reader is not always and only

that of an interpreter. We return to these considerations in
Chapter 8. For the moment, however, we are primarily
concerned to establish the fields of ideological meaning within
which the reading of 'the texts of Bond' has been situated.

To do so, it will be necessary to take account of the
determinations which have organised the reading of the Bond
novels. (The same is true of the films, but in the interests of
clarity of exposition, we shall address these problems
primarily in relationship to the novels.) This entails that
these texts be conceived as having no existence prior to or
independently of the varying 'reading formations' in which
they have been constituted as objects-to-be read. By 'reading
formations' here, we have in mind not the generalised cultural
determinations of reading considered by David Morley, but
those specific determinations which bear in upon, mould and
configure the relations between texts and readers in
determinant conditions of reading. It refers, specifically, to
the inter-textual relations which prevail in a particular
context, thereby activating a given body of texts by ordering
the relations between them in a specific way such that their
reading is always-already cued in specific directions that are
not given by those 'texts themselves' as entities separable
from such relations.[22]

The text that is read, according to such a conception, is an
always-already culturally activated object just as, and for the
same reasons, the reader is an always-already culturally
activated subject. The encounter between them is always
culturally, ideologically and − which is to say the same
thing − inter-textually organised in such a way that their
separation as subject and object is called into question. The
reader is conceived not as a subject who stands outside the
text and interprets it any more than the text is regarded as
an object the reader encounters. Rather, text and reader are
conceived as being co-produced within a reading formation,
gridded on to one another in a determinate compact unity.
Of course, such a reading formation is not self-generating.
Rather, it is the product of definite social and ideological
relations of reading composed, in the main, of those
apparatuses − schools, the press, critical reviews, fanzines −
within and between which the socially dominant forms for

the superintendence of reading are both constructed and contested.[23] Neither texts nor readers, according these formulations, exist prior to or independently of the processes through which the struggle for textual meanings is socially enacted. This is not to suggest that texts have no determinate properties – such as a definite order of narrative progression – which may be analysed objectively. But it is to argue that such properties cannot, in themselves, validate certain received meanings above others; they do not provide a point of 'truth' in relation to which readings may be normatively and hierarchically ranked, or discounted. Nor are we suggesting that readers do not have determinate properties. They most certainly do, but complexly varying ones which, rather than being attributable to the reader as a subject independent of the text, are the product of the orders of inter-textuality which have marked the reader's formation.

It will be useful, in order to lend some substance to these arguments, to consider the problems associated with the analytical strategies most commonly used in attempts to stabilise texts as objects of study 'in themselves'. There are, in the main, four such devices. First, as we have seen from Foucault's comments, the figure of the author may be invoked to provide a stabilising context which may serve as a warrant for particular readings. The key difficulty here is that the figure of the author is clearly a malleable construct which may be discursively related to the same set of texts in different ways within different regions of textual distribution. As itself a variable, the figure of the author thus cannot furnish the fixed point of support which such analysis requires. An examination of the functioning of the figure of Fleming in this respect reveals, as we shall see, not one, nor two but several Flemings, related to the Bond novels in different ways and with different effects.

Secondly, analysis may focus on the originating moment of a text's existence or, as in many Marxist formulations, on the conditions of its production, seeking, in these, a point of anchorage in relation to which a given reading may be fastened down as, in some way, the true or original meaning of the text concerned. Analysis of the way in which a text functioned and was received in the historical relations of its

time is thus claimed to reveal its 'original' and therefore
'true' meaning. An instance of this approach is provided by
Umberto Eco's analysis of Eugene Sue's *Les Mystères de Paris*.
Relying on the 'cultivated' codes that were supposedly
shared by the author and his contemporary critics to
establish the 'fixed codes' of Sue's novel, Eco interprets
popular readings of the same period as a series of distortions
and incomprehensions which abstracted only 'the most
obvious meanings' from the 'total message'.[24]

A number of problems coalesce here. First, there are no
good reasons for privileging the originating exchange between
an author and his contemporary critics, even if these did
constitute the author's intended public, as a means of
establishing the 'fixed codes' of a text. Indeed, in the case of
popular texts, there are good reasons for not doing so since
the reactions of critics may have precious little bearing on
the cultural business that is transacted around, through and
by means of such texts in the socially predominant forms of
their distribution and circulation. To conceive the readings
produced within these as a lack or distortion in relation to
the readings of the 'cultivated' public is merely to connive in
the process whereby the cultural values which animate the
reading practices of dominant social groups are habitually
reified in being presented as the properties of 'texts
themselves'. The second problem consists in Eco's assumption
that there is, in the lives of texts, an originating exchange or
founding moment – the 'moment of emission' – which can be
fixed as singular. This may or may not be the case. It usually
is only when there is a clearly bounded context – most often
a performance of some kind – which defines a text's initial
conditions of existence: the staging of Racine's tragedies at
the court of Louis XIV, for example. However, it is rarely
the case with texts which are produced, initially, in multiple
form and circulated via the mechanisms of the market. And
it is least of all the case with texts which come to be classified
as popular since, from the very beginning of their lives, these
may circulate in different forms for both the 'cultivated' and
'mass' publics and thus be ushered forth, simultaneously,
into different social and ideological relations of reading. The
social destinies of texts are thus often pluri-dimensional

rather than singular from the very first moment of their publication, and not just subsequently. In such cases, there is no unique, founding set of text–reader relations which can serve as an anlytical device with which to decipher the 'fixed code' of a text.

We need merely mention that 1100 prints of *Goldfinger* were distributed during the first two weeks of the film's release for the force of this point to be felt. Where, given such a system of distribution, would it be possible to locate a sender–receiver exchange or a text–reader relationship which might be constituted as a privileged point of origin? The première showing of the film in New York? Or its première in London? Or its first showings in Paris, Berlin or Tokyo or, for that matter, Wanganui? Clearly, the construct of an originating moment of emission is impossible to sustain. Likewise, it would be both misleading and singularly inconsequential, in studying the Bond novels, to privilege the exchange between Fleming and his contemporary 'cultivated' public and to conceive other readings as a distortion or misrepresentation of the 'fixed codes' through which that exchange was regulated. As we have seen, there *was* such a moment in the history of the Bond novels, a moment marked by the critical production of a culturally knowing reader. However, little would be served by basing our discussion of the novels on this moment when, quite clearly, they have had their most significant impact within social and ideological relations of reading of a different kind.

Thirdly, as in E. Hirsch Junior's work, a particular genre may be invoked to provide criteria of relevance which can be used to limit the range of valid interpretations.[25] The problem here, quite simply, is that genre frameworks prove relatively indeterminate and thus cannot fulfil the stabilising function assigned to them. Finally, an attempt may be made to construct a particular figure of the reader as a means of determining the 'fixed codes' of a text. The practical consequence of this, however, is that it proves impossible to analyse the reading practices of empirically diverse groups of readers to the degree that the role of the reader turns out to be always-already occupied by an abstract and ideal figure of the reader of the analyst's own construction.

Although different in other respects, all these procedures produce, as their object, 'the text itself' only by arbitrarily privileging one set of text–reader relations above others, sometimes contending ones. The consequence of this is to establish a hierarchical ordering of the relations between different reading practices such that some are conceived as more valid – and therefore more worthwhile, more objective, more deserving of analysis – than others, which are thereby ignored, written off as marginal, aberrant, quixotic or whatever. The devices used to stabilise texts as objects of analysis 'in themselves' thereby have the effect of disabling analysis of the ways in which their functioning within history is incessantly modified.

Fortunately, we may pursue these problems in greater detail and, at the same time, commence our discussion of the Bond novels since, in his classic study of these, Umberto Eco uses a number of the devices we have enumerated in order to determine their 'fixed codes'.[26] (Page references in brackets throughout the rest of the chapter are to this work.) Eco approaches the Bond novels as instances of what he calls 'closed texts'; that is, texts which 'apparently aim at pulling the reader along a pre-determined path', which seem 'to be structured according to an inflexible project' (p. 8). In so far as they have been designed for the 'average reader' and are thus 'potentially speaking to everyone', Eco argues, such texts 'can give rise to the most unforeseeable interpretations, at least at the ideological level' (p. 8). They are 'in the last analysis randomly open to every pragmatic accident' (p. 7). Although internally closed, such a text is randomly opened up from without by the contingent irruptions of history.

This would seem fine. Everything is allowed for. As Eco concludes his essay:

> Since the decoding of a message cannot be established by its author, but depends on the concrete circumstances of its reception, it is difficult to guess what Fleming is or will be for his readers. When an act of communication provokes a response in public opinion, the definitive verification will take place not within the ambit of the book but in that of the society that reads it (p. 172).

The difficulty is that 'the society that reads it' is left with little option but to deviate marginally from the position of the 'average reader', a category which, in Eco's use, limits all possibilities in advance of their actually been taken.

Plotted pleasures and the pleasures of culture and knowledge

The Bond novels, Eco argues, exhibit an invariant plot structure consisting of a series of moves through which the relationships between the principal characters are developed. Likening this plot structure to a 'narrating machine' which narrates 'not the Unknown, but the Already Known', Eco contends that the 'average reader' derives pleasure 'simply from following the minimal variations by which the victor (i.e. Bond) realizes his objective' (p. 160). There are, however, additional pleasures available to the 'sophisticated reader' who is privy to the system of literary and cultural allusions which are at work (or can be read into) the novels: 'Fleming also pleases the sophisticated readers who here distinguish, with a feeling of aesthetic pleasure, the purity of the primitive epic mischievously translated into cultural terms and who applaud in Fleming the cultured man, whom they recognize as one of themselves, naturally the most clever and broadminded' (p. 163).

Here, the text–reader encounter is conceived as one between a culturally operated text and a culturally operated reader. We are dealing with pleasures produced within the system of cultural references which animates the reader's practice. The pleasures of the 'average reader', by contrast, are conceived as purely 'plotted pleasures', the direct and unmediated effects of the plot mechanisms attributed to the novels. No space is allowed for the effects of what might be *different* systems of cultural reference operative within the exchange between text and reader in the sphere of demotic readings.

Exclusion of such considerations follows necessarily from the steps Eco takes to constitute, as the object of his analysis, the plot structure of the novels and its effects on the 'average reader'. First, however, a note on terminology, since our own departs somewhat from that proposed by Eco.[27] We propose to use the concepts of *plot*, *story* and *narrative* as follows:

1. *Plot* will refer to the regular and repeatable elements which recur across the Bond novels; to the types of events, characters and situations, the 'story-stuff', from which the story is made.
2. *Story* will refer to the way in which, in a particular novel, such elements are organised into a temporally and causally coherent sequence. Similar plot elements may thus be ordered into different stories depending on the way they are combined and logically developed.
3. *Narrative* will refer to the way plot and story are formally manipulated by the use of specific narrative (or 'ways of telling') devices. Thus, the 'same story' may be told differently according to whether narrative and real time are coincident or whether flashback techniques are used, whether the narrator is present or absent and so on.

Eco's purpose is to look below variations in story and narrative to detect a set of underlying rules governing the organisation of plot elements in the Bond novels. Just as Vladimir Propp argued that 'all fairytales are of one type in regard to their structure',[28] so Eco argues that, at the level of plot, the Bond novels are structurally uniform. Indeed, he further contends that the 'Bond formula' is merely a variant of the archetypal structure of the traditional fairytale. According to Propp, the basic plot elements of the fairytale consists in the functions performed by its central protagonists – the hero, the villain, the princess – in developing the course of action within the story. Likewise, Eco argues that the main characters in the Bond novels are motivated by the functions assigned to them, functions which he likens to a series of moves required by the rules of a game. He identifies nine such moves, present in all the novels but not necessarily in the same sequence:

A. M gives a task to Bond.
B. The villain appears to Bond (perhaps in vicarious form).

C. Bond gives a first check to the villain, or the villain gives a first check to Bond.
D. 'The girl' shows herself to Bond.
E. Bond possesses 'the girl' or begins her seduction.
F. The villain captures Bond and, either simultaneously or at different moments, 'the girl'.
G. The villain tortures Bond and, sometimes, 'the girl'.
H. Bond beats the villain, killing him or his representatives, or helping at their killing.
I. Bond, convalescing, possesses 'the girl', whom he then loses; she either leaves him or is killed by the villain.

Dr No provides a convenient illustration of these moves. The novel opens with a move on the part of the villain in the form of the destruction of the Caribbean station of the British Secret Service and the murder of its principal officer, Strangways, and his assistant, Mary Trueblood (move B). M then assigns Bond his mission: to investigate the mystery of Strangways's disappearance (move A). This results in a series of moves and countermoves between Bond and the villain in which the latter is represented vicariously – by the Chinese girl who photographs Bond, first at Kingston Airport and, later, at a nightclub; by the unknown assassin who places a poisonous centipede in Bond's bed (move B). It is through his response to these moves, by confiscating the film of the photographer and by surviving the assassination attempt, that Bond gives a first check to the villain by thwarting his plans (move C). Move D occurs on Bond's first morning on Crab Key when Honeychile Rider makes her appearance on the beach. The next move is taken by the villain, again in vicarious form, as Dr No's henchmen machine-gun the beach, destroying Honeychile's canoe (move B). This results in Bond assuming responsibility for Honeychile, offering her protection from Dr No as they seek to escape from their pursuers, this initial move resulting in a series of moves and countermoves between Bond and Honeychile which function as a prelude to Bond's possession of Honeychile, deferred until the end of the novel. Both Bond and Honeychile are then captured and taken to Dr No's headquarters (move F). Their capture is followed by a second series of moves and countermoves between Bond and Honeychile as, ensconced in the 'mink-lined prison' of the luxurious quarters provided them, they await their meeting with Dr No. Move B then recurs in the direct encounter between Bond and Dr No, followed by move G as both Bond and Honeychile are subjected to trial by torture. Bond, having triumphed over the obstacle course of pain constructed for him by Dr No, averts the villain's conspiracy – to interfere with the guidance systems of Western nuclear missiles – and kills Dr No (move H). The novel closes with Bond's possession of Honeychile (move E), whom he is destined to lose (move I), although this takes place outside the confines of the novel – we learn, in *The Man with the Golden Gun*, that she subsequently marries and has two children.

Eco combines this plot analysis with a Lévi-Straussian analysis of a series of binary oppositions which governs the relations between the principal characters and provides the structural co-ordinates for the system of ideological meanings at work in the novels. These binary oppositions take the form of a series of opposing values which are superimposed or 'gridded' on the relations between the various characters: Free World/Soviet Union; Great Britain/non-Anglo-Saxon countries; duty/sacrifice; cupidity/ideals; love/death; chance/planning; luxury/discomfort; excess/moderation; perversion/innocence; loyalty/disloyalty. Eco's primary interest centres on the way these opposing values are organised around the relations between Bond and the villain. Bond represents all those values which are positively ranked. He stands for Great Britain and the Free World, places the service of ideals above self-interest (cupidity), is sexually 'normal' (i.e. innocent), embodies the virtues of loyalty and duty, relies upon chance and improvisation in his contest with the villain, is willing to subordinate his taste for luxury to discomfort when his mission demands it, and so forth. Not only is the villain, at least in the novels up to and including *Goldfinger*, in the service of the Soviet Union; the geographical and racial distribution of villainy is also such that the villain is always a member of a non-Anglo-Saxon race. He (or she) may be Russian (Rosa Kleb in *From Russia, With Love*), German (Hugo Drax in *Moonraker*), of Jewish ancestry (Le

Chiffre in *Casino Royale*), Chinese–German (Dr No) or Slav (Blofeld). The villain, furthermore, typically accumulates within himself all those values which are negatively ranked. He is sexually perverse (i.e., is impotent, neuter or homosexual), places self-interest above all ideals, does not recognise any claims of duty or loyalty, carries a taste for luxury to excess, relies unduly on bureaucratic planning at the expense of personal initiative and improvisation and, of course, embodies the principle of death, usually in the form of a conspiracy directed against the peace and security of the Western world.

These contrasting qualities are also subject to a distinctive ideological organisation in that all the positive values, through their association with Bond, are thereby also associated with England and, more generally, the West whilst all the negative values, through their association with the villain, are thereby connected with the Soviet Union and/or non-Anglo-Saxon races. The contest between Bond and the villain is thus always more than that. It is also a contest between the Free World and the Soviet Union, between Anglo-Saxon and non-Anglo-Saxon racial characteristics and the contrasting qualities – chance versus planning, loyalty versus disloyalty – which are connected, through Bond and the villain, to these political/national/racial oppositions. The consequence is that, as the contest between Bond and the villain is worked through and resolved, a series of collateral ideological contests is also worked through and resolved as all the positive values, articulated to the Free World/Anglo-Saxon axis of signification, triumph over the negative values articulated to the Soviet Union/non-Anglo-Saxon axis of signification. It is by thus working a set of contemporary ideological references into the system of elementary oppositions governing the structure of the fairytale, Eco argues, that the Bond novels achieve their considerable ideological potency.

Eco interprets the Bond–M pair as a dominated–dominant relationship. M assigns Bond his task and, thereby, sets events moving. M also represents knowledge in relation to Bond's (relative) ignorance. He 'has a global view of events, hence his superiority over the "hero" who depends on him and who sets out on his various missions in conditions of inferiority to the omniscient chief' (p. 147). Finally, M represents those values which most forcefully articulate an ideology of Englishness: the values of duty, country, method and measure. Whilst Bond also represents the first two of these, his exceptional abilities and his reliance on improvisation distinguish him from the dependency on methodicalness which characterises both M and the villain. This distinction is accentuated by the love–hate ambivalence which governs the relationship between Bond and M.

Finally, Eco construes 'the girl' as a (potential) mediator between Bond and the villain. Initially in the service of the villain, and thus on the 'wrong' side in the contest between good and evil, 'the girl' is also, again initially, the subject of a 'deviant' or 'dislocated' sexuality. In winning 'the girl' from the service of the villain and, in the process, into his own bed, Bond 'repositions' her both sexually and ideologically. In embodying values which are otherwise split between Bond and the villain – she embodies both perversion and innocence, both loyalty and disloyalty, both luxury and discomfort – 'the girl' also personifies the possibility of mediation between values which are otherwise construed as polar opposites. To the degree that her death, real or symbolic, constitutes her return to the domination of the negative (the villain, as the representative of death), her mediation remains putative, always cancelled out at the end of each novel so that the system of opposing values organised around Bond and the villain remains in operation – for the next novel – as a set of unmediated contraries.

Such, then, are the plot elements of the Bond novels. It is, according to Eco, the foregone nature of their conclusion that explains the particular nature of the pleasure the Bond novels afford the 'average reader'. He likens the position of such a reader to that of a football spectator who knows not only the rules of the game but also, and in advance of the start of play, the outcome of the particular match concerned. Narrative mechanisms enter into Eco's analysis only through the role accorded them in discriminating between the pleasures of the 'average' and the 'sophisticated' reader. This entails viewing such narrative mechanisms as 'signifying frills', inessential aspects of the novels' organisation which pass unnoticed by the 'average reader'. Indeed, it is through the detection of such 'signifying frills' that the 'sophisticated reader' is distinguished, interpellated as a subject of culture and knowledge. The Bond novels thus become, for such a reader, a medium for the exchange of cultural values between author and reader. For Eco, however, the values exchanged are counterfeit, a stock of second-hand, well-worn and distinctly down-market cultural clichés.

In his comments on Fleming's literary techniques, Eco thus argues that Fleming writes with a cunning artifice which simulates literature by combining a series of experimental literary techniques. He focuses particularly on the way Fleming paces the development of the action within the novels, alternately speeding up and slowing down the narrative, dwelling languorously on detailed descriptions of objects and events which are 'apparently inessential to the course of the story' whilst hastening through the key plot moves with a 'feverish brevity' (p. 165). This 'technique of the aimless glance' is produced by superimposing on the 'narrative machine' designed for the masses a clever montage of literary styles; the terrors of the Gothic novel combined with the apparently purposeless description of objects which characterises the *nouveau roman*, for example. Such technical virtuosity may provoke 'the thrill of poetic emotion' (p. 172) in the 'sophisticated reader'. Such a reader, however, is deluded. The 'sophisticated reader' feels himself 'a malicious accomplice of the author, only to become a victim, for he is led on to detect stylistic inventions where there is, on the contrary . . . a clever montage of *déjà vu*' (p. 163).

The unwary reader may also derive an extra 'thrill of poetic emotion' by reading into the Bond novels a series of references to earlier literary sources. It is possible, Eco allows, to do so almost without limit. 'Fleming is,' he argues, 'more literate than he gives one to understand' (p. 169). If one looks hard enough, it is possible to see in the Bond novels echoes of Goethe's *Faust* (the opening chapter of *From Russia, With Love*), of Baudelaire (in the exploitation of the erotic potentialities of torture), and so on. Again, however, the reader whose 'extra appreciation' is produced by recognising these allusions is merely a dupe, taken in by 'a tongue-in-cheek bricolage' which 'hides its ready-made nature by presenting itself as literary invention' (p. 172).

Questions of genre and inter-textuality

Eco's strengths and weaknesses are, ultimately, those of his mentors: Propp and Lévi-Strauss. The product of the hey-day of structuralism, the considerable rigour of his approach results, in the end, in an abstract schematisation of the novels which does not adequately encompass the full complexity of either their internal relations or their connections with the cultural and historical processes of which they have formed a part. For all that, it still stands as a landmark in the history of Bond criticism. Whatever its shortcomings, Eco's account of the pleasures of the 'sophisticated reader' counts as one of the few attempts to illustrate the ways in which the reading of popular fiction may be culturally stratified. In thus pointing to the way in which relations of cultural superiority/inferiority may be organised in relation to popular fiction, rather than solely in the form of a distinction between 'literature' and popular fiction, he opened up an area of inquiry which has not subsequently received the attention it deserves.

Our interest here centres on the principles governing the way Eco constitutes the Bond novels as objects of analysis. Our criticisms might be summarised by saying that, whereas in his approach to the pleasures of the 'average reader' Eco takes into account less than the text, his analysis of the 'sophisticated reader' encompasses more than the text. The 'average reader', as we have seen, is represented as encountering the plot mechanics of the Bond novels as if these could be abstracted from the processing of reading produced by their narrative organisation. The encounter between the Bond novels and the 'sophisticated reader', on the other hand, is conceived as taking place within the frameworks of inter-textual, ideological and cultural reference which determine the latter's formation as a reading subject. The pleasures of culture and knowledge are produced not by the reader's direct encounter with 'the Bond novels themselves', but in the context of a culturally mediated relationship to those novels produced by the systems of cultural reference which animate the reader's practice. His approach to the 'average reader', however, assumes that it is possible to identify the basis of his/her pleasure without any reference to the frameworks of inter-textual reference which animate his/her reading practice. These, as it were, come after; cultural variables which may be erected on top of the basic pleasures afforded by the novels' plot mechanics but which cannot efface or reorganise those pleasures. It is in this sense, as we argued earlier, that the 'role of the reader' can never be adequately theorised because it is always-already occupied by the 'average reader'. This reader is, in effect, a construct, and one which Eco is obliged to posit in order to sustain his own analysis of the Bond novels. It supplies the anchorage point in relation to which their 'fixed codes' are tied down. Teresa de Lauretis has commented usefully on this aspect of Eco's work. Arguing that the reader Eco posits is one who 'co-operates with the text's own construction of meaning, its "generative structure" ', she contends that this reader

is presented as a *locus* of logical moves, impervious to the heterogeneity of historical process, to difference or contradiction. For the Reader is already contemplated by the text, is in fact an element of its interpretation. Like the Author, the Reader is a textual strategy, a set of specific competencies and felicitous conditions established by the text, which must be met if the text is to be 'fully actualized' in its potential content. Such a theory of textuality, in short, at one and the same time invokes a reader who is already 'competent', a subject fully constituted prior to the text and to reading, *and* poses the reader as the term of the text's production of certain meanings, as an effect of its structure.[29]

In brief, Eco's concept of the 'average reader' is both an effect of and guarantees the text's closure. It is the model of the reader required by an abstract structuralism which must foreclose the text against history in order to conceive its

object: the text's invariant structure. This is disguised by
Eco's illegitimate equation of 'the average reader' (an effect
of the text's structure) with the mass audience (seemingly a
particular group of readers). The problems this poses become
clear if one attempts to interpret the 'average reader' as
anything other than an effect of the text's structure, for it
soon becomes evident that there is no such creature.

Eco's equation of the 'average reader' with the mass
audience, for example, reflects the *a priori* assumption that
the 'horizontal' stratification of reading produced by the
uneven distribution of cultural capital has a prior and greater
social and cultural weight than those 'vertical' divisions
produced by the operation of such factors as race, gender,
nation and region. It would be equally plausible to argue
that gender divisions produce a clustering and patterning of
reading practices which both cut across and are socially and
culturally more consequential than those produced by the
sophisticated/average reader distinction. A more telling
problem is that, in order to maintain his construction of the
'average reader', Eco is obliged to disallow any role to the
systems of cultural reference which may organise popular
readings, differentiating them from one another as well as
from 'sophisticated reading'. While placing considerable
emphasis on the 'literary' references which may be read into
the Bond novels, Eco neglects entirely those cultural
references – implicit or explicit – which have a more
distinctively popular association. Indeed, he not only neglects
these but, where he does notice them, denies them any
relevance. Having posited a connection between the episode
in *You Only Live Twice* in which Bond escapes Blofeld's castle
by clinging to a balloon and the exploits of a Chinese
revolutionary poet, Eco makes the following observation: 'It
is true that Bond hung onto the balloon remembering having
seen Douglas Fairbanks do so, but Fleming is undoubtedly
more cultured than his character is' (p. 169).

This use of the figure of Fleming the author to disallow
such an explicit popular cultural reference in favour of a
more obtuse and esoteric connection which, so far as we have
been able to ascertain, only Eco has 'noticed', is, of course,
illegitimate. Moreover, the Bond novels positively bristle

with such references. In *On Her Majesty's Secret Service*, for example, Bond likens his situation at Piz Gloria to that of 'one of those comic film stars who get snarled up in a girls' school. You know. Sort of Saint Trinians' (p. 90). (All page references to the Bond novels are to the Pan paperback editions.) Similarly, in the same novel, Fleming reactivates the reader's memory of the film of *Dr No* in having Ursula Andress visit Blofeld's mountain-top health clinic. In *You Only Live Twice*, David Niven makes an appearance as the only actor to befriend Kissy Suzuki during her stay in Hollywood. In *From Russia, With Love*, Tatiana Romanova models her self-image on Greta Garbo whilst, in the same novel, an entire narrative sequence – the assassination of Krilencu – is orchestrated around an advertising hoarding dominated by the image of Marilyn Monroe.

In short, there are cultural references at work in the Bond novels other than those which Eco detects, references which equally imply and produce a 'culturally knowing' reader who thus, albeit 'down-market', also experiences the 'pleasures of culture and knowledge'. Nor is this merely conjecture on our part. It is clear from the publications of the various James Bond fan clubs that the energies of a good many readers have been invested precisely in tracking down such references as we have described. The contradictions within Eco's approach to these questions is the product of a simple, but near universal, oversight. He construes sophisticated reading as being subject to a distinctive form of social and cultural organisation because he is familiar with the determinations which organise it. Lacking such familiarity with the determinations which mould and configure popular reading, such reading is conceived as being socially and culturally unorganised. The differences between two different systems for the organisation of reading are thus conceived according to the logic of presence/absence; popular reading is conceived as a mere lack, characterised by the absence of the determinations which mould sophisticated reading.

At the same time, Eco assumes that popular reading is organised within particular inter-textual co-ordinates in analysing the Bond novels in terms of their similarity to/differences from the hard-boiled detective novel as represented by Mickey Spillane. His general argument is that the Bond novels develop the 'narrating machine' which characterises this genre one step further. Arguing that there is 'no basic variation' in the plot of the detective novel, 'but rather a repetition of a habitual scheme' (p. 160), Eco concedes that, within this habitual scheme, unexpected events – particularly the revelation of the identity of the criminal – may occur. In the Bond novels, by contrast, the invariant scheme of the plot 'even dominates the very chain of events' in the respect that 'the identity of the culprit, his characteristics, and his plans are always apparent from the very beginning' (p. 160).

A number of problems coalesce here. The assumption that the reader is located in a position of knowledge concerning the identity and conspiracy of the villain is certainly questionable. While true of *From Russia, With Love*, this is hardly the typical pattern. The reader is more usually moved from a position of ignorance to one of revealed knowedge as the nature of the villain's conspiracy, initially withheld in being represented in the form of an enigma – the inexplicable disappearance of large amounts of gold in *Goldfinger*, for example – is progressively unfolded. Perhaps more to the point, the construction and resolution of such problems of knowledge play a largely incidental role in the Bond novels. Whereas, in the detective story, the resolution of the enigma which founds and motivates the narrative usually constitutes the end of the story, the revelation of the identity of the villain and of the nature of his conspiracy in the Bond novels serves merely as a prelude to and as a means of establishing the main source of narrative tension in the Bond novels. These revolve around questions of action. Will Bond defeat the villain and avert his conspiracy? Will he conquer the girl? This would suggest, to use the terms posited by J. G. Cawelti, that the Bond novels are more readily classifiable as adventure stories, where interest centres on the character of the hero and the obstacles he has to overcome in fulfilling his quest, than as instances of the detective story where interest centres on the problems of knowledge the hero has to resolve.[30]

This is not to suggest that Eco is imply mistaken in the genre comparisons he makes. To do so would be to concur with Eco in assuming that a genre can be defined as a body of conventions which recur, with minimal variations, across a specifiable range of texts. Recent work on genre has called this view into question. Stephen Neale has thus argued that 'genres cannot, in fact, be systematically characterised and differentiated one from another' on the basis of abstracted formal properties as if such properties 'constituted specific generic essences'.[31] Rather, he argues, genres can more usefully be viewed as sets of expectations through which the possibilities of reading are organised. Such expectations, he contends, are neither lodged within nor produced by the properties of individual texts or even groups of texts viewed in isolation. Rather, he suggests, texts are drawn into genre relationships only through the frameworks of inter-textual reference which animate readers' practices. To the degree that such frameworks are culturally specific, the same text may, in different social and ideological relations of reading, be drawn into association with different genres. The determination as to which genre rules will be operative in organising the possibilities of reading is thus, in the last instance, cultural and variable rather than textual and fixed.

It is thus not so much a question of disputing the genre classification Eco proposes as of recognising its cultural specificity. It may make perfect sense within the Italian situation, and even more so in America where the spy-thriller is not usually recognised as a distinct category. Whereas, in Britain, police procedurals, masculine adventure stories, classic and hard-boiled detective stories are usually shelved, along with spy-thrillers, as separated categories under the generic heading of 'thrillers', American bookshops more typically group what are classified as spy-thrillers in Britain under the headings of 'crime' or 'mystery'. American critics, too, tend to merge what would usually be regarded as distinct genres in Britain. Dennis Porter, for example, offers an expanded definition of detective fiction which includes the Bond novels:

'Detective novel' will therefore be employed here as a generic term for all novels whose principal action concerns the attempt by a specialist investigator to solve a crime

and to bring a criminal to justice, whether the crime
involved be a single murder or the endeavour to destroy a
civilization. Neither the type of crime committed nor the
type of legal or extralegal agent involved in pursuing the
criminal determines a given novel's relation to the formula.
It is the course of the action alone that does that.[32]

There is little doubt, then, that the hard-boiled detective
novel *did* provide the relevant genre framework against which
the Bond novels and, indeed, films were initially read/viewed
in the United States. When *Dr No* opened in New York, for
example, the review of the film in the *New York Times* opened
as follows: 'If you haven't yet made the acquaintance of Ian
Fleming's suave detective, James Bond, in the author's fertile
series of mystery thrillers akin to the yarns of Mickey
Spillane, here is your chance to correct that misfortune in
one quick and painless stroke.'[33]

While the novels of Spillane, Hammett and Chandler were,
of course, influential in Britain by the late 1950s, this
potential point of genre reference was eclipsed by the earlier,
distinctively British tradition of the 'imperialist spy-thriller'
which provided by far and away the most influential textual
backdrop against which the novels were initially read. This
tradition, which had its roots in the spy novels which
flourished in the 1890s and the period immediately prior to
the First World War, while of scarcely any consequence
outside Britain, was extremely important within it in
achieving, as Michael Denning has shown, a popularity
which cut across class divisions in a way that detective
fiction singularly failed to do.[34] It was and is, moreover,
perceived as distinct from detective fiction. Denning argues
that the development of the spy-thriller was clearly associated
with the reorganisation of British publishing and the system
of bookselling which characterised the late nineteenth century.
These developments, leading to the production of cheap,
single volume novels distributed by such chains as Boots and
W.H. Smith, created a working-class readership for the spy-
thriller. The classical detective story of the same period, by
contrast, was circulated via middle-class literary magazines

and journals, whereas the detective fiction of the inter-war period was distributed largely through the public library system and was consciously 'literary' in its ambitions, defining itself in opposition to the populist vulgarity of the spy-thriller.

The novels comprising the tradition of the 'imperialist spy-thriller' typically concerned the exploits of an English gentleman who, engaged in espionage work on an amateur basis, wards off a threat to Britain represented by a foreign villain – usually French or German, and always in some way connected with anarchism, socialism or communism. Le Queux's Duckworth Drew and Oppenheim's Hardcross Courage – 'Saxon to the backbone' – are perhaps the best known heroes within the earlier phases of this tradition.[35] Rather better known, perhaps, and belonging to a later period – the 1920s and 1930s – are Cyril McNeile's Bull-Dog Drummond stories and, as the 'literary' consummation of the whole tradition, John Buchan's Richard Hannay stories. Yet these are only the visible peaks of a vast but now largely subterranean tradition of popular reading – nowhere more powerfully operative, as E. S. Turner has shown, than in the boys' comics of the period – which continued to contribute to the reading formation of boys and male adolescents until well into the post-war period.[36]

There can be little doubt that this tradition provided the most influential grid of intelligibility through which the Bond novels were initially read, in Britain, by adult male readers of all classes. We have found no evidence which might suggest that British detective fiction provided a relevant point of textual comparison for any group of readers. However, the American detective novel may have provided an influential inter-textual backdrop for male working-class readers; as Ken Warpole has shown, the writings of Chandler, Hammett and Spillane were quite popular with working-class readers in the 1940s and 1950s, well before they acquired a cult value for the middle-class intelligentsia.[37] There are, moreover, a series of both overt and covert references to the tradition of the imperialist spy-thriller within the Bond novels. The most explicit of these is the taunt with which Red Grant warns Bond in *From Russia, With Love*: 'Careful, old man. No tricks. No Bulldog Drummond stuff will get you out of this one' (p. 190).

Other references to the tradition are rather more indirect. The boredom and lassitude to which Bond periodically succumbs in the 'dog days' between missions, for example, is a recurrent theme in the earlier tradition.[38] When first introducing his hero in *Bull-Dog Drummond*, McNeile portrays him as languishing in the inactivity forced on him by the end of the war. He finds 'peace incredibly tedious, and would welcome diversion'.[39] Similarly, Bond is introduced to the reader in *From Russia, With Love* as follows:

> The blueberry arms of the soft life had Bond round the neck and they were slowly strangling him. He was a man of war and when, for a long period, there was no war, his spirit went into decline. In his particular line of business, peace had reigned for nearly a year. And peace was killing him (p. 78).[40]

Our concern in pointing to these similarities is not with the question of influences, although we have it on Pearson's authority that Fleming read the novels of Buchan and McNeile whilst he was at preparatory school. Nor are we concerned with Fleming's intentions although, again, there are sufficient grounds for assuming that these references to the tradition of the imperialist spy-thriller were neither casual nor of a purely incidental significance. Eric Ambler has stated that his purpose in writing within the framework of the spy-thriller was both to intellectualise it and to turn it 'upside down and make the heroes left-wing and popular front figures'.[41] We know from Fleming's interviews that Ambler served as his most immediate point of reference as a writer, and his novels are sprinkled with references to Ambler's work. In *From Russia, With Love*, for example, Bond chooses Ambler's *The Mask of Dimitrios* to read on his flight to Istanbul. It would thus not be implausible to argue that Fleming's purpose was to write against Ambler, to place the spy-thriller 'right side up' again and, in the process, to modernise it; to create a hero who would stand as the antithesis to Ambler's left-wing, popular front heroes but who, whilst echoing to the tune of his predecessors, would also be distinguished from them by his more modern, more liberated outlook. The case for this view has been argued by David Cannadine who regards Fleming's portrayal of Bond as an attempt to counter the 'decline of England' by refurbishing the values of its élite, retaining the virtues bred on the playing fields of Eton while simultaneously reforming them, purging them of their association with archaic and outmoded styles of cultural leadership.

Whatever Fleming's intentions, our concern here is to establish that the tradition of the imperialist spy-thriller formed the most influential culturally active textual backdrop against which the Bond novels were initially read. This is not to say that this tradition has continued to perform this role or, indeed, that it ever did so unambiguously in the same way for all groups of readers. It is, as we have seen, more likely to have informed the reading of men than women. It is also likely that the precise way in which this framework of inter-textual reference animated reading practices varied with class and cultural determinations. The evidence of reviews from the late 1950s, for example, suggests that, for 'middle-brow' readers, its most immediate consequence was the production of yet another set of 'pleasures of culture and knowledge' in which the reader, by spotting the appropriate allusions, demonstrated his conoisseurship of the spy-thriller genre. The works of Nevil Shute may have provided a more 'literary' point of inter-textual comparison. These, as D. Lammers has argued, sought to modify imperialist virtues, disarticulating them from their earlier racist base in portraying foreign peoples as embodying the drive and loyalty of which empires are made at the same time as, in Britain, such qualities were being sapped by welfare socialism.[42] It would thus be possible to construe Fleming as writing alongside Shute, but in a more populist vein, constructing, in Bond, a still-loyal Briton, a representative of imperialist virtues who rearticulated them to their Anglo-Saxon racial base. Whatever the detailed and specific patterns of response, however, it is only in relation to the organisation of reading possibilities produced by this point of genre reference that it is possible to identify the specific ideological and cultural co-ordinates within which – in Britain – the Bond novels were initially read.

Given this, an analysis which accepted the point of genre comparison proposed by Eco would yield relatively little insight into the cultural and ideological business that has been conducted around and through the Bond novels in Britain. Equally, given that the imperialist spy-thriller has had scarcely any cultural purchase outside Britain, insistence on this as the uniquely valid framework of genre reference for the Bond novels would prove just as disabling. It would shed virtually no light on the ways in which the Bond novels have been read or been culturally active outside Britain. Rather, if the varying history of the signifying functioning and effects of the Bond novels is to be understood, one must accept the necessary interdeterminacy of their genre location. The consequence of doing so is to undermine Eco's contention that it is possible, first, to analyse the 'fixed codes' of the Bond novels and only then to consider the ways in which these have been variantly decoded. For there is no space in which such 'fixed codes' might be constituted which is not already organised by the operation of some framework of inter-textual reference.

Further consideration of the distinction we proposed at the beginning of this chapter between the concepts of *intertextuality* and *inter-textuality* may help to underline the significance of this point. The former concept refers to a set of signifying relations that is alleged to be manifest within a text, the product of the permutation of texts it deploys. The latter refers to the ways in which the relations between texts are socially organised within the objective disposition of a reading formation. This is not merely to reassert that the two concepts are different. It is also to argue that the latter overrides and overdetermines the former. *Intertextualities*, that is to say, are the product of specific, socially organised *inter-textualities*; it is the latter which, in providing the objective determinants of reading practices, provide the framework within which inter-textual references can be produced and operate.

Again, these are matters we return to. Meanwhile, it is worth noting that, if Eco's account of the pleasure of the 'average reader' labours under considerable difficulties, his approach to the 'sophisticated reader' is no less suspect. This is not to deny its pertinence. It's certainly not difficult to find examples of readings which multiply the network of 'literary' associations into which the Bond novels may be drawn. In his *Anatomy of the Spy Thriller*, Bruce Merry construes the spy-thriller as a modern analogue of the Homeric epic and posits a series of parallels between the characters in the Bond novels and the mythic protagonists of the *Illiad* (M and Nestor; Bond and Odysseus, for example) and their respective narrative functions. The production of such 'literary' reference points for the Bond novels, however, does not necessarily function in the way Eco suggests. In their intriguing article 'The Bond Game', David Ormerod and David Ward posit a series of correspondences between characters and events in the Bond novels and those of classical mythology.[43] Their purpose in doing so is clearly to parody, to puncture as pretentious any attempt to dignify the novels with any degree of superior literary or cultural value precisely by doing so to excess. The same is true of Kingsley Amis's *Colonel Sun*, self-consciously and playfully parodic in the range of 'literary' and cultural references it openly deploys.[44]

Furthermore, it could be argued that this was precisely Fleming's intention, thereby disqualifying Eco's account of the pleasures of the 'sophisticated reader' as a response to a cynically contrived literariness on Fleming's part. Bruce Merry convincingly argues that whilst 'espionage fiction trips over itself to play the game of culture', it does so only to debunk that game, to deflate the signs of culture and knowledge which the text displays precisely by foregrounding them as a 'paraded literariness'.[45] According to this view, Fleming's simulation of literature could be read as a subtle anti-literarising device, a parading of signs of value which simultaneously reveals itself as valueless and, more aggressively, calls into question their more general cultural currency by saying, in effect: 'Look anyone can do it.' Perhaps more to the point, whatever Fleming's intentions on the matter, there is no doubt that the figure of Fleming has been manipulated to precisely this end. Boris Tomashevskii, the Russian Formalist critic, argued that the biographical construction of any author is a 'literary fact' and that, accordingly, the literary historian must consider how a writer's 'biography operates in the reader's consciousness'.[46] It is important to add that such constructions may be plural and variable, particularly as between different regions of textual distribution. It is, as Eco suggests, true that attempts have been made to establish Fleming as a significant literary figure. In the socially preponderant form of their distribution, however, Fleming's views on the subject of writing have been used to produce precisely the opposite effects.

The key text here has been Fleming's essay, 'How to Write a Thriller'. Whilst, in this, Fleming confessed that it was possible to write 'thrillers designed to be read as Literature', he also disavowed any claim to be competing for 'the Shakespeare stakes' and deprecated any attempt to read the Bond novels for their cultural or intellectual significance by defining the aims and effects of his style in exclusively sensual terms:

> I write for warm-blooded heterosexuals in railway trains, aeroplanes and beds.

> The target of my books . . . lay somewhere between the solar plexus and, well, the upper thigh.

> . . . my contribution to the art of thriller writing has been to attempt the total stimulation of the reader all the way through, even to his taste buds.[47]

Unsurprisingly, perhaps, these remarks and their like have predominated in the constructions of Fleming which have prevailed in the popular press, fanzines, and so on. One of the more vivid illustrations of this is Frederick Sands's 'Simenon and Fleming discuss the Thriller Business' in which the figures of both Fleming and Simenon are manipulated so as to elevate the thriller above 'literature' as a consequence of its anti-literariness. Here is Fleming, allegedly quoted by Simenon purportedly recalling an earlier conversation with him:

> There is no top limit to writing well. I try to write neatly,

concisely, vividly, because I think that that's the way to write. I think that approach largely comes from my training as a fast-writing journalist under circumstances under which you damned well had to be neat, correct, concise and vivid. My journalistic training was far more valuable to me than all the English literature education I ever had.

I think that communicating enjoyment is a very good achievement even in the fairly modest seam of literature that comprises thriller writing.

I think a writer should try to get an accurate ear for the spoken word and not, so to speak, put on a top hat when he sits down at his typewriter. He mustn't make the mistake of thinking that literature has to be literary.[48]

The modesty Fleming expresses here can only be described as vaunting. In extolling the virtues of solid craftsmanship over those of a paraded literariness, he inverts the usual hierarchy of values between thriller writing and writing 'literature'. The 'culturally knowing' reader implied and produced by this exchange is not one who, as Eco has it, would be drawn into the game of reading the Bond novels as a means of validating his/her cultural capital but, to the contrary, one who would know better than to look – in the Bond novels, or anywhere else for that matter – for any values beyond the solid craftsmanship of a story well told.

The more general point, however, is that the figure of the author is a variable which may be constructed so as to support a variety of exchanges between 'author' and reader. Eco's analysis deals with the effects of only one of these author constructions. Outside the academy, the figure of Fleming has more typically functioned as merely one more site for the incarnation and expanded reproduction of the figure of Bond. Various fragments of Fleming's biography have assisted greatly in this. His coverage of the Moscow show trials for Reuters in 1933; his wartime service as deputy to the Director of Naval Intelligence; the assistance he is said to have rendered American Secretary of State Dulles in establishing the CIA – these associations with the real world of espionage have greatly facilitated the construction of Bond as a quasi-real person. Biographies and reminiscences of Fleming have thus, as it were, 'Bondianised' his life in order that the figure of Bond might thus, in being 'Flemingised', be constructed on a real-life support.[49]

Analysing the Bond phenomenon

Our purpose in this chapter has been to examine the conditions of existence of the Bond phenomenon and, in doing so, to identify some of the problems involved in its analysis. It is clear, from the foregoing, that there is no place – no cultural space – in which the individual 'texts of Bond' can be stabilised as objects to be investigated 'in themselves', except by abstracting them from the shifting relations of inter-textuality through which their consumption has been regulated. As an instance of the connections between texts and social processes, the Bond phenomenon makes it clear that such connections are not made once and for ever, for all time. To the contrary, the various 'texts of Bond' have been connected to, disconnected from and reconnected to diverse cultural and ideological concerns at different moments in the Bond phenomenon. It is thus not possible to locate a fixed context in relation to which, taken either as a whole or individually, the signifying function of 'the texts of Bond' – their meaning in history – can be stabilised, at least not without arbitrarily privileging one set of text–reader relations above others. Nor, of course, are these considerations unique to the 'texts of Bond', although their peculiar composition does serve to highlight them. It is clear that the figure of the author, through which reading practices are organised in other regions of textual distribution, is subject to processes of cultural remodelling similar to those we have outlined for the figure of Bond and is thus, despite appearances, just as unstable a point of reference. In brief, texts never come on to or are active on the stage of history except as always-already inscribed within particular and changing frameworks of inter-textuality, particular and changing social and ideological relations of reading. A text, in short, is never 'there' except in forms in which it is also and always other than 'just itself', always-already humming with reading possibilities which derive from outside its covers.

Given these considerations, to proceed, as we now turn to develop our discussion of the novels, as if these were self-contained texts that are, or ever have been, available to be read 'on their own terms' would be a singularly fruitless undertaking. It will rather be necessary to take account of the inter-textual relations through which the actual reading and specific social uses of the novels have been modulated. This, in turn, entails that such inter-textual relations should not be construed as secondary phenomena but as determinations which actively press in upon and powerfully reorganise the specific texts which fall within the orbit of their activity. Rather than producing a reading of the Bond novels that we would defend as 'more correct' than other readings, our aim is to produce a reading that will 'hover' midway between the novels and the other 'texts of Bond' and wider reading formations which, in various ways at various moments, have reorganised the field within which the novels have been culturally active. Our aim in what follows, therefore, is not to reveal the 'true meaning of the Bond novels', but to net analytically the spheres of meaning in which they have been floated as a result of the different regions of ideological and cultural concern to which they have been yoked by virtue of the changing orders of inter-textuality in which they have been inscribed.

However, it will clearly not be possible to keep all the variables which have borne on these processes in the air at the same time. In order to establish a point of reference in relation to which, however provisionally, the terms of the discussion can be pinned down, we shall consider the Bond novels largely in terms of their similarities to/differences from the earlier tradition of the imperialist spy-thriller. This is not to suggest that, when the chips are down, this *really is* the correct genre location for the Bond novels. Nor is it to suggest that this particular tradition should be privileged as the most important influence on Fleming; the evidence that he was influenced by Chandler, Hammet and Spillane is equally strong and compelling. Rather, we have determined on this point of comparison for the *historical* reasons we have outlined rather than for *essentialist* ones. Our concern is less with the logic of influences bearing on the Bond novels through their author than with the inter-textual co-ordinates which animated reading practices within what was, for British male readers in the 1950s and 1960s, the culturally dominant reading formation organising the cultural terrain on which the Bond novels were initially read. Frederic Jameson has argued that genres function as literary institutions, establishing a particular contract between readers and texts.[50] Viewed in this light, our purpose is to decipher the particular kind of contract produced by the imperialist spy-thriller for early readers of the Bond novels. This will then serve as a reference point in relation to which the contrasting readings produced from within other reading formations can be located.

Chapter 4

Bonded Ideologies

'I must confess,' Fleming once said of Bond, 'I quite often get terribly excited myself at his adventures. There are times when I can hardly wait to turn the next page.'[1] In this sense, perhaps, Fleming was his own ideal reader, the reader who would want, as he put it, to 'turn the page', to find out what happens next.[2] Although in itself no more than a happy coincidence, this symmetry between Fleming's account of his experience of the process of writing and his description of the urge towards narrative completion he aimed to produce in the reader suggests a further respect in which Eco's approach to the Bond novels needs to be qualified. For Eco, as we have seen, the pleasures of the 'average reader' are accounted for solely in terms of the operation of the novels' plot mechanics. This is to suppose that the reader has access to such plot mechanics independently of the specific formal or 'ways-of-telling' devices which condition the mode of their narrative realisation. This is clearly not the case. Whilst plot and narrative mechanisms are logically separable for the purpose of analysis, the reader encounters the plot only in the form of a 'plot-in-the-text', indissociable from the forms of its narrative organisation.

These considerations have an important bearing on the organisation and processing of the reader's energies. There is, of course, a sense in which Eco is right to argue that the reader knows in advance that Bond will conquer the villain and to maintain that this foreknowledge constitutes an important ingredient in the reader's pleasure. But this is truer for the reader outside the text – the reader who is just about to start or who has just finished reading – than it is for the reader actually immersed in the text. For the latter, the functioning of this element of foreknowledge can be accurately assessed only in relation to the processes of narrative suspense which work to check and call it into question. It is the dialectic between certainty and uncertainty, knowledge and ignorance, produced by the ways in which 'ways-of-telling' devices position the reader and organise the realisation of the plot which account for the peculiar pleasurable excitation experienced by the reader. Who is the villain? What is the nature of his conspiracy? Will Bond conquer the villain? Will he resolve the enigma posed by 'the girl' and successfully respond to the challenge she represents? It is these questions, placed in suspense by the organisation of the narrative, which, for the reader immersed in the text, motivate his/her energies, propel him/her to 'turn the page' in order to put an end to the troubling excitation produced ‾by such uncertainties. On the other hand, it is the reader's foreknowledge – culturally derived from his or her experience of similar narrative types – that, in the end, all will be well which renders this troubling excitation securely enjoyable.

The pattern of the reader's psychic investment in the process of narrative completion which results from these conflicting tendencies of narrative organisation is also crucial in understanding the ideological dimensions of the reader's pleasure. In view of the ideological co-ordinates which govern the relations between Bond and the villain and Bond and 'the girl', the production of suspense in relation to these two centres of narrative interest also places into suspense the imaginary orderings of real relations produced by Cold War, imperialist and patriarchal ideologies. In this way, the narrative effects a 'putting into suspense' of the reader as a subject formed within these ideologies. The reader's pleasure, we might thus say, is produced by the contradictory ways in which he/she, as a subject within ideology, is 'rubbed' by the processes of narrative. It is located within the dialectic between those narrative tendencies which place the subject positions and identities produced within Cold War, imperialist and patriarchal ideologies into fictitious crisis and those narrative tendencies which work towards the resolution of such fictitious crises.

Contrary to reductive accounts of popular fiction, the Bond novels thus do not merely reflect or pass on, unmodified, a series of contemporary ideologies. Nor do they simply narrate a series of pre-existing tensions within and between such ideologies. They rather narrate such ideologies into, and then out of crisis, producing a series of fictitious abysses within those ideologies but only so as to 'bond' them back into place – but not necessarily the same place. The consequence, for the reader, is the initiation of a certain movement in relation to ideology as he/she is dislocated from the ideological places and subject positions the narrative puts into crisis, but only to be relocated, replaced as a subject, within a modified set of ideological places which, for brevity's sake, can perhaps be characterised as 'Bonded ideologies'. The nature and direction of this movement, however, is not determined solely by such intra-textual narrative processes; account must also be taken of the inter-textual set through which the expectations of the reader are organised. In what follows, we seek to identify the ways in which these 'internal' and 'external' considerations interacted in structuring the reading practices of male readers of the Bond novels in the 1960s. While this involves taking the imperialist spy-thriller as our point of departure, we shall also comment on the respects in which, in the British context, spy-thrillers and detective fictions have been perceived as distinct.

Narrative and ideology in the imperialist spy-thriller

The process of narrative, Steve Neale has argued, consists in 'the interruption of an initial equilibrium and the tracing of the dispersal and refiguration of its elements'.[3] As we saw in the previous chapter, Neale regards genres as too fluid to be susceptible to a precise determination. They are, he argues, culturally variable systems of expectations circulating between texts and readers rather than fixed categories into which texts can be neatly pigeon-holed. None the less, he argues that what might be loosely called the 'generic leanings' of narratives can be specified in terms of the ideological preoccupations which the narrative works across in its movement from the introduction of disequilibrium to its final resolution. Such leanings, Neale suggests, are discernible less in the specific range of ideological discourses across which the narrative works than in the relative weight and specific articulation of the relations between such discourses. The discourses which are worked across in the western, the gangster film and the detective film are thus substantially the same: discourses concerning crime, the law, justice, social order, and so on. Where they differ is in terms of the ways in which the relationships between these ideological preoccupations are ordered and developed in relation to the equilibrating/disequilibrating tendencies of the narrative. It will be possible, using this perspective, to identify the respects in which the Bond novels and the earlier tradition of the imperialist spy-thriller might be regarded as both similar and yet distinct, as well as to identify those in which, in Britain, both have usually been distinguished from detective fiction.

With regard to the latter question, Michael Denning has suggested that the main difference between the spy-thriller and the detective story consists in the contrasting ways in which they organise the relations between questions of knowledge and questions of action. In the detective story, the two are, in effect, equated: the resolution of the crime and the revelation of the guilty party is the principal action accomplished during the course of the narrative and usually brings it to a close. In the spy-thriller, by contrast, the series of disturbing events which motivate the narrative form part of a pattern which can be traced back to an evil source which must not only be revealed but also destroyed. Yet the spy-thriller does not so much dispense entirely with the narrative strategies which characterise detective stories as subordinate them to its own dominant organising principles. Thus, the villain's conspiracy is often portended by a series of threatening enigmas, mysteries which have to be resolved before the identity of the villain and the nature of his conspiracy can be revealed. In Buchan's *The Three Hostages*, for example, the founding disequilibrium which motivates the narrative takes the form of the mysterious disappearance of 'the daughter of the richest man in the world, the heir of our greatest dukedom, the only child of a national hero'.[4]

However, the resolution of such founding enigmas merely paves the way, in the spy-thriller, for the fulfilment of the hero's mission, search or quest. Attention thus focuses less on problems of knowledge than on problems of action – on what the hero must do in order to defeat the villain and frustrate his conspiracy.

So far as the ideological preoccupations of the imperialist spy-thriller are concerned, Denning contends that these typically centre on discourses of nation and nationhood. The villain is invariably foreign and his conspiracy constitutes a direct threat to England or England's interests. In McNeile's *Bull-Dog Drummond*, for instance, Carl Peterson co-ordinates a syndicate of foreign businessmen (including one American) who conspire to forment a revolution in Britain for the sake of the fortunes they might reap as a result of the subsequent lapse of Britain's trading agreements. Rather more typically, the threat to the nation takes the form of a threat to the ruling class and is usually registered as a disturbance in the smooth and regular running of its institutions – a disturbance which ripples through the world of London clubs and England's (and sometimes Scotland's) country houses, and which the narrative works to efface or cancel out. It is this implicit equation between the ruling class and the nation which perhaps best accounts for the peculiar ideological potency of the spy-thrillers in this period. In Denning's view, this aspect of the genre enabled the spy-thriller to play a key role in constructing a vision of the nation and of national loyalties which overrode the claims of class and other sectional interests. The hero of the imperialist spy-thriller, invariably ruling class, imaginarily unifying the people of Britain 'in a contest with supra-national dynasties, international financiers, or "tub-thumpers of the world revolution"', was, he suggests, 'both a sign of and a reason for the effectiveness of these thrillers in constructing a popular "national" readership, across and against class'.[5]

In many respects, the narrative organisation of the Bond novels conforms to the model Denning proposes for the spy-thriller. Questions of knowledge, although not absent, are typically subordinated to, and serve merely as a prelude to, questions of action. The reader, that is to say, is typically less interested in what Bond knows or doesn't know than in what he does.

Nevertheless, there are also important differences. The narrative organisation is considerably complicated by the interaction between a number of overlapping disequilibrating/equilibrating tendencies which work across a series of interwoven ideological preoccupations and co-ordinate a set of interacting problems of both knowledge and action.

These differences can be grouped into three main sets. The first concerns the ways in which the discourses of nation and nationhood are articulated with discourses of class and the manner in which the disequilibrating/equilibrating tendencies of the narrative are worked across these. The second concerns an additional series of narrative tensions, centred principally on the relations between Bond and 'the girl', which are worked across discourses of gender and sexuality alongside those of nation and nationhood. Alongside but not separate from: the distinctive narrative and ideological economy of the Bond novels consists in the way these two sources of narrative and ideological tension are imbricated on to and worked through in relation to one another. The means by which this overlapping is effected are supplied by the references to the Oedipus complex which are present in all the novels. While these have usually been regarded as of a purely incidental significance – as either a crude means of titillating the reader, or as an over-obvious and heavy-handed parody of the Oedipus myth – they in fact play an important role in organising the narrative structure of the novels. Operating in the relations between Bond and M, Bond and the villain, and Bond and 'the girl', these references to the Oedipus complex produce a further set of narrative tensions centring on the threat of castration and its avoidance. The crucial significance of these tensions, however, consists in their co-ordinating role in articulating the tensions worked across discourses of gender and sexuality, principally in the unfolding of the relations between Bond and 'the girl', and those worked across discourses of nation and nationhood, principally in the unfolding of the relations between Bond, M and the villain, into a complex unity.

We have already considered, in the previous chapter, the

Cold War or, depending on the period, détente aspects of the Bond novels. We shall therefore limit our attention here to the functioning of discourses of nation and sexuality within the novels. Initially, we shall deal with each of these separately. In the final section of this chapter, we consider the ways in which phallic imagery and references to the Oedipus complex serve to connect these different aspects of the novels' ideological economy.

Bond and England

'With Mr Fleming,' Kingsley Amis has argued, commenting on the differences between Bond's world and that of a Bull-Dog Drummond, 'we move beyond the situation in which you only had to scratch a foreigner to find a villain, but you still don't need to scratch a villain to find a foreigner.'[6] While this is true, the differences between the Bond novels and those of Buchan and McNeile are rather more far-reaching than this suggests. Most obviously, perhaps, whereas the heroes of Buchan and McNeile typically represented the singular and unique virtues of Britain (especially England) acting alone against some evil foreign conspiracy, in turn directed solely against Britain, Bond can be read as a hero of the NATO alliance. Acting in unison with either the American CIA (represented by Felix Leiter) or the French Deuxième Bureau (represented by René Mathis), Bond represents not just Britain – and, again, especially England – but the West in general, just as the villain's conspiracy is usually directed against the West as a whole. It is arguable that one of the reasons the Bond novels were able, via the films, to break out of the specifically British market, to which the earlier tradition of the imperialist spy-thriller had been limited, and recruit an international readership consists in this construction of Britain as a stand-in for the interests of the West as a whole.

Bond was, however, first and foremost an English hero. Indeed, the system of NATO alliances, as represented in the novels, typically functions as a means of placing Bond – and thereby England – imaginarily at the centre of the world stage. It is Bond and not Leiter – and, thereby, the British Secret Service and not the CIA, England and not America – who engages in the decisive contest with the villain. Leiter's role is always structurally subordinated to that of Bond. He supplies Bond with technical support and hardware, added muscle where needed and money (he finances Bond's gambling contest with Le Chiffre in *Casino Royale*). He never takes the initiative against the villain or, when he does, in *Live and Let Die*, is (literally) cut down to size (he loses an arm and half a leg to Mr Big). Amis pinpoints Leiter's function for British readers precise

> The point of Felix Leiter, such a nonentity as a piece of characterization, is that he, the American, takes orders from Bond, the Britisher, and Bond is constantly doing better than he, showing himself, not braver or more devoted, but smarter, wilier, tougher, more resourceful, the incarnation of little old England with her quiet ways and shoe string budget wiping the eye of big global tentacled multi-billion-dollar-appropriating America.[7]

England is similarly imaginarily placed at the centre of the world stage in being chosen as the target of the villain's conspiracy. This is particularly the case in *From Russia, With Love*. When the intelligence chiefs of SMERSH meet to determine on a conspiracy that will strike 'at the heart of the Intelligence apparat of the West' (p. 35), their deliberations as to an appropriate target come to settle on a choice between the British Secret Service and the CIA:

> 'England is another matter altogether. I think we all have respect for her Intelligence Service,' General Vozdvishensky looked around the table. There were grudging nods from everyone present, including General G. 'Their Security Service is excellent . . . Their Secret Service is still better. They have notable successes. In certain types of operation, we are constantly finding that they have been there before us. Their agents are good. They pay them little money – only a thousand or two thousand roubles a month – but they serve with devotion. Yet these agents have no special

privileges in England, no relief from taxation and no special shops such as we have, from which they can buy cheap goods. Their social standing abroad is not high, and their wives have to pass as the wives of secretaries. They are rarely awarded a decoration until they retire. And yet these men and women continue to do this dangerous work. It is curious. It is perhaps the Public School and University tradition. The love of adventure. But still it is odd that they play the game so well, for they are not natural conspirators . . . Of course, most of their strength lies in the myth – in the myth of Scotland Yard, of Sherlock Holmes, of the Secret Service. We certainly have nothing to fear from these gentlemen. But this myth is a hindrance which it would be good to set aside.'

'And the Americans?' . . .

'The Americans have the biggest and richest service among our enemies. Technically, in such matters as radio and weapons and equipment, they are the best. But they have no understanding for the work. They get enthusiastic about some Balkan spy who says he has a secret army in the Ukraine. They load him with money with which to buy boots for his army. Of course, he goes at once to Paris and spends the money on women. Americans try to do everything with money. Good spies will not work for money alone – only bad ones, of which the Americans have several divisions' (pp. 38–9).

Rather more important is the fact that whilst, in the early novels, the villain's conspiracy may echo to the ideological tunes of the Cold War in being directed against the peace and security of the Western world in general, this conspiracy is often enveloped within and overshadowed by a set of disequilibrating/equilibrating tendencies which centre specifically on England and the ideology of Englishness. In *Moonraker* and *Dr No*, for instance, the founding disequilibria which motivate the narratives take the form of enigmas, mysterious and threatening disturbances registered against the quiet and orderly background of English institutions which symbolise the defining strengths and virtues of Englishness. Posed initially as a problem of knowledge which

Bond, at M's behest, must resolve, it is by tracing these disturbances to their source that Bond reveals the nature of the villain's conspiracy. In the case of *Moonraker*, the narrative is motivated by M's discovery that 'Sir Hugo Drax cheats at cards' (p. 19). Drax is represented as a 'possible saviour of the country' (p. 74) as a consequence of his having donated the Moonraker project to Britain, thereby offering her the possibility of 'an independent say in world affairs' (p. 68), and as a popular hero, a classic example of the self-made man made good. His behaviour therefore constitutes an ideological scandal (he cheats at Blades, the last thing an English gentleman would do!) which threatens to assume major proportions should it become public knowledge. Assigned the task of teaching Drax a lesson, Bond is able, in time, to resolve the enigma of Drax's behaviour and to efface the ideological disturbance which it represents (he is, it turns out, German). In doing so, he unearths Drax's conspiracy which portends an even greater ideological disturbance. An ex-Nazi in the pay of the Soviet Union, Drax's Moonraker – a rocket armed with a nuclear warhead – is targeted to land not in the North Sea nor even in the provinces (which, it appears, would have been bearable) but in London, a hundred yards from Buckingham Palace, striking right at the ideological heart of the nation. The Cold War aspects of Drax's conspiracy pale into insignificance compared with its assault on the ideology of Englishness as the nation faces the prospect of being both blown up and belittled by a foreign imposter. Drax makes his motives clear:

'I loathe and despire you all. You swine! Useless, idle, decadent fools, hiding beneath your bloody white cliffs while other people fight your battles. Too weak to defend your colonies, toadying to America with your hats in your hands. Stinking snobs who'll do anything for money. Hah!' he was triumphant, 'I knew that all I needed was money and the facade of a gentleman. Gentleman! *Pfui Teufel*! To me a gentleman is just someone I can take advantage of. Those bloody fools in Blades for instance. For months I took thousands of pounds off them, swindled them right under their noses until you came along and upset the apple-cart' (p. 161).

In short, in *Moonraker*, the primary disturbance which the narrative works to efface centres exclusively on the nation, first in the form of what appears to be an internal disturbance as constituted by Drax's breach of the codes of gentlemanly conduct, a disturbance which, in turning out to be externally motivated, none the less continues to trouble that ideology in threatening the nation's destruction and humiliation. Much the same is true of *Dr No*. The initial disturbance which motivates the narrative here takes the form of the murder of Strangways, head of the Secret Service in Jamaica, and his assistant, Mary Trueblood. This disturbance is registered against an evocation of the quiet and orderly world of the colonial institutions which dominate the centre of Kingston: Richmond Road with, at one end, King's House, the Governor's residence, and, at the other, Queen's Club, 'the social Mecca of Kingston' (p. 1). This disturbance also constitutes an enigma. We do not know who killed Strangways or why. Nor, for that matter, does M and the task that is initially set for Bond is to resolve the enigma by discovering what happened to Strangways and why. These questions are answered roughly two-thirds of the way through the narrative when Bond is captured by Dr No. It is not until this point in the novel that the Cold War dimensions of the plot are introduced via the revelation of Dr No's conspiracy – a Soviet-financed threat to the guidance systems of American missiles. Once the nature of this conspiracy has been revealed, the centre of narrative interest shifts away from questions of knowledge (who is Dr No? what are his designs?) towards questions of action (can Bond withstand the trial of courage and pain Dr No inflicts on him, avert his conspiracy and save the Free World?). The completion of this task, however, does not bring the narrative to a close; nor does it resolve the tensions which had motivated the preceding parts of the narrative. Apart from the narrative tensions associated with Honeychile Rider, which we shall consider later, there remains the task of correcting the disturbance wrought by

the disappearance of Strangways, of restoring an equilibrium
to the unsettled colonial institutions of Kingston. It is only in
the final chapter that this disturbed world of kings and
queens is put back into order. Back at the Governor's
residence, beneath a portrait of King George VI at one end
of the room and, at the other, a portrait of the Queen,
looking down on the table 'with grace and good humour',
Bond's thoughts turn to England:

> His mind drifted into a world of tennis courts and lily
> ponds and kings and queens, of London, of people being
> photographed with pigeons on their heads in Trafalgar
> Square, of the forsythia that would soon be blazing on the
> bypass roundabouts, of May, the treasured housekeeper in
> his flat off the King's Road, getting up to brew herself a
> cup of tea . . . (p. 182).

The specific functioning of these narrative tensions focusing
on the nation is conditioned by the interpellative devices, or
'hailing mechanisms', through which the reader is called in
to occupy or be placed at the very centre of the ideology of
Englishness which is imaginarily put into the crisis as it is
worked across by the narrative. We have in mind here those
aspects of the novels which, in specifying Bond's place and
function in the world, also putatively stitch the reader into
the subject positions produced by dominant ideologies of
Englishness. The process of interpellation is one through
which individuals come to inhabit, to take as their own, the
subject positions and identities made available to them by
the forms in which they are addressed. These subject positions
receive their coherence from the centres of interpellation,
higher and self-subsistent principles of meaning and identity,
in relation to which they are constructed.

We might illustrate these processes by examining the
mechanisms through which Bond is enlisted in the services of
his country. The 'dog-days' to which he succumbs in the
periodic bouts of inactivity to which he is subjected between
missions are, for Bond, periods of an often acute ideological
crisis: he harbours hostile and rebellious attitudes toward M,
occasionally considers resigning (in *On Her Majesty's Secret*

Service, for example) and is sometimes impotent (as in *You Only Live Twice*). In such moments, in effect, Bond is a 'drifting subject' ideologically speaking, unsure of his place in the world and of his goal in life. Invariably, such crises are terminated when Bond is 'called up' by M (his office in the Secret Service is above Bond's) or, more usually, by his Chief-of-Staff. The following exchange in *From Russia, With Love* is typical of the way in which many of Bond's missions commence:

> Bond picked up the receiver. '007.'
> 'Can you come up?' It was the Chief-of-Staff.
> 'M?'
> 'Yes. And it looks like a long session' (p. 84).

It is, moreover, important that on such occasions Bond is addressed by or responds in his official capacity, by his number, as it is this alone which inscribes him in the position of a subject bound by the requirements of duty, relinquishing the burden of individual responsibility in being called to the service of his country:

> 'What do you think, 007?'
> James Bond's heart leapt and he felt a new urgency coursing through his veins. It was a long time since M had addressed him as 007, and it signified that he could well be off into the unknown again. He could almost smell the possibilities (*Licence Renewed*, p. 32).

To be addressed in any other way is a bad omen:

> 'Good morning, James. Sorry to pull you along a bit early in the morning. Got a very full day ahead. Wanted to fit you in before the rush.'
> Bond's excitement waned minutely. It was never a good sign when M addressed him by his christian name instead of his number. This didn't look like a job – more like something personal (*Thunderball*, p. 10).

To appreciate the significance of such 'calling up'

sequences, it is necessary to understand the position M occupies within the novels' representation of England and Englishness. He is, in effect, the go-between between Bond and the centres of interpellation in relation to which Bond is recruited in the service of England. As we noted in the previous chapter, M is a potent representative of England himself. An ex-Admiral embodying the strength of England's naval traditions, M is comfortably at home in the world of London clubs and is acquainted with all the powerful forces in the land. However, M is also the point of contact between the Secret Service and the Prime Minister (who is always, as David Cannadine observes, 'aloof, olympian and supreme – the steward of Her Majesty's affairs, rather than a calculating, partisan politician, temporarily enjoying the fruits of office') and, beyond the Prime Minister, the monarchy itself, the supreme and absolute embodiment of Englishness.[8] M's place in the order of things is made particularly clear in *From Russia, With Love* which orchestrates an elaborate series of relations between the figures of M, Churchill, the monarchy and Bond. In determining on a target for their conspiracy, the intelligence chiefs of SMERSH consider and reject the Queen and Churchill before choosing Bond; Darko Kerim's office is decorated with Annigoni's portrait of the Queen and Cecil Beaton's wartime photograph of Churchill (looking 'like a contemptuous bulldog', p. 120), and Kerim has taught his men that M is 'just below God' (p. 114). As for Bond, he is granted a precarious toe-hold on this chain of interpellations in the singular mark of respect accorded him by his housekeeper in her customary morning greeting:

> 'Good morning-s'. (To Bond, one of May's endearing qualities was that she would call no man 'sir' except – Bond had teased her about it years before – English kings and Winston Churchill. As a mark of exceptional regard, she accorded Bond an occasional hint of an 's' at the end of a word) (p. 79).

God, the Queen, Churchill, M, Bond and (potentially) the reader: during his 'dog-days', Bond is dislocated from this chain of interpellations just as M's call, enlisting him in the service of the nation, resolves his identity crisis by stitching him back into place within that chain of interpellations, giving him a mission and an identity, set into motion as the delegated representative of all that stands behind M. It is through the operation of this chain of interpellations that the place which Bond and, through identification with Bond, the reader is called in to occupy is, ultimately, that of England. Bond becomes the figurative stand-in, for the reader, of the centres of interpellation in relation to which the rights, duties and self-conception of the English subject are constructed. As a consequence, if the reader takes up this position – which, of course, he/she need not – the narrative tensions centring on the nation are likely to produce an internal troubling of the subject position into which the reader has thus been called, a troubling that is all the more disquieting for the fact that it is often associated with and worked through via the threat of castration directed against Bond and, thereby, the reader.

Something of the significance of this aspect of the Bond novels can be gauged from the consequence of its absence. *Colonel Sun* is a case in point. The fact that the villain's conspiracy here first manifests itself in the kidnapping of M means that M is not able to fulfil any linking role within the chain of interpellations through which, in most of Fleming's novels, Bond is recruited as an emissary of the crown. Rather than assigning Bond his mission, M is its cause; rather than being put into motion by M, Bond has to put himself into motion in assigning himself the task of rescuing M. Structurally subordinated to Bond in being helpless and incapacitated, reduced to fulminating against Colonel Sun like a feeble dotard, M is unable to insert Bond's contest with the villain in a wider ideological context with the result that his duel with Colonel Sun becomes little more than a personalised feud.

The functioning of this chain of interpellations is all the more important in the respect that the target of the villain's conspiracy is sometimes, purely and simply, the myth of Englishness itself as personified by Bond. Where this is not the case, that myth is none the less conspicuously on trial, to be validated or exposed as, indeed, a myth depending on the way in which Bond conducts himself. In *From Russia, With*

Love, SMERSH's aim is to secure a propaganda victory over England – and, thereby, over the West as a whole – by discrediting Bond, selected as a target because it is judged that he most consumately incarnates the myth upon which the alleged strength of the Secret Service – and, thereby, of England – depends. Red Grant drives the point home:

> 'So what's the story, in the papers – the Left Wing ones that will be tipped off to meet the train? Old man, the story's got everything. Orient Express. Beautiful Russian spy murdered in Simplon tunnel. Filthy pictures. Secret cipher machine. Handsome British spy with career ruined murders her and commits suicide. Sex, spies, luxury train, Mr and Mrs Somerset . . . ! Old man, it'll run for months! Talk of the Khoklov case! This'll knock spots off it. And what a poke in the eye for the famous Intelligence Service! Their best man, the famous James Bond. What a shambles. Then bang goes the cipher machine! What's your chief going to think of you? What's the public going to think? And the Government? And the Americans? Talk about security! No more atomb bomb secrets from the Yanks' (p. 193).

Everything hinges on whether Bond, in validating the myth, can secure for England a position that is still at the centre of world affairs. Similarly, in *You Only Live Twice*, Bond's task is to prove that there is still an élite in Britain, still a backbone to the English character, that merits her being regarded as a worthwhile ally by the Japanese. Tiger Tanaka informs Bond of the Japanese view of Britain's deterioration:

> 'Bondo-san, I will now be blunt with you, and you will not be offended, because we are friends. Yes? Now it is a sad fact that I, and many of us in positions of authority in Japan, have formed an unsatisfactory opinion about the British people since the war. You have not only lost a great Empire, you have seemed almost anxious to throw it away with both hands. All right,' he held up a hand, 'we

will not go deeply into the reasons for this policy, but when you apparently sought to arrest this slide into impotence at Suez, you succeeded only in stage-managing one of the most pitiful bungles in the history of the world, if not the worst. Further, your governments have shown themselves successively incapable of ruling and have handed over effective control of the country to the trade unions, who appear to be dedicated to the principle of doing less and less work for more money. This feather-bedding, this shirking of an honest day's work, is sapping at ever-increasing speed the moral fibre of the British, a quality the world once so much admired' (pp. 76–7).

Bond responds in spirited fashion:

'Balls to you, Tiger! And balls again! . . . Let me tell you this, my fine friend. England may have been bled pretty thin by a couple of World Wars, our Welfare State politics may have made us expect too much for free, and the liberation of our Colonies may have gone too fast, but we still climb Everest and beat plenty of the world at plenty of sports and win Nobel prizes. Our politicians may be a feather pated bunch, and I expect yours are too. All politicians are. But there's nothing wrong with the British people – even though there are only fifty million of them' (pp. 77–8).

Tanaka's reply places the burden of proof on Bond's shoulders. Only if Bond succeeds in the task Tanaka sets him – to slay Dr Shatterhand, who turns out to be Blofeld – will the Japanese Prime Minister regard Britain as being worthy of the top-grade secret material which M had requested and entrusted to Bond to secure. This overt foregrounding of Bond's role in embodying the myth of Englishness contrasts markedly with the earlier tradition of the imperialist spy-thriller. In the novels of Buchan and McNeile, the villain's conspiracy is usually targeted directly against Britain's economic, political or military interests; the innate superiority of English character is never seriously put into question. The reflections of Derek Vane, the hero of McNeile's *Mufti*, adequately communicate the confidence of the genre in this respect:

> Before the war Derek Vane had been what is generally regarded as a typical Englishman. That is to say, he regarded his own country . . . whenever he thought about it at all – as being the supreme country in the world. He didn't force his opinion down anyone's throat; it was simply so. If the other fellow didn't agree, the funeral was his, not Vane's. He had to the full what the uninitiated regard as conceit; on matters connected with literature, or art, or music, his knowledge was microscopic. Moreover, he regarded with suspicion anyone who talked intelligently on such subjects. On the other hand he had been in the eleven at Eton, and was a scratch golfer. He had a fine seat on a horse and rode straight; he could play a passable game of polo, and was a good shot . . . He belonged, in fact, to the Breed; the Breed that may find its members in London and Fiji; in the lands that lie beyond the mountains and at Henley; in the swamps where the stagnant vegetation rots and stinks; in the great deserts where the night air strikes cold. They are always the same, and they are branded with the stamp of the Breed. They shake your hand as a man shakes it; they meet your eye as a man meets it.[9]

By contrast, the Bond novels positively bristle with allusions – such as those in *You Only Live Twice* – to Britain's declining power and status. This subtly modifies the nature of Bond's task and of what he accomplishes, ideologically speaking, in fulfilling it. Buchan's Richard Hannay and McNeile's Bull-Dog Drummond tend, by and large, to reconfirm effortlessly a substantially uncontested ideology of Englishness, and to do so by sheer character, by virtue of a superiority which is naturally, rightly and indisputably theirs. Bond has an altogether harder time of it. Required to vindicate a myth of Englishness which has been put into question by the tide of history (as represented by the allusions to Britain's declining power and status), he does so not by sheer force of personality or by means of naturally acquired aptitudes; instead, he relies on the assistance of technological gadgetry, does regular target practice and trains for physical fitness, especially when an arduous task awaits him:

> They ate their breakfast while Bond fixed his training routine – up at seven, swim a quarter of a mile, breakfast, an hour's sunbathing, run a mile, swim again, lunch, sleep, sunbathe, swim a mile, hot bath and massage, dinner and asleep by nine (*Dr No*, p. 61).

David Cannadine has argued that such aspects of the novels reflect Fleming's concern to reaffirm the virtues of the public school tradition. This is, in our view, unlikely. When Buchan's Hannay or, in *Prester John*, his David Crawford need to exert themselves they call upon an athleticism and a physical resilience which they possess simply because they are of true British stock and which, therefore, does not need to be fine-tuned by training. Rather, the stress Bond places on training and preparation relates to the fact that, whereas the heroes of Buchan and McNeile are gentleman amateurs, reluctantly pressed into the service of their country when the need is great, Bond is a professional, working in a bureaucracy with all its back-up services at his disposal and in association with fellow professionals. Ultimately, the code he lives by is not that of his antecedents: if he encounters a cheat, he cheats in turn (his game of golf with Goldfinger, for example) if doing so will help to secure his objective. Nor is his class position the same. Buchan's central characters are unequivocally members of the leisured ruling class; his Edward Leithen, as Richard Usborne puts it, 'talked about his bankers in the plural'.[10] Bond's economic position is more precarious: he has a private income, but it is minimal, and he depends on his salary to supplement it. It secures him 'the good life' but not the staid, solid respectability of the traditional ruling class; a flat off the King's Road, but not a country house. He has access to the world of Blades and to the most powerful in the land via M, but he is not of that world – it is not his natural habitat as it was for Hannay.

In short, Bond's lifestyle, views and attitudes depart

significantly from those of his predecessors. His social views are, of course, anything but egalitarian. His attitudes towards trade unions are (or should be) unprintable and when, on the one occasion he encounters a member of the British working class who does not conform to the model of a faithful old retainer – a fly young taxi-driver – he regards his teddy-boy appearance as 'typical of the cheap self-assertiveness of young labour since the war' (*Thunderball*, p. 16). Unequivocally commited to élite values, Bond seeks to distinguish himself from the common mass – by the Bentley convertible he drives, his special cigarettes and hand-tailored suits. But his élitism lacks the usual class articulation of the hero of the earlier imperialist spy-thriller. Indeed, he is sharply distinguished from traditional representations of the ruling class within this tradition. His attitudes towards sex, gambling and pleasure in general are distinctly liberal and his tastes and lifestyle have a decidedly international and cosmopolitan flavour. In a word, Bond is not old fashioned. M is, and it is in the relations between Bond and M that a space is opened up between, on the one hand, earlier fictional representations of the lifestyle and ethos of the traditional British ruling class and, on the other, the projection of a new set of élite values and styles. Bond belongs not to the Breed but to a new élite – international rather than parochially English in its orientation – committed to new values (professionalism) and lifestyles (martini). This tension between the old and the new is most clearly expressed in Bond's capacity for improvisation, his ability to take risks and bend the rules for, in doing so, he breaks with the constraints of the traditional code and embodies a new one: success, no matter what the means, but by relying on an individual flair which distinguishes him from the villain, not ethically, but instrumentally, in terms of the means by which he acts rather than the ends he pursues.

It is in this respect that, so far as their functioning in relation to ideologies of nation and nationhood is concerned, the Bond novels can be regarded as having initiated a process of the reformation of more traditional fictional representations of Englishness. Their significance in relation to readers formed within such fictions was to promote a certain ideological shift in facilitating an adjustment from one mythic representation of Britain's ruling élite to another and from one mythic conception of Englishness to another. This is not to say that all readers made this movement. Indeed, a part of the reason for the popularity of the Bond novels consists in the degree to which they were able to co-ordinate a range of responses to the crisis of nation and nationhood which characterised the late 1950s and early 1960s. The space they opened up in relation to traditional myths of Englishness in enabling a popular scepticism to bubble up to the surface and find expression may, in the long term, have proved more enduringly important in explaining the novels' popular appeal than any widespread credence given to their positive refashioning of such myths. This is especially the case if the influence of the films is taken into account, since these have consistently widened this space, exploiting to the full the humorous potential of the laughing-gaps in an ideology exposed as redundant. The point we are concerned to make here, however, concerns the ways in which the Bond novels actively reworked an inherited repertoire of ideological themes rather than reproducing them. This, in turn, means that their effects must be understood in terms of the part they played, in association with other ideological phenomena, in constructing a new set of ideological positions and identities rather than simply passing on ideologies already formed and determined elsewhere.

We shall return to these considerations later. Meanwhile, we consider another – and perhaps the most crucial – respect in which the Bond novels departed from their predecessors. J. G. Cawelti has argued that in the adventure story, where interest centres on the hero, 'the erotic interests served by attendant damsels are more in the nature of frosting on the cake'.[11] In the case of the imperialist spy-thriller, even this frosting was often lacking. Erotic interests, at least in so far as these concern the relations between men and women, are at a minimum in the novels of Buchan and McNeile. More important, they do not constitute a source of tension that is in any way imbricated with the national and political tensions which motivate the narrative in these novels. Whilst there are women characters who connote both a sexual and a political deviancy, they do not function as a source of erotic attraction for the hero. They are usually older women and, like Irma Peterson in *Bull-Dog Drummond*, too completely associated with the villain and too grotesque in both physique and mentality to be even potentially redeemable: in short, characters like Fleming's Irma Bunt and Rosa Klebb. The typical 'girl', by contrast, is, as Richard Usborne put it, 'the open-air type always, clean-run, boyish and a sportsman'.[12] Such women do not pose any threat of sexual otherness because they are all 'good chaps' anyway, albeit carrying the markers of a 'correctly' attuned feminine identity in being married or about to be married, mothers or about to be mothers. Equally important, they are always, and unswervingly, on the same side as the hero. Instead, although in a repressed way, erotic interest centres on the relations between men: those between Richard Hanney and his 'boon companion', Sandy Arbuthnot, for example. This repressed homosexuality is particularly clear in Buchan's *The Three Hostages* where Hannay is obliged to submit himself – reluctantly, but also half-willingly – to the villain's hypnotic power in order to avert his conspiracy. The ambiguity implicit in this is made clear by the characterisation of the villain, Medina, as a man who fascinated Hannay 'as a man is fascinated by a pretty woman' and whose eyes 'would have made a plain-headed woman lovely', as a man for whom women held no charm and whose motto was *Hominum dominatus*.[13] Echoes of this aspect of the Buchan–McNeile tradition survive in the Bond novels: Bond's true spiritual companions are always other men – Darko Kerim in *From Russia, With Love*, for instance. In incorporating a major erotic interest centring on the relations between Bond and 'the girl', however, Fleming both broke with the previous tradition and enormously enriched its potential.

Bond and 'the girl'

In *Thunderball*, shortly after his first encounter with Domino Vitali, Bond reflects: 'This was his first sniff at the town and already he had caught hold of the girl' (p. 108). At this point,

Bond has no reason to suppose that Domino is in any way connected with his mission. Yet, there she is, 'the girl', already met and, did she but know it, well on the way to meeting her come-uppance. An odd piece of carelessness on Fleming's part, this is, none the less, a symptomatic slip. That Bond should encounter a girl in the course of his mission is foreordained, a necessity of the formula. It is, moreover, always a girl he encounters, never a woman, and, when not directly present, she is invariably referred to, in the exchanges between Bond and the villain, Bond and M, or Bond and his helpers as 'the girl'.

What, then is the function of 'the girl' within the narrative? Usually, she furnishes a source of narrative tension in two related respects. First, she constitutes a problem of knowledge, a troubling enigma which Bond must resolve. This enigma takes the form of a disturbing 'out-of-placeness' in the respect that, to varying degrees and in different ways, 'the girl' departs from the requirements of femininity as specified by patriarchal ideology. The 'place' which 'the Bond girls' are 'out of', so to speak, is that alloted to them – that which, ideologically, they should occupy – in a patriarchal order, defined, socially and sexually, in relation to men. This 'out-of-placeness' may take the form of a challenging aggressiveness (Vesper Lynd in *Casino Royale* and Domino Vitali in *Thunderball*), a resisting frigidity (Gala Brand in *Moonraker*) or lesbianism (Tilly Masterton and Pussy Galore in *Goldfinger*) and is sometimes symbolised by a physical deformity – Domino Vitali's limp, for example, or Honeychile Rider's broken nose.

The enigma surrounding 'the girl's' sexuality is usually resolved as her biography is progressively unfolded. This accounts for her 'out-of-placeness', usually in one of two ways: she has either been orphaned from an early age (Domino Vitali) or has suffered a childhood experience which has damaged her sexually (Tiffany Case, in *Diamonds are Forever*, and Pussy Galore were raped). In some cases – that of Honeychile Rider, for example – the two circumstances are combined. Either way, the effect is the same: 'the girl' has been either insufficiently or faultily positioned sexually. It is the absence of men in her life (the lack of a father) or the overburdening presence of men of the wrong sort (in the form of rape) that accounts for her skewed positioning in relation to traditional, patriarchal orderings of sexual difference. This, in turn, in some novels, accounts for her skewed positioning in the ideological divide between good and evil, West and East, symbolised by her working in the service of the villain. Lacking a clear anchorage in the ideological ordering of the relationships between men and women, 'the girl' – like Bond in his 'dog-days' – often functions as a 'drifting subject' within the sphere of ideology in general: unsure of her place sexually, she is also insufficiently attuned to the distinction between right and wrong.

Once the mystery of 'the girl's' displaced sexuality has been accounted for, the problem she poses is one of action: will Bond successfully respond to the challenge of effecting her sexual readjustment and, thereby, 'correctly' realigning her within the patriarchal sexual order? Usually, of course, he does. In thus responding to the challenge posed by 'the girl', putting her back into place beneath him (both literally and metaphorically), Bond functions as an agent of the patriarchal order, refurbishing its imaginarily impaired structure by quelling the source of the disturbance within it. In the event that Bond fails in this task, the narrative and ideological tensions constructed around 'the girl' are effaced, and equilibrium finally restored, by means of her death – as is the case with Vesper Lynd in *Casino Royale*. There is, however, a third scenario. In *Moonraker*, Bond misinterprets Gala Brand's reserve – not, it turns out, a sign of resisting frigidity so much as of her engagement, and to a police inspector no less, so that, since she is already 'correctly' in place both sexually and ideologically, Bond's services are not required after all.

Stephen Heath has offered an interesting discussion of *Goldfinger* which combines the first two of these narrative strategies:

Hero James Bond – whose concentration of stereotypes of 'the man' needs no description – confronts two women. First, Tilly Masterson: 'She was beautiful – physically desirable. But there was a cold, hard centre to her that

Bond couldn't understand or define.' The woman-enigma, the woman-problem. But, of course, Bond *can* understand and define the cold, hard centre: she is 'one of those girls whose hormones had got mixed up' (the result of 'fifty years of emancipation'), one of 'a herd of unhappy sexual misfits – barren and full of frustrations'. Men are men, women are women (or should be); Tilly is a hysteric, neither one nor the other or both, aggressive and masculine (acts like a *son*, not a daughter); a misfit, she is unhappy and frustrated in her failed femininity (what she really wants and needs is a *master* – Masterson should be master's daughter). Since she cannot place herself correctly to Bond as woman to man, she gets killed: 'Poor little bitch. She didn't think much of men . . . I could have got her away if she'd only followed me.' Second, Pussy Galore, leader of a lesbian criminal gang, a natural challenge: Bond 'felt the challenge all beautiful lesbians have for men'. Tilly falls for Pussy, Pussy falls for Bond, 'I never met a man before'. QED. It then only remains to *explain* her lesbianism: she is anti-men (lesbianism is being anti-men) because of a traumatic childhood rape by an uncle (shades exactly of Freud's seduction theory of hysteria); and to prescribe treatment from practising sexologist Bond: ' "All you need is a course in TLC . . . Tender Loving Care Treatment . . ." "When's it going to start?" Bond's right hand came slowly up the firm, muscled thighs, over the flat soft plain of the stomach to the right breast. Its point was hard with desire. He said softly, "Now." His mouth came ruthlessly down on her's.' So she fits in the end, finally cured, identity established, his and hers, in her place, name confirmed – pussy galore.[14]

While substantially correct, there is a revealing slip in Heath's analysis: Tilly's surname is, in fact, Masterton, not Masterson. It's also worth adding that, in repositioning Pussy Galore sexually, Bond also repositions her ideologically, detaching her from the service of the villain and recruiting her in support of his own mission. When Bond orders her into bed ('She did as she was told, like an obedient child', p. 222), she speaks to him 'not in a gangster's voice, or a

Lesbian's, but in a girl's voice' (p. 222), and is thus simultaneously doubly repositioned, back 'in place' as a woman and back on the right side in the contest between good and evil. While, in this respect, representative of the Bond novels as a whole, *Goldfinger* is somewhat untypical in the degree of explicitness which characterises its construction and resolution of narrative tensions surrounding the place of 'the girl'. Compared with the challenge of 'complete conversion' which he faces in relation to Pussy Galore, the task Bond more usually has to respond to is one of 'fine-tuning', of adjusting a sexuality which, although basically 'on the right lines', is significantly awry in some particular respect or which has yet to be fully formed. As a consequence, the narrative tensions relating to 'the girl' are usually more subtley constructed and differently worked in at least two respects. First, in some novels, Bond does not so much reposition 'the girl' as furnish the point of reference, the norm of a 'pure masculinity', in relation to which she repositions or reinterpellates herself into a 'correctly tuned' female sexed identity. Secondly, in putting 'the girl' back into place, the Bond novels also typically refashion the place she is thus put back into. They do not simply confirm established ideologies and fictional representations of femininity but reform them, fashioning a new construction of femininity tailored to the requirements of a promiscuous male sexuality in being set free from the restraints of marriage and fidelity. Released from the constraints of social inhibition and from the hypocrisy of the double-standard, the only (!) restriction placed on the Bond girl – the model, once finely tuned, of a free and independent sexuality – is that she should submit to the regime of the phallus in the ordering of her desires.

In *Thunderball*, for example, Domino Vitali's qualities of independence are ones Bond admires:

> This was an independent, a girl of authority and character. She might like the rich, gay life, but so far as Bond was concerned, that was the right kind of girl. She might sleep with men, obviously did, but it would be on her terms and not on theirs (p. 109).

She is, however, over-masculine ('But this girl drove like a man ... she took a man's pleasure in the feel of her machine ...', p. 110) and, in her excessive aggressiveness and over-dominating bearing (her full name is Dominetta; 'little dominator'), constitutes a threat to the 'proper distribution' of phallic attributes between men and women:

> The general impression, Bond decided, was of a wilful, high-tempered, sensual girl – a beautiful Arab mare who would only allow herself to be ridden by a horseman with steel thighs and velvet hands, and then only with a curb and saw bit – and then only when he had broken her to bridle and saddle. Bond thought that he would like to try his strength against hers (pp. 110–11).

An Italian, brought up in England until her parents were killed in a train accident, Domino has had to make her own way in the world, using only 'a woman's weapons' (p. 151). A rough schooling, the experience has bruised and damaged her sensibilities ('I don't expect they're very far underground', Bond tells her 'They certainly haven't atrophied. They've just lost their voice because you wouldn't listen to them', p. 151) although her limp suggests another, more vulnerable side to her nature (Bond 'found it endearing, a touch of childish sweetness beneath (her) authority and blatent sex appeal', p. 150). She is also disillusioned with men, except for one, the picture of the sailor which used to adorn the Player's cigarette packet:

> 'And I would like a packet of Players' – she laughed – 'Please, as they say in the advertisements. I am fed up with just smoking smoke. I need my Hero.'
> Bond bought a packet from the cigarette girl. He said, 'What's that about a hero?'
> She had entirely changed. Her bitterness was gone, and the lines of strain on her face. She had softened. She was suddenly a girl out for the evening. 'Ah, you don't know! My one true love! The man of my dreams. The sailor on the front of the packet of Players ... This man,' she pointed, 'was the first man I ever sinned with. I took him

into the woods, I loved him in the dormitory, I spent
nearly all my pocket money on him. In exchange, he
introduced me to the great world outside the Cheltenham
Ladies' College. He grew me up. He put me at ease with
boys of my own age. He kept me company when I was
lonely or afraid of being young. He encouraged me, gave
me assurance' (p. 152).

'He grew me up': the only man to provide a point of reference
in relation to which the feminine side of her nature was
cultivated (but in secret) was an imaginary one – until she
meets Bond, who takes the place of the sailor ('My hero' is
what Domino subsequently calls him) and, through
lovemaking, once again softens and tempers her hardness
('The lines of authority had been sponged away by the
lovemaking and the face had a soft, sweet, bruised look',
p. 186).

Similarly, in *Dr No*, Bond's role is that of a tutor, and a
somewhat reluctant one, in relation to Honeychile Rider
whose sexuality is, in part, unformed and, in part, deformed –
or, more accurately, deformed in the respect that it has never
been completely formed. From the very first, Honeychile
represents a confusion of sexual categories, a combination of
male and female characteristics aptly captured in Bond's
description of her as an 'extraordinary Girl Tarzan' (p. 99).
The problem which this displacement constitutes, a problem
which Bond accepts as his task to resolve ('There could be no
dropping the leash until he had solved her problems for her.
He knew it', p. 99) is precisely expressed in the ambivalence
which characterises Bond's own erotic attraction to
Honeychile, who herself alludes to what she fears might be a
displaced sexuality on Bond's part in referring to his
fascination for her behind. When Bond tells her she's a
wonderful girl ('I thought so directly I saw you'), she
immediately replies: 'Saw my behind you mean' (p. 99) – a
behind which is described, when Honeychile first appears on
the beach at Crab Key, as 'almost as firm and rounded as a
boy's' (p. 67). Similarly, when Bond refuses her invitation to
join her in her sleeping bag, she seeks both to reassure him
that she won't make any demands of him whilst also covering

all the available options: 'If you're thinking . . . I mean –
you don't have to make love to me . . . we could go to sleep
back to front, you know, like spoons' (p. 100).

There is, however, another dimension to Honeychile's
sexual 'out-of-placeness'. Emerging naked from the sea at
Crab Key, she responds to her awareness of Bond's presence
not by covering her breasts and groin. Instead:

> One hand flew downwards, but the other, instead of hiding
> her breasts, went up to her face, covering it below the eyes,
> now wide with fear (p. 68).

When Honeychile turns to face Bond, her behaviour is
explained:

> He looked up at her face. Now he realized why her hand
> had instinctively gone to it . . . for the nose was badly
> broken, smashed like a boxer's. Bond stiffened with revolt
> at what had happened to this supremely beautiful girl. No
> wonder this was her shame and not the beautiful firm
> breasts that now jutted towards him without concealment
> (pp. 68–9).

This introduces a theme that is to figure prominently in
the relations between Bond and Honeychile: the question of
her nose. We learn, subsequently, that Honeychile's parents
were killed when she was five and that, as a consequence, she
had, in effect, to 'grow herself up'. With only her black
nanny to look after her, she ran wild. Becoming a creature of
nature with a curious affinity with animals, her sole education
consisted in the encyclopaedia she had laboriously worked her
way through – 'as far as the middle of T' (p. 93) – from the
age of eight. Left entirely on her own when her nanny died,
Honeychile is raped by Mander, the overseer of a neighbouring
sugar plantation who, in overcoming her resistance, hits her
so violently that her nose is broken. The visual legacy of this
assault, Honeychile's nose thus functions as a sign of her
damaged sexuality, impaired at the very time of its awakening
(she was fifteen at the time, her encounter with Mander
being her first and, we learn later, only sexual experience).

Obsessively concerned with her facial disfigurement, Honeychile herself views her nose as a sign of deformity: 'I know some of me's alright, but when I look in the glass I hardly see anything except my broken nose. I'm sure it's the same with other people who are, who are – well – sort of deformed' (p. 94).

Moreover, she views the correction of her nose, sign of her 'out-of-placeness', as necessary if she is to be put back into place and resume the interrupted trajectory of her feminine career in becoming 'rich enough to find a nice husband and have some children' (p. 98). Her ambitions are conventional enough, but her nose stands as sign and visual reminder of a history that has placed her outside the conventions in disrupting the unfolding of a 'properly attuned' female sexuality. It is thus that she risks visiting Crab Key for the sake of the rare shells that can be found there for she hopes, by selling these to a dealer in Miami, to raise enough cash in order to have her nose – and, thereby, herself – put back into place by means of plastic surgery.

Honeychile's nose thus symbolises her anxieties that her feminity has been impaired by rape. Further, given that in the psychoanalytic study of dreams an undue degree of concern with the nose is often interpreted as a displaced reference to the penis, Honeychile's obsession with her over-prominent nose might also be interpreted as a displaced expression of anxieties centring on her tomboyish characteristics. However, Honeychile is also represented as the subject of an essentially *untutored* sexuality. She is, in effect, an innocent (Honey/chile = sweet and childlike), the subject of a sexuality that has yet to be fully awakened and properly positioned. This is made clear when she reveals her plan to be a call girl ('she said it as she might have said "nurse" or "secretary"', p. 98). Put simply, she doesn't know the forms of behaviour and expression appropriate to womanhood. No one has taught her. The two previous men in her life failed to support the construction of a properly positioned sexuality on Honeychile's part. Her father, who died when she was a child, represents an insufficiency of the male principle in this respect, whereas Mander represents male sexuality carried to excess. A Girl Tarzan who has yet to become fully a woman, anxious lest her assault has deformed her irreparably, Honeychile looks to Bond to complete her education. Throughout the novel, it is thus Honeychile who takes the initiative in relation to Bond, offering herself to him, inviting him to possess her, to talk about and teach her the ways of love. For reasons we shall consider shortly, Bond is unable to respond to this task until the very end of the novel. However, although it is clear that Bond, the first 'real man' she has met, supplies a valid norm of male sexuality in relation to which she might correctly define her own sexuality, Honeychile's approach to her education is anything but submissive:

> The girl let go his hand and climbed into the sleeping-bag. She looked up at him. She said, practically, 'I bought this today. It's a double one. It cost a lot of money. Take those off and come in. You promised. You own me slave-time.'
> 'But . . .'
> 'Do as you're told' (p. 188).

In short, the mould in which the Bond girl is cast is not archetypally feminine. Constructed according to the formula 'equal but yet subordinate', her destiny is not to be a housewife – in *Diamonds are Forever*, Tiffany Case flirts with this possibility, but only to reject it – but a free and equal partner, neither dependent on Bond nor encumbering him with duties and responsibilities, but who none the less, when it comes to the crunch (in bed) knows her place. Freed from the codes of romance and chivalry, the subjects of mature and frank sexualities, Bond and 'the Bond girl' are, in effect, pure cock and cunt, stripped of all pretence and inhibitions, but with the role of the latter being defined in relation to the former. If 'the Bond girl' abandons the traditional restraints, and claims, of a sexuality confined to the marriage bed, it is often to become merely the fantasy object of the male reader, licensed, through Bond, to go whoring by proxy – and with good conscience. In *On Her Majesty's Secret Service*, Tracy thus cuts short Bond's attempt 'to protect her, to solve her

problems, make her happy' in terms which correspond
entirely to stereotyped male fantasies of the nature of female
desire:

> 'I said "no conversation". Take off those clothes. Make
> love to me. You are handsome and strong. I want to
> remember what it can be like. Do anything you like. And
> tell me what you like and what you would like from me.
> Be rough with me. Treat me like the lowest whore in
> creation. Forget everything else. No questions. Take me'
> (p. 36).

There is, however, an exception to the rule: 'the girl' in
You Only Live Twice is not a source of narrative and ideological
tensions such as we have described them. And for good
reason. When Bond allows some women to precede him in
getting on to a bus, Tiger Tanaka chastises him: 'First
lesson, Bondo-san! Do not make way for women. Push them,
trample them down. Women have no priority in this country'
(p. 83).

While this extreme subordination of women clearly makes
Bond feel uncomfortable, he is fortunate in meeting, in Kissy
Suzuki – a Japanese girl who has learned the ways of the
West in Hollywood, but who retains her respect for Japanese
traditions – an ideal blend of tradition and modernity, of
subordination and independence. 'You don't have to bow to
me,' she tells Bond when they first meet, 'and I shall never
bow to you' (p. 124). Bond is delighted. 'Thank God,' he
reflects, 'for a straightforward girl at last' (p. 124). She is, in
short, the ideal Bond girl – natural, unaffected, totally lacking
in deference, independent and self-reliant, yet also caring,
loving, solicitous for Bond's well-being and willing to cater to
his every need without making any demands in return.
Already fashioned in Bond's image, he does not need to do
anything to or for her.

Indeed, the relations between Bond and 'the girl' are
reversed in *You Only Live Twice* in the respect that, at the end
of the novel, Kissy has the task of reawakening and tutoring
Bond's sexuality. The fact of the matter is that Bond is not
himself in *You Only Live Twice*; nor, for that matter, is he

properly equipped. At the opening of the novel he is in the deepest and most acute of his 'dog-days' crises. Deranged by the loss of Tracy – killed, shortly after marrying Bond, at the end of *On Her Majesty's Secret Service* – Bond is a physical wreck. Disinterested in his work (He told his doctors: 'I feel like hell. I sleep badly. I eat practically nothing. I drink too much and my work has gone to blazes. I'm shot to pieces. Make me better', p. 25), he is suffering from impotence, visits prostitutes in an attempt to 'regain his manhood by having a woman' (p. 25) and harbours feelings of deep resentment toward M ('Anyway, who's afraid of the Big Bad M?', p. 27). Sent to Japan by M (basically to see if the challenge of a mission will jolt him out of himself), Bond is sent as other than himself. Deprived of his 007 prefix and, with it, his licence to kill and carry a gun ('there won't be any strong-arm stuff', M gave a frosty smile, 'none of the gun-play you pride yourself on so much', p. 30) Bond is sent on his mission symbolically castrated (the link between gun and phallus is made clear later when Bond, visiting a Japanese whorehouse, 'remembered his interview with M and M saying that he could leave the hardware behind on this purely diplomatic assignment; and the lines of irony round Bond's mouth deepened', p. 81). He is, moreover, subject to a process of renaming so that, in the course of the narrative, his identity is progressively dissolved: M gives him a new number (7777), Tiger Tanaka rechristens him Bondo-san and, later, he assumes the disguise of Taro Todaroki, a deaf and dumb coal-miner from, incredibly enough, Fukuoka. Indeed, at the end of the novel, Bond's identity is dissolved completely. Suffering from amnesia after his terrible ordeal at Blofeld's Castle of Death, he stays on with Kissy Suzuki, living the life of a simple fisherman, and is presumed dead in London (an obituary is printed in *The Times*). Nor is his name all that he forgets – 'he had forgotten how to perform the act of love' (p. 186) until Kissy procures a pillow-book: 'We'll start at page one', Bond exclaims when he gets the general idea.

In short, in *You Only Live Twice*, Bond is living through a peculiarly acute phase in his ever-ongoing, never-to-be-resolved Oedipal crisis. Indeed, between them, *You Only Live*

Twice and its sequel, *The Man with the Golden Gun*, offer a fairly explicit rehearsal of the Oedipus myth. In *You Only Live Twice*, Bond is sent away to a foreign land, is given another name, loses his memory so that, like Oedipus, he lacks a knowledge of his true identity and parentage, eventually leaves those who have adopted him (Kissy) and journeys back to his homeland where (having been captured and brainwashed by the KGB *en route*) he attempts, in the opening pages of *The Man with the Golden Gun*, to kill M. Moreover, having been symbolically castrated by M at the beginning of *You Only Live Twice* (M takes away Bond's gun and his licence to kill), Bond is subsequently exposed to the threat of real castration by the villain. Blofeld thus forces Bond to sit on a throne placed above a mud geyser set to erupt at fifteen minute intervals, calling to mind Tiger Tanaka's earlier regret that Bond had not had time to learn the art of testical retraction practiced by the Japanese *suma* wrestlers:

> It is a great pity that it is now too late for you to practice this art. It might have given you more confidence on your mission. It is my experience that agents most fear for that part of the body when there is fighting to be done or when they risk capture. These organs, as you know, are most susceptible to torture for the extraction of information (p. 103).

All things considered, throughout *You Only Live Twice*, Bond is in no fit condition, nor is he equipped (he is always unarmed), to respond to the challenge of a Honeychile Rider let alone the more exacting calls on his masculinity made by Domino Vitali or Pussy Galore. He is not 'in place' himself and unable to risk the extension of phallic prowess which his relations with 'the girl' usually require. An adventure of the phallus on one front only, the novel is, in this respect, untypical.

To appreciate why more fully, we now turn to consider the respects in which phallic imagery performs a connecting role within the ideological economy of the novels. We argued earlier the respects in which, through identification with

Bond, the reader is 'called' into the place of England and, accordingly, disposed to respond to the villain's conspiracy as a threat to the integrity of the subject position of Englishness which the novels construct. It is through the superimposition of this ideological position on to a textual position that the reader (may) come to be implicated in the narrative in the sense of having a subjective stake in the success of Bond's mission. Similarly, we have also suggested, in this section, that Bond, in constituting a reformed model of male sexuality, also supplies the point of reference in relation to which female sexuality is to be adjusted. The reader who takes the place of Bond is thus implicated in the narrative processes through which two related subject identities are constructed, put into crisis and, ultimately, confirmed. It is through the functioning of phallic imagery that these two aspects of the novels' narrative organisation are, potentially, related to one another.

Adventures of the phallus

Terry Eagleton has remarked that, enriched by the work of Lacan, psychoanalytical criticism nowadays is able to 'do more than hunt for phallic symbols'.[15] While this is true, it would be mistaken, in the case of the Bond novels, to ignore the part which such symbols – and the wider system of references to the Oedipus myth of which they form a part – play in the construction and organisation of the narrative. Nor is there any need to hunt for them: they positively leap from the page and there can be little doubt that Fleming's use of phallic imagery was quite carefully calculated. This is particularly true in his later novels which positively parade this aspect of their organisation. In *The Man with the Golden Gun*, for example, the file on Scaramanga includes a psychoanalytic assessment of his obsession with guns:

> It is a Freudian thesis, with which I am inclined to agree, that the pistol, whether in the hands of an amateur or of a professional gunman, has significance for the owner as a

symbol of virility – an extension of the male organ – and
that excessive interest in guns . . . is a form of fetishism
(p. 39).

Whilst most commentators have noted these aspects of the
novels, opinions have differed as to their significance.[16]
Umberto Eco and Kingsley Amis tend to regard them as
inconsequential. On the other hand, R. Trahair has offered
an elaborate Freudian reading of the novels, arguing that
their appeal consists in the opportunity they offer, via Bond,
of once again resolving the universal dilemma of infantile
history, the dilemma of both loving and hating father and
mother.[17] More commonly, and inevitably, the novels have
been regarded as an expression of Fleming's own unresolved
infantile psycho-drama – his excessive fondness for his
mother, his hostility towards his father, his generally
contemptuous attitudes towards women and his preference
for male companions being interpreted as a sign of his failure
to pass through the castration anxieties of the Oedipal phase
to assume a position of genitally-centred, female-directed
sexuality.[18]

Our own view is somewhat different: that is, that the use
of phallic imagery, the allusions to the Oedipus myth and
the castration complex fulfil an important signifying role in
the Bond novels in respect of the ways in which they play
into, connect with and reinforce the troubling of sexual
difference posed by 'the girl' and articulate these aspects of
the novels to the ideological and narrative tensions that are
worked through in relation to images of England and
Englishness. They are no more and no less than signifying
devices which add an extra dimension to the tensions that
are set up and resolved in the course of the narrative. An
extra dimension but not a marginal one in that in supplying
the means through which the different sources of narrative
tension meet, are overlapped on to one another and worked
through in a complexly organised system of interrelations,
they occupy the centre of the novels' ideological economy.
Nor is this surprising in view of the twofold functioning of
the phallus within the structure of the Oedipus complex in
serving as the privileged signifier of sexual difference in

relation to which male and female sexed identities are formed and, through the interdiction placed on incest in the name of the Father, in representing the world of the Law, the moral authority of the world of social institutions introjected in the form of the super-ego.[19]

We return to these more abstract considerations later. First, we examine the ways in which the 'phallic code' at work in the novels informs the relationships between the various principal characters, particularly M, the central axis around which this system of signification revolves, and Bond. It is clear that M functions as a surrogate father in relation to Bond and that the relations between the two are worked through in terms of the Oedipus complex. In M's person, the father principle is split as his attitudes towards Bond veer from the stern, demanding and unsympathetic – expressed in his 'frosty voice', his 'steel grey eyes', in his code-name for the cyphers (Mailedfist) – to expressions of fatherly care and solicitude (the exceptional regard he shows for Bond in forgiving him his assassination attempt and giving him a chance to win back his spurs in *The Man with the Golden Gun*). This quality of ambivalence is mirrored in Bond's attitudes toward M. Usually ones of excessive filial respect and obedience ('the man who held a great deal of his affection and all of his loyalty and obedience', *Diamonds are Forever*, p. 15; 'Bond felt a quick warmth of affection for this man who had ordered his destiny for so long', *You Only Live Twice*, p. 32), Bond also frequently rebels against and, at times, rejects the paternal authority vested in M:

> A sudden wave of anger poured through him. This was all M's fault. M was mad. He would have it out with him when he got back to Headquarters. If necessary he would go higher – to the Chiefs of Staff, the Cabinet, the Prime Minister. M was a dangerous lunatic – a danger to the country. It was up to Bond to save England (*Thunderball*, p. 34).

However, M does not function merely as a father in relation to Bond. The entire Secret Service is represented as an imaginary household with M at its head, Miss Moneypenny as a mother figure, Bond's fellow 00 officers as brothers and his secretaries – Mary Goodnight and Leolia Ponsonby – as sisters. Miss Moneypenny thus functions as an object of desire, chiefly because she basks in the power that radiates from M – 'the desirable Miss Moneypenny, M's all-powerful private secretary' is how she is introduced in *Diamonds are Forever* (p. 13) – but, since she belongs to M, she is placed under an interdiction (Bond's playful flirtation with her is destined to remain forever playful). Miss Moneypenny, moreover, mediates the relations between Bond and M. Guarding the portals to Bond's office, she warns Bond of M's moods, frets when Bond is ill or neglects his duty and, as the occasion demands, takes the side of the father or that of the son. In *You Only Live Twice*, she responds to Bond's disparagement of M with the 'ill-concealed hostility' (p. 27) of motherly reproof whereas, in *Thunderball*, she tries to reassure Bond that M's insistence that he visit a health clinic merely reflects his concern for Bond's health and well-being:

> Miss Moneypenny gave a secret smile. 'You know he thinks the world of you – or perhaps you don't. Anyway, as soon as he saw your medical he told me to book you in.' Miss Moneypenny screwed up her nose. 'But James, do you really drink and smoke as much as that? It can't be good for you, you know.' She looked up at him with motherly eyes (p. 14).

However, the incest prohibition applies to all the women in the Service (in Fleming's novels, that is; John Gardner makes bedfellows of Bond and Ann Reilly – or Q'ute – the Armourer's assistant, in *For Special Services*). Little mothers/big sisters to a woman, they are either out of play or put themselves out of play. In *Moonraker*, we are told that Bond and two others members of the 00 section had, at various times, made determined assaults on Leolia Ponsonby's virtue: 'She had handled them all with the same cool motherliness (which to salve their egos, they privately defined as frigidity) and, the day after, she treated them with small attentions and kindnesses to show that it was really her fault and that she forgave them' (p. 8).

Unable to form a relationship within the Service, she seemed destined to a spinster's life:

> But, for the women, an affair outside the Service automatically made you a 'security risk' and in the last analysis you had a choice of resignation from the Service and a normal life, or of a perpetual concubinage to your King and Country ... (but) every day it seemed more difficult to betray by resignation the father-figure which The Service had become (p. 8).

Interestingly enough, the only exception to this rule occurs in *The Man wiht the Golden Gun* in which, having tried to assassinate M, Bond subsequently possesses Mary Goodnight – in Jamaica, far away from the stern eye of M – in an episode that is replete with allusions to the incest prohibition: 'Bond put his hand under the soft chin and lifted up her mouth and kissed her full on the half-open lips. He said, "Why didn't we ever think of doing that before, Goodnight? Three years with only that door between us! What must we have been thinking of?"' (p. 52).

M's significance, however, is not merely that of serving as a surrogate father to Bond and the Secret Service household. He also functions as the Symbolic Father defined, by Lacan, as he who is capable of saying 'I am who I am';[20] the source of an identity that is complete and full in relation to itself, in no need of external supports, and in relation to which other identities and roles may therefore be constructed. M is just that: M – a place of pure being, complete and final, the originating source of all action and the centre of meaning. As Symbolic Father, M represents the phallus as the privileged signifier in relationship to which sexual difference is defined just as he represents the authority of the Law and of Knowledge ('Only M and his Chief of Staff know absolutely everything there is to know', *The Man with the Golden Gun*, p. 7). Yet M also, as we have seen, represents Englishness. He is the point around which there cluster all those references to England's greatness, the virtues of tradition and duty, and the strengths of the national character. He is also, as we argued earlier, the stand-in, in the texts, for those institutions –

most notably, the monarchy – which constitute the points of interpellation in relation to which Bond is called to the service of England and sent forth as its delegated representative.

M thus fulfils a number of signifying and narrative functions. He is central to the structure of signification within the novels in the sense that, as Symbolic Father – as representative of both England and of the phallus as the privileged signifier of sexual difference – he is the point in relation to which the tensions worked through in the relations between Bond and England and Bond and 'the girl' are overlapped on to one another. The system of differences – national, sexual and racial – at work in the novels radiate out from M as the point of reference in relation to which the defining characteristics of the principal characters (the racial characteristics of the villain, for example) derive their differential signifying value by virtue of being contrasted with the qualities accumulated in M's person (the qualities of Englishness, for example).

M is also central to the structure of action within the novels. Everything begins and ends with M: he sets Bond off on his mission and is the point to which, at the end of the novel – or the beginning of the next one – Bond again refers himself. Sent forth against a target of M's choosing, Bond furthermore derives his power and authority – his 'licence to kill', and his gun – from M. Licensed possessor of the gun-cum-phallus, Bond, as well as functioning as the delegated representative of England, is also, and at the same time, the delegated representative of the phallic power and authority that is accumulated in M's person. He is thus employed in the service of both King and Country and of the phallus in being sent forth to quell the disturbances – the conspiracy of the villain, the 'sexual deviance' of both the villain and 'the girl' – which threaten both. It is thus that, in *You Only Live Twice*, Blofeld refers to Bond as 'a blunt instrument wielded by dolts in high places' (p. 171), while, in *The Man with the Golden Gun*, Bond expresses his resentment against M in similar terms: 'And for most of my adult life you've used me as a tool' (p. 22). But he that giveth may also taketh away: if M gives Bond his gun, he also – repeatedly – takes it away again with the result that Bond is never secure in the possession of the phallus, never, so to speak, has one of his own but only one which he holds conditionally, which he must earn the right to and which he may therefore lose. He is, in short, always in the place of the son and never that of the father. It is through the part that guns play in mediating the transactions between Bond and M that the never-to-be resolved castration anxieties of Bond's endless Oedipus complex are worked into the structure of the narrative.

Thus, stripped of his gun – and his 007 prefix – in *You Only Live Twice*, the task that is assigned to him in *The Man with the Golden Gun* in order to redeem his revolt against the Father and earn the right to resume his place in the Service is to kill Scaramanga, possessor of the gleaming phallus ('the golden gun') and 'the most efficient one-man death dealer in the world' (p. 168):

> James Bond would not possess the Double-0 prefix if he had not high talents, frequently proved, as a gunman. So be it! In exchange for the happenings that morning, in expiation of them, Bond must prove himself at his old skills. If he succeeded, he would have regained his previous status. If he failed, well, it would be a death for which he would be honoured (p. 30).

By contrast, at the end of *Moonraker*, M sends Bond a gift of two guns as a mark of his exceptional appreciation while, at the beginning of *Dr No*, Bond, in being stripped of his Beretta, is subject to a symbolic castration which, as we shall show in due course, constitutes one of the primary disturbances which the narrative works to correct. Reprimanding Bond for having been bested by Rosa Klebb at the end of *From Russia, With Love*, M attributes this to Bond's unprofessional fondness for his Beretta and insists that he change his gun ('we'll have to change your equipment' p. 18), threatening to withdraw his 00 prefix if he refuses: 'Your gun got stuck, if I recall. This Beretta of yours with the silencer. Something wrong there, 007. Can't afford that sort of mistake if you're to carry an 00 number. Would you prefer to drop it and go back to normal duties?' (p. 17).

His Beretta having been belittled as a 'ladies gun' (p. 18), Bond is re-equipped with the heavier and more powerful Smith and Wesson, although he clearly resents being forced to part with his Beretta in a passage whose masturbatory and castratory references are clear enough to require no further comment:

> His eyes slid to the gun and holster on the desk. He thought of his fifteen years' marriage to the ugly bit of metal. He remembered the times its single word had saved his life – and the times when its threat alone had been enough. He thought of the days when he had literally dressed to kill – when he had dismantled the gun and oiled it and packed the bullets carefully into the springloaded magazine and tried the action once or twice, pumping the cartridges out on to the bedspread in some hotel bedroom somewhere round the world. Then the last wipe of a dry rag and the gun into the little holster and a pause in front of the mirror to see that nothing showed . . . Bond felt unreasonably sad. How could one have such ties with an inanimate object, an ugly one at that, and, he had to admit it, with a weapon that was not in the same class as the ones chosen by the Armourer? But he had the ties and M was going to cut them. M swivelled back to face him. 'Sorry, James,' he said, and there was no sympathy in his voice. 'I know how you like that bit of iron. But I'm afraid it's got to go. Never give a weapon a second chance – any more than a man. I can't afford to gamble with the double-0 section. They've got to be properly equipped. You understand that? A gun's more important than a hand or a foot in your job.'
>
> Bond smiled thinly. 'I know, sir. I shan't argue. I'm jusy sorry to see it go' (pp. 20–1).

In the majority of cases, then, Bond is sent on his mission either symbolically castrated, without a gun, or as the bearer of a gun-cum-phallus donated by M and heavily invested with his phallic authority. The threat which the villain articulates is that of real castration. In *Casino Royale*, Le

Chiffre beats Bond's testicles with a carpet beater ('Say good-bye to it, Bond', p. 127); Hugo Drax threatens Bond's vitals with a blow-torch (which is no match for Bond: its pressure runs out so that it eventually 'gave a quiet plop and went out', p. 164); Goldfinger directs a circular saw at Bond's genitals, whereas the menace which Dr No embodies is always phallically articulated – as in the poisonous centipede his agent directs against Bond's groin, or in the threat of castration represented by his claws, especially when he surveys the vulnerability of Bond's sleeping nakedness. Of course, in such instances, it is not merely Bond's vitals that are threatened, but Bond himself and everything that has been invested in him. The threat posed by the villain is that Bond, as emissary of the English phallus, extended for 'overseas duty', might be cut off.

The villain also alludes to the Oedipal relations between Bond and M by way of inverting them. He thus stands opposed to M as an alternative embodiment of the. father principle. Bond views Mr Big, for example, 'with awe, almost with reverence' (*Live and Let Die*, p. 218) whilst Le Chiffre speaks to Bond 'like a father' (p. 120). Equally important, the villain serves as a counterpoint to Bond's excess of filial obedience, and as a possible model for his rebellious tendencies, in the respect that his biography usually evidences a complete lack of respect for the father and, accordingly, for all forms of authority. Dr No is the classic example. 'I changed my name,' he tells Bond, 'to Julius No – the Julius after my father and the No for my rejection of him and of all authority' (p. 134). Finally, the villain is always, in some way, sexually aberrant. He signifies either an insufficiency of sexuality – he is either impotent or neuter – or, as is the case with Mr Big, an excess of sexuality. At the same time, however, the villain's phallic authority is indisputable, indeed, overwhelming. Bond is overawed by Hugo Drax's rocket, 'his eyes dazzled by the terrible beauty of the greatest weapon on earth' (p. 84), and, when outgunned by Dr No's dragon-vehicle, reflects on how ineffective his Smith and Wesson is against 'the glowing red filament of the firer deep inside the big tube' and asks himself: 'Why had he been so

insane as to take on this man with his devastating armoury?
Why hadn't he been warned by the long finger that had
pointed at him in Jamaica?' (p. 103).

In these ways, the villain threatens to undermine Bond's
certainty of the distinction between right and wrong, good
and evil, male and female, in constituting a rival source of
phallic authority, a phallus articulated to social, political and
sexual deviance. The villain, in short, in striking at the very
centre of Bond's being, threatens to de-centre him, to pull
him out of the ideological places into which he has been
stitched in being enlisted in the service of England and the
patriarchal phallus. It is no small wonder, therefore, that if,
in the 'dog-days' prior to his enlistment by M, Bond
frequently functions as a drifting subject, his contest with
the villain often induces bouts of ideological derangement.
Thus, in *Casino Royale*, when Bond is in hospital recovering
from the injuries inflicted on him by Le Chiffre, worried lest
he has been made impotent, and with the mark of SMERSH –
described, interestingly enough, as an inverted 'M' (rather
than a 'W') – branded on his hand, he outlines his reasons
for considering resigning to Mathis:

> 'The hero kills two villains, but when the hero Le Chiffre
> starts to kill the villain Bond and the villain Bond knows
> he isn't a villain at all, you see the other side of the medal.
>   The villains and heroes get all mixed up.'
>   'Of course,' he added, as Mathis started to expostulate,
> 'patriotism comes along and makes it seem fairly alright,
> but this country-right-or-wrong business is getting a little
> out-of-date. Today we are fighting Communism. Okay. If
> I'd been alive fifty years ago, the brand of Conservatism
> we have today would have been damn near called
> Communism and we should have been told to go and fight
> that. History is moving pretty quickly these days and the
> heroes and villains keep on changing parts' (p. 143).

As Mathis replies: '"Anyone would think from the rot you
talk that he had been battering your head instead of your
. . ." He gestured down the bed' (p. 143).

It can now be seen why 'the girl' constitutes such a

problem for Bond. In the midst of the Oedipal phase herself, looking for a man who can compensate for the absence of her father (Honeychile Rider), or having failed to pass through it to assume a female sexuality 'correctly positioned' within the regime of the phallus, she threatens to divert the phallic power Bond needs in his contest with the villain ('Doesn't do to get mixed up with neurotic women in this business,' M warns in *From Russia, With Love*. 'They hang on to your gun-arm, if you see what I mean', p. 86) or to over-extend Bond-as-phallus and thus expose him to risk.

Thus, in the novels in which Bond is subject to a symbolic castration, he is able to give his full attention to 'the girl' only after the villain has been vanquished. Although, in *Live and Let Die*, Bond's abduction of Solitaire constitutes 'a dent in The Big Man's machine' (p. 86), Mr Big has likewise symbolically disabled 'Bond's machine' (by breaking his little finger) so that he is unable to make love to Solitaire. The most he can do is to threaten literally to impale her into her proper place when he is recovered: 'And then one day when you're playing your little game you'll suddenly find yourself pinned down like a butterfly' (p. 114).

Again, however, this theme is most clearly developed in *Dr No*. If Bond is unable to respond to Honeychile's overtures, this is because he has been unmanned, symbolically by M and literally by Dr No (he takes Bond's gun away). Honeychile herself taunts Bond on the question of his manhood on the second occasion he resists her advances:

> I wonder why he's frightened. Of course if I wrestled with him I'd win easily. Perhaps he's frightened of that. Perhaps he's really not very strong. His arms and chest look strong enough. I haven't seen the rest yet. Perhaps it's weak. Yes, that must be it. That's why he doesn't dare take his clothes off in front of me (p. 118).

Bond is only able to turn his attention to Honeychile once he has defeated Dr No and, in the process, reacquired his phallic authority in regaining possession of a gun which, tried and tested in action, he has made his own. This occurs after Bond passes through the trial of pain and courage Dr

No sets for him – a trial which constitutes a symbolic rebirth which counterbalances and cancels out the symbolic castration with which his mission is inaugurated. For the form of Bond's trial – imprisoned in a womb-like cell, he has to climb a narrow vertical shaft, then work his way through a long, heated, uterine like passage, filled with tarantula spiders, before being jettisoned into a pool inhabited by a giant squid – arguably mimics the various stages in the process from inception to birth and the perils the foetus encounters on the way. Bond's first act, after passing through this ordeal, is to repossess a gun – a Smith and Wesson, but not exactly the same as that with which he was equipped by M (he acquires a 'Smith and Wesson .38, the regular model' (p. 172) rather than the Smith and Wesson Centennial Airweight provided by M). Having acquired the gun, Bond puts it where it belongs – 'He slipped it down inside his waistband. It was fine to feel the heavy cold metal against his skin' (p. 172). It is only after this point in the novel that Bond, now the possessor of a gun-cum-phallus won by his own deeds, becomes the initiator of action in his struggle with Dr No and is able to respond to the task of tutoring Honeychile's sexuality. The nearest he ever comes to passing through the Oedipal phase, Bond communicates his rejection of the gun-cum-phallus donated him by M in the signal he sends him at the end of the novel: 'KINDLY INFORM ARMOURER SMITH AND WESSON INEFFECTIVE AGAINST FLAME-THROWER ENDIT' (p. 186).

In other cases, it is 'the girl' who draws Bond out, exposing him to the villain's threat of castration. In *Casino Royale*, Bond is thus lured to Le Chiffre's hideout through the kidnapping of Vesper, trussed up with her skirt above her head so that the lower part of her body is exposed – cunt-bait set to trap a cock. Indeed, the very plot of *From Russia, With Love* is organised around this conception. Bond, as we have argued earlier, is selected as a target by SMERSH as a consequence of his being deemed the most consummate embodiment of the myth of England. Bond is thus enticed to Turkey by the prospect of acquiring a Spektor decoding machine which a Russian cipher clerk (Tatiana Romanova, a member of the State Security working to the orders of Rosa

Klebb) has promised, but only if Bond collects it and, at the same time, her (she has allegedly fallen in love with him from his picture). Bond's instructions are clear: he is sent forth 'to pimp for England' (p. 93) and, when he expresses concern that Tatiana might be disappointed in him, M warns firmly: 'It's up to you to seē that you *do* come up to her expectations' (p. 90). Understandably enough, Bond has acute performance anxieties:

> Would he able to act the part? Perhaps he could make the right faces and say the right things, but would his body dissociate itself from his secret thoughts and effectively make the love he would declare? . . . Perhaps there was an erotic stimulus in the notion that one was ravishing a sack of gold. But a cipher machine? (p. 94).

Tatiana's role, however, is not merely that of cunt-bait set to trap the English cock (and smelly bait, too: Bond 'will be available to go after our bait when they get the scent', Kronsteen remarks, p. 76); she is also the centre of the enigma within the narrative, a disturbance in the world of signs, a point where word and meaning fail to coincide. Subject to the domination of Rosa Klebb – a phallic mother ('You must learn, my dear Tania, to treat me as you would your mother', p. 67) who stands in relation to Tatiana as M stands in relation to Bond – Tatiana promises to supply the key to meaning (the Spektor decoding machine) but is herself a riddle (knowledge of the true nature of the conspiracy, in which she is a mere pawn, is withheld from her). Her behaviour constitutes an enigma which Bond has to resolve and, as his reply to Darko Kerim shows, he knows how to do so:

'There is only one way of telling if a woman really loves you, and even that way can only be read by an expert.

'Yes,' said Bond dubiously. 'I know what you mean. In bed' (p. 106).

Drawn forth from England, then, solely in order to be killed in circumstances that will compromise England as he withdraws with his prize, Bond frustrates the villain's conspiracy by an unexpected piece of phallic improvisation.

Red Grant – opposed to Bond as the body that doesn't respond to women versus the body that must – makes his mistake in relying unduly on the power of the gun, apparently unaware of the fact that, in this particular novel, knives and swords are constructed as the true centre of phallic authority. The equation between sword or knife and the phallus is first established when Bond, prior to being enlisted into service by M, reflects on his tendency to carelessness, the result of months of enforced inactivity ('Now, from months of idleness and disuse, the sword was rusty in the scabbard and Bond's mental guard was down', p. 80) and is reinforced at various subsequent points in the novel (Darko Kerim advises Bond not to indulge himself too fully with the dancing girls at the gipsy camp: 'You must keep your sword sharp', p. 123; and Tatiana looks out of the Orient Express at 'the tall figure of James Bond, straight and hard and cold as a butcher's knife, coming and going', pp. 172–3). Thus, although Red Grant disarms Bond and shoots at him, with his own gun, from the groin, Bond is able to turn the tables with his knife, driving it into Grant's groin: 'The fist with the long steel finger, and all Bond's arm and shoulder behind it, lunged upwards. Bond's knuckles felt flannel. He held the knife, forcing it in further' (p. 199). Unexpectedly, however, the role of domination returns to the phallic mother as, at the very end of the novel, Rosa Klebb stabs Bond in the calf with a poisoned knife protruding from her boot.

To conclude, the narrative function of the 'phallic code', so clearly in evidence in the Bond novels, is that of overlayering the tensions which the narrative constructs and works across in relation to ideologies of nation and nationhood, sexuality and gender – and, of course, those of the Cold War period or détente – adding to these sources of narrative and ideological suspense an extra dimension of excitation organised around the threat of castration and its avoidance. Ultimately, the threat of ideological disruption embodied in both the villain's conspiracy and 'the girl's out-of-placeness' is avoided because Bond – as delegated representative of M, the holding centre of England and the patriarchal order – proves 'man enough' for the task. It is also by the operation of the 'phallic code' that the two centres of narrative tension constituted in the relations between Bond and the villain and Bond and the girl are connected: figuratively speaking, their interconnection might be expressed by saying that Bond puts England back on top at the same time as he places 'the girl' back in place beneath him. Finally, the Oedipal tensions which characterise the relations between Bond and M support the respects in which, as father and son, they are differentiated as representatives of England and Englishness in their old and new styles, as well as opening up a space in which Bond can function as a model of sexual readjustment.

Situating the analysis

Our analysis of the Bond novels in this chapter has been implicitly directed against reductionist accounts of popular fiction which typically construe such works as no more than containers for ideology, passing it on unmodified or subjecting it to a formulaic reproduction. We have sought, to the contrary, to stress the respects in which the Bond novels initiate a set of intersecting processes in relation to a number of interacting ideologies, subjecting them to a reformation in view of the ways in which they are worked across by the establishment and resolution of a series of imbricated narrative tensions. In doing so, our account has had in mind, as its implied reader, the male reader of the early 1960s when, as we argued in Chapter 2, Bond functioned as a hero of modernisation, facilitating an adjustment from one image of nationhood to another and from one model of sexuality to another, particularly when viewed against the backdrop of the earlier tradition of the imperialist spy-thriller as the most immediately relevant point of inter-textual comparison bearing on the formation of male British readers in this period.

It should be clear, however, that we do not offer this analysis as though it revealed the true meaning of the Bond novels or constituted a scientifically neutral description of their objective structures. On the contrary, we have contended that neither the meanings nor the meaning-producing structures of texts can be specified independently of the reading formations which regulate reading practices. Our purpose, in focusing on the culturally dominant reading formation of the earlier and distinctively British phases in Bond's career as a popular hero has been to throw some light on the ways in which, read in this context, the Bond novels were able to assume a position of central significance within a number of closely interacting cultural and ideological processes. Our intention in choosing this as the starting point for our analysis has not been to fix it as a moment of truth or origin in relation to which the inter-textual co-ordinates which have regulated the reading of the Bond novels in other reading formations should be discounted or disparaged. Quite the opposite: as we turn now to consider the Bond films our purpose is to examine the respects in which, in adding to 'the texts of Bond', they contributed to a reorganisation of the inter-textual relations in relation to which both the films and the novels were read.

Chapter 5

The Transformations of James Bond

The period of the production of the early James Bond films involved a crucial transformation in the texts of James Bond. At one level, the form of that transformation seems relatively simple. A number of Ian Fleming's books were made into films, beginning with *Dr No* in 1962 and continuing on an annual basis with *From Russia, With Love* (1963), *Goldfinger* (1964) and *Thunderball* (1965). There was nothing new in this. The translation of literary or dramatic fiction could be said to be commonplace in film history. Both Hollywood and the British film industry had ruthlessly looted popular and classical fiction and many heroes of popular fiction, such as Sherlock Holmes and Bull-Dog Drummond, had already made their successful screen appearances. Discussions of this process have tended to devolve upon questions such as whether or not film versions of a book or play remain true to the original author's intentions or to concentrate on the respective merits of films and the literary texts from which they have been derived.

The relationship between the Bond novels and the Bond films has certainly generated this order of comment. Earlier, Fleming's authorship had been both attacked and celebrated. 'Without a doubt the nastiest book I have ever read,' Paul Johnson wrote with his customary moral fervour about *Dr No*, 'incorporating the sadism of a schoolboy bully, the mechanical two dimensional sex-craving of a frustrated adolescent and the crude snob cravings of a suburban adult.'[1] Amis, on the other hand, threw himself into Fleming's defence. Fleming's proper place, he argued, lies 'with those demi-giants of an earlier day, Jules Verne, Rider Haggard, Conan Doyle'.[2] With the production of the films, the centre of gravity of Bond criticism shifted as the relative merits of the films and the novels were weighed in the balance. Here, again, opinion was divided. Kingsley Amis, for example, suggested that the parodying and joking elements of the films destroyed the real mythic power of the Bond figure as displayed in the books.[3] Shana Alexander similarly argued that the films inadequately translated the qualities of the novels, in that the films became 'caricatures of the caricatures' and James Bond became 'the put-on's put-on'.[4]

Likewise Zorzoli, in an early book of critical essays on Bond, commented that the use of a circular saw to threaten Bond in the novel of *Goldfinger* was 'simple and efficacious' while 'in the film a laser is employed in an entirely gratuitous exhibition'.[5] Dow, writing of the same sequence, took a completely different view:

> Only by comparing the novels with the films can one appreciate the film-maker's art behind *Dr No*, *From Russia, With Love*, *Goldfinger* and *Thunderball*, in that the transfer from the novel to film has been highly successful in each case and with thoroughly conventional film techniques. Almost without exception the books have been made more topically pertinent, more melodramatic and certainly more visually suitable. In the novel, *Goldfinger*, for example, the villain ties Bond down in a spread eagled position on a work bench and activates a large buzz saw with which he threatens to saw Bond in two; in the film the buzz saw is discarded for a menacing industrial laser, which threatens Bond with its bright red beam of intense light. The very modernity of the device renders it all the more awesome and sidesteps a very stereotype situation through its updated technology.[6]

In this chapter, we want to explore the transformation of Fleming's novel *Goldfinger* into the film of *Goldfinger* in a slightly different way, focusing rather less on questions of authorship, value and morality than on the shifts within the mythology of James Bond established by the films. In the first place, we want to consider the formal differences between the two texts of *Goldfinger* in terms of character, plot and narrative organisation. In the second place, we shall examine the ways in which the film of *Goldfinger* marked a significant change in the system of inter-textual relations through which the figure of James Bond was constructed and put into broader social circulation. By the time Penelope Houston attended the London press showing of *Goldfinger*, the conventions of the Bond film genre had been established. Penelope Houston addressed an audience familiar in the ways of James Bond:

> The pre-credits sequence of *Goldfinger* ends, as everyone knows, with an impromptu electrocution. Caught for a moment without his revolver (the trusty Beretta? or the Walther with the tailored holster?) Bond catches a glimpse of an advancing assailant reflected in the eyeball of a lady with whom he is temporarily engaged. Casually, he gets her out of the way by flinging her in the path of his opponent. Scuffle: villain tipped into bath, but still clutching Bond's pistol firmly above the waterline: the electric fire is hurled across the room with a movement reminiscent of a slip fielder shattering the bails; and exit in a cloud of steam another emissary of SMERSH or SPECTRE. At which moment, the audience of the London press show gave that concerted yell of innocent happiness, that collective sigh of satisfied expectation, which has become the standard accompaniment to the exploits of 007.[7]

The respects in which, by this period, the currency of Bond had changed, however, cannot be understood solely in terms of the reworking of the novels by the films. The period of the first three Bond films also saw important changes in the audience for Bond, in the forms of production of 'the texts of Bond' and in the general cultural pressures moulding and organising reading practices. To say that the inter-textual relationships of Bond had altered is to point not only to changes between the novels and the films, but also to the changes in the ideological discourses and formations against which the Bond texts were both produced and read.

Beginnings

What are the main differences between the novel and the film of *Goldfinger*? Broccoli and Salzman suggested that the early Bond novels were tailor-made for film-making and required little in the way of adaptation. 'When I first read the Bond books,' Broccoli remarked, 'they appealed to me as good films because in the early ones that he [Fleming] wrote, they were practically scripted.'[8] The differences between even the openings of the two texts of *Goldfinger*, however, suggest that the transition from novel to film was by no means a smooth or merely mechanical process. The novel of *Goldfinger* begins with a moment of introspection on the part of its hero: 'James Bond with two double bourbons inside him, sat in the final departure lounge of Miami airport and thought about life and death' (p. 7).

The passage establishes Bond's character and credentials quickly. This was after all the seventh James Bond novel, written in 1958 and published in 1959. Bond's 'reflections in a double bourbon', occasioned by his assassination of a Mexican involved in an international heroin racket take up a further six pages. Time for brief philosophising:

> What an extraordinary difference there was between a body full of person and a body that was empty! Now there is someone. Now there is no one. This had been a Mexican with a name and an address, an employment card and perhaps a driving licence. Then something had gone out of him, out of the envelope of flesh and cheap clothes, and had left him an empty paper bag waiting for the dustcart. And the difference, the thing that had gone out of the stinking Mexican bandit, was greater than all Mexico (p. 7).

But the philosophising is cut short:

Bond looked down at the weapon that had done it. The cutting edge of his right hand was red and swollen. It would soon show a bruise. Bond flexed the hand, kneading it with his left. He had been doing the same thing at intervals through the quick plane trip that had got him away. It was a painful process but if he kept the circulation moving the hand would heal more quickly. One couldn't tell how soon the weapon would be needed again. Cynicism gathered at the corner of Bond's mouth (p. 8).

The introduction to the novel of *Goldfinger* is characterised by what Kingsley Amis refers to as the 'Fleming effect', an imaginative use of information which gives realism to the essentially fantastic nature of Bond's world. Amis outlines the pedigree of the technique:

> It [the information] provides motives and explanations for action and the information itself is valuable, not simply as information, but in the relish and physical quality it lends to the narrative. A gun-boat in a well written boys' book can't just be a gun-boat, it must be (say) of the *Zulu* class with five 4.7's arranged in two pairs for'ard and aft and a single one amidships, not, again, just to be believable or because we need to understand about the guns for later or because we like guns, but also so that the gun-boat shall be fully *there*. To mention boys' books doesn't denigrate this interest, it merely helps to define it.[9]

Eco similarly identifies the opposition in Fleming's style between a story concerned with wicked, violent and often fantastic acts and a narrative that proceeds through the description of ordinary and trifling events:

> In fact what is surprising in Fleming is the minute and leisurely concentration with which he pursues for page after page descriptions of articles, landscapes and events apparently inessential to the course the story; and conversely the feverish brevity with which he covers in a few paragraphs the most unexpected and improbable

actions. A typical example is to be found in *Goldfinger* with two long pages dedicated to a casual meditation on a Mexican murder, fifteen pages dedicated to a game of golf, twenty five occupied with a long car trip across France, as against the four or five pages which cover the arrival at Fort Knox of a false hospital train and the *coup de théâtre* which culminated in the failure of Goldfinger's plan and the death of Tilly Masterton.[10]

In contrast to the opening of the book, the preliminary sequences of the film contain no moments of self-reflection and this form of realism is not invoked. In the course of these sequences, a man is killed, an installation blown up and reference is made to the breaking of a heroin racket. There, however, the resemblance ends. The beginning of the film involves three key sequences, which are worth looking at in some detail.

1. *The James Bond sequence*

The film begins in the manner established by the film of *Dr No*. Across the black screen and to the accompaniment of the James Bond theme, we see the double 00 roll across the screen and one 0 becomes the camera lens through which we see James Bond who turns and shoots directly into the camera. As he does so, a wave of red spreads across the screen.

2. *The pre-credits sequence*

Shot 1: A long shot of guards walking around a large installation at night. The camera pans across to a small harbour with a sea bird resting on the water. Bond emerges from the water to reveal that the sea gull is part of his head-gear.

Shot 2: Bond walks out of the water throwing off diving equipment and sea gull, and shoots a rope and clamp up the wall.

Shot 3: A guard is knocked out by Bond who runs on to a circular building.

Shot 4: Bond enters a circular room by a small side door. The room is full of dramatic curves including a huge circular sky light. Bond proceeds to squeeze out plastic explosive on to two large drums marked NITRO.

Shot 5: Bond sets the detonator and runs out.

Shot 6: Close-up of detonator.

Shot 7: Bond unzips his diving suit to reveal himself in full evening dress and puts a red carnation in his buttonhole.

Shot 8: The camera rests on the exposed body of a cafe dancer. She looks up at Bond.

Shot 9: Bond lights a cigarette and looks at his watch (a Rolex).

Shot 10: The installation explodes.

Shot 11: The camera focuses on Bond's calm face as people flee from the cafe in response to the explosion.

Shot 12: Bond walks down to the bar where a man is still drinking.

Shot 13: The man congratulates him.

Shot 14: The dancer flounces out of the door with a backward glance at Bond.

Shot 15: The man at the bar warns Bond to leave for Miami on the next plane. Bond replies tossing a set of keys casually, 'I'll be on it but first I have some unfinished business to attend to.'

Shot 16: Shot of a girl in the bath.

Shot 17: Bond enters and throws a towel at the girl, takes off his jacket and embraces the girl, who exclaims at the feel of the gun, 'Why do you always wear that thing?' Bond replies, while taking the shoulder holster and gun off, 'I have a slight inferiority complex', and resumes the embrace.

Shot 18: The camera focuses on a man advancing behind Bond with a raised club.

Shot 19: The girl's eyes look away from Bond in mid-kiss.

Shot 20: The man advances further.

Shot 21: A close-up of Bond's face looking suspicious.

Shot 22: The camera focuses on a reflection of the advancing villain in the girl's eyes.

Shot 23: Bond turns the girl he is holding to take the blow intended for him.

Shot 24: Bond throws his assailant against the wall and knees him in the groin.

Shot 25: A reaction shot of the thrown man who then hurls a stool at Bond.

Shot 26: A close-up of Bond's face followed by a struggle between the two which ends with Bond throwing his attacker backwards.

Shot 27: The man lands in the bath.

Shot 28: A close-up of Bond's face expressing amusement and triumph, which quickly changes to worry.

Shot 29: The man in the bath reaches for Bond's gun in the shoulder holster hung by the bath.

Shot 30: Bond looks around desperately and then throws the electric fire.

Shot 31: The fire lands in the water between the man's legs with a great sizzling.

Shot 32: The man's whole body stiffens.

Shot 33: A close-up of Bond's satisfied face. Bond then collects his shoulder holster and puts it back on, coolly commenting, 'Shocking.' He turns at a moaning noise.

Shot 34: The girl comes round on the floor and sits up, still rather miraculously clad in her towel. Bond puts on his coat to leave and repeats, 'Positively shocking!'

3. *Titles sequence*

In time with the theme song of *Goldfinger* we see a series of shots of a girl in a bikini, both made up and lit to look gold-coloured against a dark backbround.

Shot 1: The back of the girl's hand with Goldfinger's face seen as if reflected within it.

Shot 2: The girl's impassive face with Bond's face drinking and talking seen within it.

Shot 3: The girl's face with Pussy Galore seen within it.

Shot 4: The girl's face and torso with Oddjob within it. The same girl's shoulder is superimposed over the shot with Bond and Jill Masterton talking intimately and drinking champagne contained within it.

Shot 5: The girl's legs with Goldfinger's men contained within them.

Shot 6: The girl's body with Goldfinger's aeroplane reflected in it.

Shot 7: The girl's face with Bond's Lotus number plates swinging round in her mouth, in place of teeth.

Shot 8: The girl's shoulder showing Oddjob and the American criminal Solo.

Shot 9: The camera moves languorously down the girl's legs following the travelling car seen through the legs.

Shot 10: The girl's body through which we see Bond walk and turn.

Shot 11: The camera focuses on Bond running and falling with a helicopter overhead, but pulls back to show the scene contained within the girl's legs.

Shot 12: A shot of the girl's armpit – into which a golf ball rolls.

Shot 13: The girl's face in which hands struggle for a gun and it goes off.

Shot 14: The camera travels down the girl's face and body.

Shot 15: The girl's back with head bent forward – containing golden lit explosions, as the song reaches the climax.

Shot 16: The girl lying flat on her back. The camera travels down her body which is lit by red and gold flames, as 'He loves only gold, he loves gold' is repeated. On the final sustained note of the word gold, the camera shifts to the final shot.

Shot 17: The girl's hand with Goldfinger's face seen within it.

The *Goldfinger* pre-credits and titles sequences are characterised by speed and rhythm of cutting, paced to the pulsating beat of the James Bond theme and the theme song of *Goldfinger*. The sequences are both witty and involve a high degree of stylisation, of self-confident and tongue-in-cheek play with film conventions. The image of Bond with which

the film opens is typical of this. It proclaims the 'imagery' of
Bond in the transition of the double 0 into camera lens and
the focus on Bond walking and shooting into camera against
a pure white background, demanding the audience's instant
complicity with the playful use of film conventions. When, in
the novel, Bond kills the Mexican, it is a sobering experience
from which Bond must recover, 'the finishing touch of a bad
assignment'. Moreover, the actual killing is described
precisely in the order of terms which Amis describes as
typical of a well-written boys' book: 'Almost automatically,
Bond went into the "Parry Defence against Underhand
Thrust" out of the book. His right arm cut across, his body
swivelling with it' (p. 11).

In the film, this strategy of realism has disappeared and,
with it, the nuances of mood with which the James Bond of
the books was so well endowed: the faint bitterness; the
endless struggle, shared by many British thriller heroes,
against *accidie*; the slightly humourless capability and
resourcefulness, and the obsessional, almost old-maidish
concern with the specifics of the 'high life'. While Sean
Connery's James Bond is just as ruthless as the Bond of the
books, his killing is followed not by cynical and bitter
reflection but by the one line joke, 'Shocking, positively
shocking'. Moreover, the organisation of the Bond pre-credits
sequences is designed to draw the spectator into an understood
joke about the excesses of the Bond figure. Hence, in
Goldfinger, the visual gags abound from the plastic sea gull
under which we first see Bond's head to the removal of his
diving suit to reveal immaculate evening dress. The latter
joke is underlined by Bond's casual placing of a carnation in
his button hole.

The relationship of the titles sequence to the pre-credits
sequence is also essential to the impact of the opening of a
Bond film. Almost all the Bond films have used a titles
sequence in which the posed figures of scantily clad or naked
women play the central part. The sequence is shot in time to
the title song. At one level, those sequences seem to be very
much a part of a long tradition in mainstream Hollywood
cinema, whereby women are constructed in terms of erotic
spectacle. In her work on visual pleasure, Laura Mulvey

argues that woman 'displayed as sexual object is the leit-motif of erotic spectacle; from pin-ups to strip-tease, from Ziegfield to Busby Berkeley, she holds the look, plays to and signifies male desire'.[11] In Mulvey's analysis, visual pleasure in the cinema is linked to the existence of two partly opposed systems of looking. On the one hand, there is the pleasure of looking at women in terms of sexual stimulation. On the other hand, there is the pleasure of identification with the hero, who makes things happen and with whom the spectator shares the pleasure and the active power of the erotic look. Mulvey points out that there is always likely to be a conflict between such systems of looking. The erotic images of women which are a vital part of the spectacle in most commercial movies, tend to work against the narrative, slowing the unfolding of the plot through which identification with the hero is largely achieved. The titles sequence in *Goldfinger* certainly operates in this way, consciously puncturing the film after the mini-narrative of the pre-credits sequence. But the same sequence, while it can undoubtedly be read simply in terms of erotic pleasure organised around the male look, also offers a troubling of that eroticism.

The woman in the titles is totally fetishised, irrelevant, in the most obvious way to the narrative. She is both passive and impassive. But it is through her image that we see a simplified version of the main characters and the plot. She is represented as the *site* of Bond's battles with Goldfinger and, in this respect, functions as a complex and contradictory signifier. At once sexually alluring and rewarding, as desirable as the gold of the title song, and finally laid on her back, in the ultimate demonstration of Bond's phallic power, she is at the same time deeply troubling and threatening to Bond in containing, within her body, the castrating threat represented by Goldfinger. The forbidding hand placed at each end of the sequence reinforces the effect. The battle is for woman's body, woman's identity and woman's sexuality. 'The pretty girl' of the sequence is constantly warned by the song not to enter 'Goldfinger's web of sin'.

Plot changes

If there are significant differences between the opening of the novel and the opening of the film of *Goldfinger*, what of the rest of the two texts? Was the film *Goldfinger* indeed, almost scripted by Ian Fleming? Or are the transformations between novel and film rather more substantial than this formulation suggests?

In the first place, there are a plethora of changes in the plot. Many of these are organised around technological devices used by either Bond or the villain. The first and most simple example of this comes in the pre-credits sequence where Bond kills not in the 'Automatic Parry Defence against Underhand Thrust', but by electrocuting his assailant. Bond is also equipped by Q, who occupies a much more prominent place in all the Bond films than he does in the books, with a car, full of ingenious gadgets: release buttons for smoke and an oil slick, two mounted sub-machine guns, an extendable scythe-like wheel reminiscent of the chariot in Ben-Hur and a passenger ejector seat. The DB III which Bond takes from the service pool in the book is rather less lavishly equipped with switches to alter the type and colour of the car's front and rear lights, reinforced steel bumpers and a long-barrelled Colt .45 in a trick compartment. Moreover, the stress of Fleming's prose is on James Bond's *driving*. 'James Bond flung the DB III through the last mile of straight and did a racing change down into third and then into second for the short hill before the inevitable traffic crawl through Rochester' (p. 61). The film stresses the spectacular *use* of the various gadgets, culminating in the chase with Goldfinger's men in which each and every gadget is successfully employed, including the passenger ejector seat, with the precision and timing of an extended joke, playing on the audience's foreknowledge of the gadgets. Goldfinger's instruments of torture, as we have already noted, change from the circular saw, beloved of so many early film-makers, to the 'industrial laser' which Goldfinger employs with such relish.

Radar is employed throughout the film although its only use in the novel is to track Goldfinger's car across Europe. In the film it is used not only to enable Bond to follow

Goldfinger but also to allow the American CIA, in the person of Felix Leiter, to keep an eye on Bond. It also serves as the basis for Bond's attempts to warn the CIA that Goldfinger intends to attack Fort Knox. In the book, sheer ingenuity and chance suffice for this purpose. Bond writes a warning note and attaches the package under the lavatory seat on Goldfinger's aircraft, a contrivance which succeeds despite, as Amis points out, the overwhelming chances of the message being found by one of Goldfinger's gang.[12] The film accords greater respect to the laws of probability. Bond's resourcefulness combined with his equipment all go for naught in the face of Goldfinger's thoroughness. Bond places his message and a homing device in the car which is to take Mr Solo from Goldfinger's ranch to the airport. The car is driven by Oddjob who shoots Mr Solo and dispenses with the evidences by having the car, a Thunderbird, reduced to a small cube of metal in a nearby scrapyard. It is Pussy Galore rather than Bond who warns the CIA.

Oddjob's spectacular death by electrocution as he catches hold of his steel bowler wedged in the bars of the Fort Knox gold vaults is a further addition of the film. Oddjob's death in the novel, by being sucked out of an aircraft window, is reserved, in the film, for Goldfinger while the long strangulation through which Bond kills Goldfinger in the book is eliminated completely. The eradication of the Fort Knox defences, to be achieved in the novel by the introduction of a nerve poison, GB, to the water supply of the local population, is planned in the film as an exercise by aeroplanes, piloted by Pussy Galore's 'Flying Circus', which spray the area with nerve gas.

However, the difference between the film and the novel are not limited to the roles allocated to technological gadgetry. The political articulations of the plot also differ significantly. In the novel, Goldfinger's aim is to seize the American gold reserves and thereby become 'the richest man in the world, the richest man in history'. His conspiracy is supported by SMERSH, interested in provoking a currency crisis in the Western world. In the film, Goldfinger's conspiracy takes the form of a nuclear threat. An atomic device, provided by Red China, is to be detonated in Fort Knox, thereby contaminating

the American gold reserves for many years to come. Thus is
the interest of China explained while Goldfinger, as a member
of SPECTRE, should, if all goes well with the plan, experience
an enormous rise in value of his own holdings in gold.

The character of the Englishness represented by Bond also
differs significantly between the book and the film of *Goldfinger*.
In the former, Bond represents a fairly extreme version of
English chauvism. Bond's loyalty is to Queen and country as
represented, perhaps rather curiously, in the patriarchal
figure of M. When Goldfinger asks how Bond and England
came to intervene in his plans, Bond replies to both
Goldfinger's and other attacks on the 'decline of England':

> You underestimate the English. They may be slow but
> they get there. You think you'll be pretty safe in Russia? I
> wouldn't be too sure. We've got people out of even there
> before now. I'll give you one last aphorism for your book,
> Goldfinger: 'Never go a bear of England'. (p. 215)

In the film, this attack is neither made nor answered
because the role Bond occupies is more widely conceived as
representing the 'Western world' in general rather than
Britain in particular. Moreover, in the novel Bond protects
American interests in a manner which is more than slightly
contemptuous of American abilities to do the same. Bond, for
example, shares friendship with the CIA in the person of
Felix Leiter but effortlessly outdoes him in every sphere from
spying to sex. In the film, by contrast, Felix Leiter is given a
quasi-paternal role in relation to Bond. M requests Leiter
and the CIA to keep an eye on Bond while he is in America
and Leiter takes on this task of watching Bond, responding
to his signals and defusing the threat to Fort Knox, partly
but not solely because of Bond. (Pussy Galore, a fellow
American, has warned Washington of the plot.) In effect, the
maintenance of *pax Americana* is leased to Britain, in the
person of Bond, but only in the context of close
American supervision and background control. The 'domestic'
associations of Bond's Englishness are also significantly
transformed. Whereas, in the book, Bond's relationship to

M carries with it some of the nuances of public school 'fagging', fear, respect and admiration, in the film, Bond combines both loyalty to M and a distinct mockery of M's views as in some essential respects, notably those concerned with sensuality, outdated.

However, perhaps the most distinctive transformations concern the position accorded to 'the girl', or girls, in the unfolding of the plot. The girls Bond encounters in the novel are either involved with the villain (Jill Masterton and Pussy Galore) sexually deviant (Tilly Masterton and Pussy Galore are lesbians) or both (Pussy Galore). Their role is to be killed in the course of Bond's battles with the villain (Jill) thereby providing Bond with a further, more personal motivation, to be wooed away from the course of villainy and sexual deviance to Bond's cause and into his bed (Pussy), or to be eliminated as irredeemable (Tilly).

In the film, neither Tilly nor Pussy are represented as lesbians. Moreover, the attraction of Pussy Galore for Tilly is made impossible by Tilly's death much earlier in the plot. The two girls never meet. Pussy Galore, despite her name and the gang of buxom pilots whom she leads, becomes a much more independent character. Unmarked by sexual deviance, she is treated with respect by Goldfinger and handles Bond with little trouble. As a consequence, her ideological conversion is a relatively understated affair. We are led to believe that she informs the CIA of Goldfinger's conspiracy as a consequence of the passionate kiss which ends the mock battle in which she and Bond engage in Goldfinger's stables.

Such changes in the characterisation of 'the girl', however, are rather less important than the transformation of the sexual economy of the novel wrought by the film's use of the three girl format. By the time of the making of *You Only Live Twice* (1967), this format had become a part of the expectations of the genre. Roald Dahl, who wrote the script for *You Only Live Twice*, summarised this format in recounting the brief he was given by Cubby Broccoli:

'So you put in three girls. No more and no less. Girl

number one is violently pro-Bond. She stays around roughly through the first reel of the picture. Then she is bumped off by the enemy, preferably in Bond's arms.'

'In bed or not in bed?' I asked.

'Wherever you like so long as it's in good taste. Girl number two is anti-Bond. She works for the enemy and stays around throughout the middle third of the picture. She must capture Bond and Bond must save himself by bowling her over with sheer sexual magnetism. The girl should also be bumped off, preferably in an original fashion.'

'There aren't many of those left,' I said.

'We'll find one,' they answered. 'Girl number three is violently pro-Bond. She occupies the final third of the picture, and she must on no account be killed. Nor must she permit Bond to take any lecherous liberties with her until the very end of the story. We keep that for the fade out.'[13]

Nor are Bond's encounters with women limited to his relations with Jill, Tilly and Pussy. In the film of *Goldfinger*, Bond's sexual attractiveness is registered with a number of other women – with the girl of the pre-credits sequence, with the girl who is sent off from the Miami hotel poolside with a pat on the bottom in order that Bond can engage in 'men's talk' with Felix Leiter, with the bewildered chambermaid Bond encounters on his way to Goldfinger's hotel suite and, of course, with Miss Moneypenny. The economy of women in the films is altered from the novels from the existence of 'the girl' to the cornucopia of women available in the films. It is also altered by means of the variables of character and performance and, more particularly, by the relay of looks between Bond, women and the spectator.

Character and performance

Characters in films are constructed not simply in terms of their function, but also through the performance of actors and actresses and the shooting and cutting of those performances. The character of James Bond in *Goldfinger* undoubtedly owes much to Sean Connery's performance. Indeed, Connery's notably sexual physical presence and voice, his youth and athleticism in the earlier films and his failure to conform to earlier stereotypes of the British thriller hero have meant that, for many people, he is *the* James Bond. When George Lazenby took the part in *On Her Majesty's Secret Service*, the producers felt it necessary to refer to and attempt to 'send up' the Connery performance.

In the pre-credits sequence, Lazenby, as Bond, attempts to rescue a girl, Tracy, from a suicidal attempt at drowning. She is then dragged away by mysterious men who also attack Bond. In the ensuing fight, Bond wins, only to find that the girl has driven away, leaving only her shoes behind. He picks them up and comments to the camera, 'This never happened to the other fellow.' Throughout the period in which Roger Moore has played Bond, he has been continuously compared with Connery and himself has told various anecdotes to the press, revealing his son's belief that although his father plays James Bond, the 'real' James Bond is Connery. It has also been suggested that audience liking for the Connery performance as Bond militated against their liking him in any other roles, as the hero in Hitchcock's *Marnie*, for example. Mayersberg suggests that the lack of box office success for *Marnie* was based on the public's inability to adjust to Connery outside the James Bond part.[14] The same point could be made of many of the non-Bond films in which Connery has played the leading role. Callan notes that *Meteor* (1979) had a recorded loss of $15.8 million two years after its release, making it one of the biggest cinematic flops of all time.[15]

By the time of *Goldfinger*, however, Connery was already confidently established in the part of Bond. In looks, he bears some resemblance to the Bond of the books. He has 'the passionate rather cruel mouth' of Bond although 'the fiercely slitted grey eyes' (Connery has brown eyes) and the famous 'comma of black hair that had fallen over his right eyebrow' are missing, as is the scar on the right cheek. He also looks physically powerful and capable of the ruthlessness of the James Bond of the novel. But there are important differences in style and behaviour. Connery's Bond does not reflect even as fleetingly as the Bond of the novels on the moral problems of his occupation. He is noticeably less obsessional about food and possessions. His attitude of respectful admiration for M and, through M, for a particular image of the English nation is contradictorily implicated in the films in his continuous one-upmanship of M. He relishes embarrassing M in the Bank of England by demonstrating a superior knowledge of brandy. Moreover, Connery's James Bond has a relentless sense of humour. It is not only that he is the centre-point of a series of visual and verbal jokes. He also combines a 'serious' playing of the Bond role, with a comic undercutting of it. The famous one-line jokes which follow a Bondian action sequence tend to be addressed directly to camera. The effect is to pull the audience into complicity with the Connery/Bond figure in shared amusement about the excesses of the Bond mythology. The desire which Amis assumes is central to a reading of the Bond novels, the desire not to have Bond to dinner, or to play golf with him or to talk to him but 'to be Bond', is only one potential form of identification likely to be produced by the textual strategy of the films.

Connery's Bond in *Goldfinger* is also compellingly sexual. In the novel, Bond continuously comes across desirable women who are described in the type of detail which lies somewhere between soft pornography and romantic fiction. 'She was very beautiful. She had the palest blonde hair. It fell heavily to her shoulders, unfashionably long. Her eyes were deep blue against a lightly sunburned skin . . . Her breasts thrust against the black silk of the brassiere' (p. 34). His own sexuality, however, tends to be signified in the text by the girl's responses to his presence. 'She had woken him twice in the night with soft demanding caresses, saying nothing just reaching for his hard lean body' (p. 43). In the film of *Goldfinger*, however, Bond's sexuality is continuously expressed in Connery's physical presence. This is not to assert that Connery in himself possesses an inherent and essential sexual charisma. Connery does not carry a transcendental meaning which exists outside the Bond and other texts in which he appears. Indeed, his image, his 'known persona', has shifted as it has traversed different films. As Pam Cook has suggested, 'stars, like all signifiers are transformed in the activity of signification'.[16] The Bond films and the surrounding publicity of Connery in the Bond role progressively transformed Connery's public persona. Moreover, Connery/Bond's sexuality is articulated in a host of sub-texts, both celebrating and condemning the role:

> In the film, indeed, he is interchangeable with Goldfinger, it requires little effort to put one in the place of another, the wonderful machines are at the service of the first as of the second. Except that we recognise the good in Bond and the evil in Goldfinger because the first is loved by women. That is to say, the good, as has already been pointed out, is the sexual biological force.[17]

Connery himself commented on the problems of playing James Bond in terms of Bond's 'absent' character. 'I had to start playing Bond from scratch – not even Ian Fleming knew much about Bond at this time. He has no mother. He has no father. He doesn't come from anywhere and he hadn't been anywhere when he became 007. He was born – kerplump – thirty three years old.' Connery's answer to the blank outline of the hero he played was to conceive him as 'a complete sensualist, his senses highly tuned and awake to everything'.[18]

Within the film, the sexuality of Bond/Connery is established in a number of ways. The first and most obvious way is through the main narrative in which Bond is sexually attractive to a number of women. The film shares this in common with the book. Here the role of women operates precisely to signify Bond's sexuality, but the Bond/Connery figure is also privileged as the object of the look. As we have already remarked, existing work in the area suggests that in the complex interaction of different looks from different places in the cinema, it is the body of the woman or women which constitutes the point of spectacle. Mulvey suggests two ways in which the spectator is implicated in the system of looks established in the cinema. In the first place, the spectator can be in direct scophilic contact with an object of desire. In the second place, he or she can be fascinated with the image of his or her like, identifying with this ego ideal and thus gaining control and possession of the desired object in the diegesis. In *Goldfinger*, while women undoubtedly constitute one direct object of scophilic desire, the Connery/Bond figure is also inscribed within the looks of the film as a direct object of desire.

At key points within the film, we see Bond immobilised, forcibly held in a passive position, either unconscious (during the killing of Jill Masterton, after crashing his Aston Martin at the end of the car chase, when shot with an anaesthetic gun at the end of the torture sequence) or imprisoned, in 'bondage'. The interplay of looks on these occasions, the camera's look as it records the pro-filmic event, the audience's look at the image and the look the characters exchange in the film, centres on Connery/Bond's face and body and the sequences are frequently differentiated by a certain eroticism. For example, in the well-known sequence in which Goldfinger threatens Bond with a laser, Bond has already been seen helpless and unconscious under Oddjob's triumphant look, and returns to consciousness under the gaze of the camera to have Goldfinger introduce his 'new toy', an industrial laser which will cut through the gold table and castrate the pinioned Bond. Dressed in black with face lit dramatically, Bond's body is the focal point not only for the threat of castration, vital though that is, but also for a threatened rape of the same symbolic order as that which overtook Jill Masterton earlier in the film, to be killed by Goldfinger's phallic power embodied in the laser. He is not expected to be tortured and to 'talk' but to be killed by the penetration of the laser. His is, momentarily, in the passive position, the object of the camera, of the villain's look and of the spectator's look. His fast talking response, threatening Goldfinger with a knowledge of Operation Grandslam, releases him from the laser threat only to be further incapacitated by a tranquilliser gun. When he returns to consciousness, it is under Pussy Galore's gaze and gun. While such moments within *Goldfinger* ensure the sexual eroticism of the Connery/Bond figure, the overall narrative renders that eroticism 'innocent' since Bond also occupies a relay position in the structure of the looks whereby the 'look' is displaced away from the hero and on to what is already defined and accepted as a 'legitimate' sex object, the 'Bond girls'.

As Bond returns to consciousness under Pussy Galore's eyes, a slightly uncharacteristic piece of subjective camera, in which Honor Blackman's face is shot in blurred focus as Bond recovers and looks at her, thus re-establishes the audience's identification with Bond and simultaneously dissolves the controlling gaze of Pussy.

Honor Blackman's role in *Goldfinger* as Pussy Galore also shifts the character of Pussy. Honor Blackman brought to the part of Pussy an established image as the redoubtable Mrs Emma Peel from the ITV series *The Avengers* in which, clad in black leather, she sorted out the villains, watched and encouraged by the hero of the series, John Steed, who offered witty asides to her judo throws. The stable judo match with Bond which ends in a long kiss was an obvious play on Blackman's existing popular image. As Honor Blackman has subsequently argued:

> 'I'm sure the appeal of a macho Bond versus kinky me was at the back of the producers' minds, and it obviously worked on screen, the strong female persona – it substituted for the lesbian aspect of the heroine Pussy, which it had been decided would be understated in the movie.[19]

Moreover, Honor Blackman's age and style meant that she could not with ease assume the quasi-childlike role allotted to Pussy Galore in the final lines of the novel. Indeed, if anything, the Pussy Galore of the film smacks of the maternal rather than the child. To Bond's warning that Goldfinger 'kills little girls like you' she responds wryly, 'Little boys too.' When Leiter tells Bond that she informed the CIA of Goldfinger's plot to contaminate Fort Knox and asks Bond what made her call Washington, he replies after a moment's reflection, 'I must have appealed to her maternal instincts.' The Pussy Galore of the film requires no sexual repositioning and in some senses is not required to 'submit' to Bond; rather she is required to 'choose' Bond as a sexual partner rather than the villain or anyone else.

The 'phallic' coding of the novel has also shifted in the sense that, in the books, Bond's phallic power must be established in relation to the villain before he can take possession of the 'girl'. In the films, and specifically in *Goldfinger*, Bond can only defeat the villain *through* his sexual possession of the girl. Although the 'formula' of the films requires that Bond's relationship to Pussy is only registered fully in the final shots of the film, Bond has already established his relationship with Pussy in the stables. It is thus Pussy's decision to side with Bond which defeats Goldfinger's plot. Clearly, this constitutes a significant reorganisation of the system of relation between Bond, 'the girl' and the villain.

Bond: spectacle, irony and narrative

Probably the most remarked upon features of the film of *Goldfinger* were its comic and spectacular qualities. 'Goldfinger is my favourite James Bond film,' remarks John Brosnan. 'It moves at a fast and furious pace but the plot holds together logically enough (more logically than the book) and is a perfect blend of the real and the ridiculous.'[20] Houston argues that it was the film producer's strategy to turn the whole thing into 'a frantic joke'.[21] The comic qualities of *Goldfinger* were held to mitigate the moral vicissitudes of Bond:

> The film people have already made the leap (that is to say into the future). But just by this, the adventures become irresistibly comic, terror is changed to laughter, the series of ingenious and atrocious deaths become play, our nightmare amusement. The public shudders and laughs. The didactic moralistic sermon no longer applies.[22]

Comedy and spectacle were recognised as the distinctive characteristics of the films. Alexander Walker suggests that the sets were aimed at keeping 'the mind boggling aimlessly at the Bond fantasy'. In *Goldfinger*, for example, Ken Adam designed the interior of Fort Knox as a spectacle. Having inspected the Bank of England gold vaults in which gold is

never stacked more than two feet high and is kept in a series
of small rooms off branching corridors, Adam designed a set
dominated by an arched and shining grille with elevators
gliding up and down it. 'In my case,' he commented, 'I
stacked gold bars forty feet high, under a gigantic roof. I had
a whole crew of men polishing the metal work so that it
would shine when we turned the lights on. And it was the
perfect place to stage the last battle with Oddjob. It was like
a gold arena and Bond was able to use gold bars as
weapons.'[23]

The comedy or irony of the film of *Goldfinger*, combined
with the concern with the spectacular and the various shifts
in plot and character which have already been noted,
produced some major shifts in the organisation of the
mythology of James Bond. In the preceding chapter we
called attention to the operations of phallic coding in the
novels, arguing that the play on phallic coding, Oedipal
references and the constant use of castration threats to the
hero, served to pull together problems of sexual difference,
the threats represented by women and certain current
ideological and narrative tensions centred on representations
of Englishness and England. The changes made in the film of
Goldfinger rather crucially altered the form of that articulation.
This is not to suggest that phallic coding is not present in the
film. It most obviously is. Phallic images and castration
threats abound in the film from the new car with which
Bond is equipped by Q to the laser aimed at Bond's genitals
by Goldfinger. Nor is it simply that the producers and
director of the film made various changes in the area of
technology in the interests of being 'up-to-date'. Rather, the
comic inflection of *Goldfinger* serves to open up contradictions
in the image of patriotism, professionalism and sexuality
established by the Bond of the novels.

Comedy is frequently held to have inherently subversive
effects and much of the recent work on comedy in film and
television is largely concerned with the identification of the
ideological effects of comedy, questioning, for example,
whether the comic use of stereotypes in comedies reinforces
prejudices or opens them up to ridicule and possible rejection.
In the case of *Goldfinger*, it could be argued that the comic

inflection of the film which was so central to the Bondian formula allowed for different strategies of identification on the part of the various audiences for Bond. The status of superhero acquired by the James Bond of the films in, say, the area of sexuality was simultaneously celebrated and mocked by the cornucopia of Bond girls in the film. Where Bond's sexuality and Englishness are taken for granted in the novel, the film comically inflates Bond's sexual prowess while stressing the spectacular in Bond's professional life. In the later Bond films, this process becomes much more obvious as, for example, in the mocking nostalgia of the title song of *The Spy Who Loved Me*, 'Nobody does it better'. In *Goldfinger*, the centrality of the phallic coding remains but the parameters of the images of Englishness and of sexuality have shifted and the organisation of the film text establishes considerable ambiguity around these areas.

There have been a number of explanations of the differences between the Bond novels and the Bond films. Brosnan suggests that the films are 'pure cinema' and that their highly visual qualities derived from stories 'conceived for cinematic purposes'.[24] Houston suggests that it was the producers of the film who, having bought themselves a 'brand-name hero, a conventional line in criminal master minds . . . a lot of skilful unassimilable detail, and the legend of sex, violence, etc.,' managed the conversion into 'box-office gold'.[25] Producers of the later Bond films refer quite consistently to the 'formula' of Bond established by the earlier films. This reference to a 'formula' is interesting since it incorporates a number of elements – plots, characterisation and strategies of identification, set design and the design of 'gadgets' – to be incorporated in the text. Unlike the structuralist formula outlined by Eco in relation to the novels, notions of style and expectations as to audience understanding are intrinsic to the producer's formula, not an overlay which certain readers may ignore and others enjoy.

Explanations of the popularity of Bond have also tended to hinge upon the characterisation of the differences and similarities between the Bond novels and films. So far, we have been concerned with the ways in which it is possible to compare the two texts of *Goldfinger*. However, many of the differences between the two texts and our established knowledge of them cannot solely be accounted for in terms of the texts' internal formal characteristics, that one is a novel rather than a film, that there are differences in plot, characterisation and narration between the two, although, of course, as we have been at some pains to point out, such differences do exist. Nevertheless, what also changes in relation to the two texts of *Goldfinger*, are the ideological formations in relation to which the novels and films were produced and read. One way into a discussion of those ideological formations is to consider *various* sets of inter-textual relations at the time of the publication of the two *Goldfingers*. We have already suggested that the boundaries of the male readership for the novels and the early films were to a certain extent formed by the generic expectations of the imperialist spy-thriller, while the parameters of romantic fiction and the image of the Byronic hero provided one inter-textual focus for women readers. The novel of *Goldfinger*, for example, certainly reworked the traditional English amateur gentleman hero-spy into a post-imperialist age and displaced the problem of male control on to women. Yet the film of *Goldfinger* was widely popular and not simply with men. It was greeted with 'the concerted yell of innocent happiness, that collective sigh of satisfied expectation' referred to by Penelope Houston at the London press showing. One reason for the film's popularity and for the undoubted pleasures of viewing the early Bond films is linked to a rather different set of inter-textual relations; those between the Bond films and certain current traditions in British and American cinema.

For example, let us consider the inter-textual relations surrounding and affecting the representation of sexuality and women in films with which the cinema-going public might reasonably be expected to have been familiar in the early 1960s. It is necessary, of course, to register that the post-war period in England had involved an attempt, both at the level of job market and ideologies, to take on the task of repositioning women into domestic labour following their use in the labour market during the war. During this period, a whole range of films reworked the ideological tensions surrounding the position of women. Within this group of films, however, it could be argued that not only were women repositioned in the family but that the sexuality of women, even within those terms, was suppressed.

Sue Aspinall argues that the British films of the years 1943 to 1953 registered substantial changes in gender roles and, in the case of women, involved 'a renewed emphasis on their subordinate domestic and feminine role'.[26] Aspinall examines a number of films but perhaps two are worth mentioning here. Both were released in 1945 and both represent rather different genres. Aspinall designates *Brief Encounter* as a 'rarity' because it combines 'women's picture material' with 'quality in its writer (Noel Coward), director (David Lean) and actors (Celia Johnson and Trevor Howard)'.[27] The film is based on the fleeting love affair of Laura Jesson. Laura is happily married with two children, a sympathetic and reliable husband and a well-off middle-class background. She then has a love affair with another man, which takes place on railway stations and in tea rooms and is, not entirely surprisingly, unconsummated. In the course of the narrative Laura reaches the painful decision to reject her lover and return to her married life. Within that decision, duty, affection and a value of middle-class material and moral standards war with her desire for sexual and emotional fulfilment and win. She cannot, for example, face the sordidness of making love in a borrowed flat. Her sexual desires are represented as painfully but rightfully suppressed.

A rather more popular film, released in the same year as *Brief Encounter*, was *The Wicked Lady* in which Margaret Lockwood plays the lady of the title, determined, manipulative, unprincipled and highly sexual, in a costume drama in which women's sexuality finds more open expression since it is safely confined to the past. Nevertheless, such activities are punished in the course of the narrative in a manner unenforced by but classically in line with the rulings of the Hollywood Production Code. Aspinall makes clear the ambiguities of the film in her summary:

> *The Wicked Lady* enjoyed enormous popularity, not because good ultimately triumphs over evil, but because the case for

pleasure is made so convincingly. Although the heroine, played by Margaret Lockwood, dies saying she wants 'a home and children, things I never thought mattered before', telling her True Love, 'If I'd met you sooner I'd never have done these things,' the images of the film that persist are those of Lockwood as a defiant wife, an energetic highway robber, an enthusiastic lover, an instigator of action. These images are more powerful than the pat ending.[28]

Interestingly, *The Wicked Lady* stands out from many other British films because, although its narrative form insists upon the punishment of women's sexuality, it is not marked by a 'poverty of desire'. Charles Barr uses this phrase as a metaphor for British cinema and for that of Ealing Studios in particular, pointing to the essential characteristic of British films as a suppression of energy and the repression of emotional and sexual desires.[29]

John Hill also suggests that the British 'New Wave' films beginning with *Room at the Top* in 1959 and including *Saturday Night and Sunday Morning*, *A Kind of Loving* and *This Sporting Life* – films which both preceded and overlapped with the Bond films in terms of period – were far from being as 'progressive' as is usually claimed. 'By and large,' he suggests, 'such films end by reproducing an ideology of marital and procreative sexuality which punishes extra-marital and unprocreative sexuality.'[30] Hill suggests that while British cinema had earlier been characterised by the presence of strong father figures and an accompanying deference to them, the new British cinema registered their absence and a subsequent search for the re-establishment of the 'law of the father'. The 'progressive realism' of the 'New Wave' is thus illusory because the representation of women and female sexuality is conceived of in terms of the need for male regulation within marriage in a world where that form of regulation and the institution of marriage is seen as being under threat.

In *A Kind of Loving* (1962) Vic has married into a family with an absent father figure. In an early scene, Vic is in the kitchen with his wife and mother-in-law. His father has sent him two tickets for a brass band concert in which he is performing and there is an argument about whether he and Ingrid will attend. Vic finally declares 'We're going anyway,' in a shot in which he is caught between Ingrid in the rear and his mother-in-law in the foreground. The following shots show the brass band with Vic's father playing a trombone solo watched by his wife and younger sons, and the two empty seats which should have been occupied by Vic and Ingrid. There is then a cut to a close-up of a television set before a cut to a shot of Vic, Ingrid and her mother watching the television. Hill perceptively notes not only the contrast between the old traditional working-class culture of the brass band with the new facile mass culture of television but the way in which its juxtaposition is effected in terms of men and women. 'While the brass band is all male, the superficial values of the new "affluence" are linked inextricably with women whose obsession with house, television, clothes and physical appearance is persistently emphasised throughout the film.'[31]

In Hill's analysis, this opposition is worked out in terms of the presence or absence of the father. While Vic's father provides the central focus for Vic's family, his new family – that of Ingrid and his mother-in-law – has no father. The absence of the father and the subsequent domination of Vic by women is castrating. Vic and Ingrid cannot make love in the house. The narrative is concerned with the reassertion of the law of the father. Vic returns to his father for advice 'and from the "natural" base of his allotment the father counsels assertive control: "She'll live where she's bloody put." '[32] As with *film noir*, Hill points out, the ideological work of such a film needs to be understood as an attempt to reconstruct a failing patriarchal order.

Rather similar themes characterise *Look Back in Anger* (1958) where the need for assertion of male sexual control is articulated with the failure of empire. Jimmy Porter (Richard Burton) is married to an upper-class woman, Alison (Mary Ure), the daughter of a retired Colonel. She is the representative of her father's social order and Jimmy's 'anger', that of the typical angry young man, at that social order is displaced into anger at and abuse of her. In *Look Back in Anger*, Hill argues 'the failed confidence in colonial certainties goes hand in hand with a failed confidence on the terrain of sexuality, and, in the process, becomes a struggle for the reassertion of "manhood" and the patriarchal principle (as Jimmy puts it to Alison, "I want to be there when you grovel")'.[33] Hill points to the way in which the 'matriarchal' defence presented in the film in Alison's relationship to Helen (Claire Bloom) is destroyed by Helen's sexual submission to Jimmy and by Alison's submissive return to Jimmy after the loss of her unborn child (a result wished upon her by Jimmy). Finally, Hill remarks that it is not surprising that the style and setting of Alison's return to Jimmy at the railway station 'should be replete with associations with *Brief Encounter*, with its similar reinsertion of female sexual desire into the "normality" of the family'.[34]

Now, of course, representations of women and women's sexuality are not confined to the films mentioned here or, indeed, simply to films. Yet it is possible to indicate an interesting pattern in both images and narratives about women in British cinema, a pattern in which women are either punished for their sexuality within the narrative and/or reinserted into a legitimate patriarchal organisation, that of marriage. American films, as in the case of *film noir*, tended to follow a rather similar pattern. Within more mainstream American cinema it is quite instructive to look at the star image of Marilyn Monroe, a key 'sex symbol' of the fifties. Richard Dyer suggests that Monroe's star image pulled together a number of theses: a child-like imagery, an implication that Monroe was a victim, dumb wit, innocence, suffering and sex appeal.[35] The orchestration of these images around Monroe's sexuality was based partly on the parts she played in various films from *The Seven Year Itch* (1955) to *The Misfits* (1962), but it was also based on the host of sub-texts, studio publicity, magazine articles and news items through which her life as a star was constructed. One of the key elements, implicit in Monroe's child–woman image, Dyer implies, is the *problem* of the father. It is possible to take this further than Dyer does and suggest that Monroe's ambivalent sexuality (ambivalent in its combination of blatency and innocence) is predicated on the *absence* of a father and the absence of patriarchal authority over her sexuality.

Throughout her publicity, her illegitimacy and deprived childhood figured strongly as did, later, her inability to have a child. Male readings of Monroe's image stress the 'incompleteness' of Monroe, her sexual desirability which 'requires' a male. Mailer points to the promise of Monroe's sexuality as essentially innocent.

> She gave the feeling that if you made love to her, why then how could you not move more easily into sweets and the purchase of the full promise of future sweets, move into tender heavens where your flesh would be restored. She would ask no price ... If your taste combined with her taste, how nice, how sweet would be that tender dream of flesh there to share.[36]

Marowitz points to the elusive and unattainable quality of Monroe's sexuality, arguing that she instilled 'in the male onlooker a powerful sense of dread'.[37] According to Marowitz, the dumb blonde image she embodied implies 'a dimension of pleasure beyond the capabilities of those nearest and (presumably) dearest to us ... she tells us there are unchartered isles of sensuality on which we could pitch our flags and claim in our own names, if we had the courage to follow our desires and submit to our lusts'.[38] It is tempting to point out how 'satisfyingly' Marilyn's life as a star follows the punitive pattern established by cinema narratives. Her 'innocent', 'untutored', 'unfathered' sexuality and her proven inability to be satisfactorily reinserted into the family and under the law of the father, witness her failed marriages and her inability to bear a child, lead logically to the tragic ending, suffering and death.

This necessarily brief exegesis of the tensions and contradictions built into representations of women in some key British and American films of the immediately preceding period may indicate why the Bond films were popular not only with men but also with women. In writing about the Bond films in the 1980s with a whole series of Bond films in view, with a more developed women's movement and with rather different inter-textual relations operating, the James

Bond films may not spring to mind as the most obvious example of women's independence.

But it is important to recollect that rather different reading formations were in play in the early 1960s when the first Bond films were produced. *Goldfinger*, for example, was characterised by certain significant repetitions of themes present in films of the 1950s and by some equally significant departures from them. The Bond girl's sexuality was 'free' in the sense that it was not tied to marriage, the family and domesticity. Of course, it was not 'free' in other ways. The Bond girls have always functioned as objects of male desire, operating within the narrative of both novels and films as the signifiers of Bond's phallic power. Nevertheless, in the light of the harshly constrained sexuality of women in earlier British films, tutored into submission to duty, the family and domesticity or to a career ending in punishment and death, the open sexuality of the Bond girls and the guilt-free but purely sexual relationship between Bond and the girl could well be seen as a welcome break with past conventions. The Bond films also offered some rather different routes through their narratives, routes which did not depend upon an unambiguous identification with the hero – that is, the desire 'to be Bond', in Amis's phrase – which provides the assumed central focus of the narrative organisation of the novels. We shall consider the ways in which such considerations may account for the rather different pleasures of male and female viewers in a later chapter.

We should stress, however, that we are *not* arguing that the Bond film's constituted, in either a relative or an absolute sense, an advance in women's freedom. Rather, they constituted a significant shift in the terrain of sexual representations, a shift which formed part of a wider cultural remodelling of sexed identities whose complex and contradictory effects cannot be calibrated on a simple, undifferentiated scale of 'liberation'. However, it will be preferable to defer a more thorough exploration of these issues until we resume our analyses of 'the Bond phenomenon' as a whole in Chapter 8. Meanwhile, our attention turns to the conditions of production of the Bond films. In examining some of the inter-textual relations of the two *Goldfingers* and the internal differences between the two texts, it should also be apparent that it is difficult and possibly misleading to think of the film of *Goldfinger* as a simple translation of the novel into a film. The film producers actively transformed the novel and the novel was, in many ways, only one part of the ideological terrain upon which they worked. In the next chapter, we consider this problem more fully by examining the relations between the industrial and the ideological conditions of the production of Bond as exemplified by the making of *The Spy Who Loved Me*.

Chapter 6

The Bond Films: 'Determination' and 'Production'

'I think that the mere fact that we were lucky enough to stumble upon Ian Fleming and Bond was a bit of good fortune. The rest was all hard work.'

('Cubby' Broccoli, 1976)[1]

The first work which we undertook on James Bond, above and beyond our rather different experiences of adolescent reading and film-going, was a study of the production of one of the later James Bond films, *The Spy Who Loved Me*, made in 1976 and 1977.[2] That original case-study raised a series of theoretical problems about some of the existing ways of analysing the texts and formations of popular culture. The case-study focused on what is usually termed the 'occupational ideologies' of people who made the Bond films. It consisted of interviews with the Bond production team combined with filmed and written accounts of a number of the planning meetings where policy decisions were made in relation to different aspects of the organisation of the film and its production. We also examined some of the shooting and editing of the film, the development of the musical score and the development of the publicity campaign which accompanied the opening of the film. In terms of its theoretical orientations, the case-study attempted to combine an analysis of the occupational ideologies of the film-makers with an analysis of the ideological economy of the Bond films generally and particularly of *The Spy Who Loved Me*. In this chapter, we examine the same period of production of *The Spy Who Loved Me* and reconsider some of the assumptions about the relationship between the views of film-makers and film texts which characterised our own and other accounts of the process of making a film.

There have been a great many accounts of film production from Lillian Ross's description of the making of *The Red Badge of Courage* onwards.[3] Finding out what happens 'behind the scenes' or 'behind the cameras' has been a continuous preoccupation of the popular press since the inception of the movies, and academics have not been immune to that particular attraction. Yet, in some important ways, film production has always occupied a space within film studies which has effectively resisted incorporation into theories of film-making. If we consider some typical approaches to film production, this contention may become clearer. Sociological studies of the film industry have either been concerned with the 'ways of life' established by film-makers, as in Hortense Powdermaker's classic anthropological account of life in Hollywood, or with the study of occupational or professional ideologies.[4] In these circumstances, the production processes of any one particular film have been of interest largely to illustrate the views and problems which media professionals hold in common. The films produced by media professionals tend to be considered only to the degree that they illustrate the conflicts and contradictions within or between specific occupational ideologies – the conflict between the requirements of creativity and those of commercialism, for example. But the film text and, indeed, the specific decisions, discussions and organisation which inform the production of any one film have been ignored to a great extent in such studies as irrelevant to an understanding of the general characteristics of media professionals. In contrast, studies of film in which ideas of authorship play the central part make a series of connections between the director's life and ideas and his films but regard the constraining institutional setting and the production processes of films as largely invisible to analysis.[5]

Early semiological studies of film texts produced an important counterthrust to this stress on occupational ideologies and authorship in their rejection of 'reductionist' accounts of film texts and their insistence upon detailed textual analysis. But while the principles of 'immanent analysis' characterised many of the early semiological accounts, the stress of later studies was on ways of conceiving the relationship between spectator and film in terms of the subject positions constructed by the film text. Valuable although these developments undoubtedly were, such studies conceived of the relationship between film and ideology mainly in terms of textual analysis. The production of films, the views of the film-makers and the institutional spaces in which they worked tended to be given a ritual genuflection before the analyst proceeded to attack 'more important' issues such as the identification of 'progressive' and 'reactionary' texts.[6] In contrast, Marxist studies, over a long period and with many different inflections, have always stressed the relationship between texts and production. Typically, however, this relationship is examined within the terms of a general theory of the determination of cultural production. Classical Marxist studies of literature, art and culture have attempted to establish a hierarchy of determinations for any particular text or set of texts in which relationships to the means of production in a society and to that society's relations of production are held to have provided the crucial determining factors. In terms of film studies, consideration of the production processes of film and the views of the film-makers concerned is limited by the ambivalent status granted to such an area within Marxist studies. Production studies are seen as necessary to an understanding of the determination of film texts but also as an area which is crucially subordinated to other, finally determining factors attributed, in the last instance, to the economic relations of cultural production.

'The Bondian' as a production ideology

Our original case-study on the making of *The Spy Who Loved Me* drew upon these theoretical traditions in a number of ways. The Bond films, and *The Spy Who Loved Me* in particular, were considered in the context of the ailing British film industry and its inter-relationship with Hollywood. The Bond films, it was pointed out, were made at Pinewood Studios in England in an industrial context characterised by a constant financial crisis in which the American film industry had played a pivotal role. The long-term problems of the British film industry, we argued, were attributable to the lack of a large enough home market to support stable and permanent film-making in Britain, while major inroads were made by large-scale expensive American productions on British screens. The 1960s saw the increased exploitation of cheap film-making facilities in Britain by American companies attracted by the conditions of the Eady Levy, through which films using mainly British production staff were eligible for a government subsidy, and by favourable exchange rates. The first Bond film, *Dr No*, was an extremely successful example of this practice. Cubby Broccoli, an American producer who had spent some time making films in England, went into partnership with Harry Saltzman who had an option on the film rights for all the Bond novels, excluding *Casino Royale*, and secured financial backing from United Artists. Broccoli recounts that

here was a series of books written by Fleming that were selling, really, you know, like hot cakes and no one really had envisaged making the films. And no distributor would put up the money for it until Arthur Krim of United Artists agreed to do it. He was primarily interested in making a film with me. For years we had talked about making films. I was making films for Columbia prior to that . . . so I flew to New York and that's where it all started and then in about forty five minutes we had a deal. I think one of the main reasons was David Picker – who was then given the job of production. He stepped in at that time. He knew about Fleming too and he was also a James Bond afficionado. He liked the idea.

The Bond films proved to be immensely profitable and United Artists continued to finance the series even when, in the early 1970s, there were major cutbacks, asset sales and write-offs in Hollywood so that American involvement in British film production substantially decreased. Only in the 1980s did the Bond films cease to have a British base. *Moonraker*, for example, was made in America with location work elsewhere and only the special effects were produced at Pinewood. Our case-study suggested that the combination of a studio base at Pinewood over a number of years and the continuing success of the series ensured the development and maintenance of a team of people who worked together on the Bond films over an extended period. Of course, there have been many changes in the members of the Bond production team. There have been many different directors involved since Terence Young first directed *Dr No*, including Guy Hamilton, Lewis Gilbert, Peter Hunt and John Glen. Broccoli and Saltzman shared producers' credits with Kevin McLory in 1965 for *Thunderball* and Broccoli bought Saltzman out of the Bond production partnership before the making of *The Spy Who Loved Me* in 1976. Nevertheless, at all levels of production, people have repeatedly returned to work on a Bond film. Such people tended to share a particular occupational ideology. At the time of the making of *The Spy*, new members of the production team (Claude Renoir, the director of photography, Christopher Wood, the writer and Barbara Bach, the 'Bond girl') were far outweighed by those who had worked on previous Bond films.

Moreover, they experienced a conscious effort on the part of Broccoli, by this time the sole producer, and other members of his team to initiate them into the world of 'Bondian' film-making. 'Bondian' was the phrase used by Broccoli and other members of the production team to mean 'in the spirit of James Bond'. To a certain extent the term 'Bondian' was used to describe the Bond films, which were seen as a distinctive formula, a specific genre of film, described by the director, Lewis Gilbert, in the following way:

> most of the things in Bond films today have kind of grown up with the picture ... they tend to keep it into the pattern they've had all along. For instance, they have an unknown leading lady. They don't like to change all the

people who are well known like 'M' and Miss Moneypenny
and there's no way in which they could be changed
because the public really wants to see them . . . they like
the pattern, the formula. I think that part of the charm of
the Bond picture (is) you know what you're going to get
. . . You're not disappointed . . . You see audiences in a
Bond film aren't looking for great acting – they want to
be overwhelmed by physical things. Well the character of
Bond, you couldn't change, of course . . . but you can
change his attitude to a certain extent . . . he doesn't find
this girl so easy – such a pushover as the other girls have
been. And so in that sense, you can change it slightly, but
it's very well laid down, the law of Bond and people want
you to abide by it . . . Bond films are very very different
from any other kind of film made. They've disproved every
law in the cinema, they've done everything wrong and
they're huge successes . . . I mean in story elements, in
characterisation elements, things like that – the anticlimactic
bit they always have at the end which you wouldn't dare
do in other pictures where they have a huge big ending
and then suddenly, the films starts up again . . . Many
things they do wrong, things which you would think get a
laugh in a normal picture, but it's a kind of sympathetic
laugh.

A great deal of discussion between members of the
production team for *The Spy* centred on the provision of
'Bondian effects' within the film, on the importance of the
sets, the gadgets, the foreign locations, the threatening
character of the villain, who must incorporate both a physical
threat and an intellectual threat to the hero, Bond's
relationship with 'the girl', the jokes and the form of the
crucial pre-credits sequence. The 'formula' of the Bond film
was understood and, to a certain extent, the term 'Bondian'
was used to refer to that formula. At the same time, people
working on *The Spy* also used the term to refer to the process
of working on a Bond picture. It was recognised and
acknowledged that this was different from working on other
films. Claude Renoir, the cameraman, listed the distinguishing
aspects of Bond picture-making as 'a lot of people, a lot of

good technicians, a lot of tricks, special effects and so on' and underlined the importance of the big budget on a Bond film, pointing out that 'it's quite rare for a French cameraman to be involved in such a big budget picture'.

The importance of the big budget was stressed by many members of the production team as a part of the 'Bondian' ethos. Christopher Wood, a newcomer to the team and one of a number of script writers used on *The Spy*, described the importance of the budget in giving rise to a particular freedom from restraint:

> I have worked on films in which people have said to me, Chris baby, it doesn't matter. The sky's the limit. You want to shoot this in Saudi Arabia, shoot it in Saudi Arabia, we don't care, as many people as you like, just don't feel there are any constraints. So I write it and then they come back and say, well, why have we got two rooms. I mean couldn't she be his uncle and his wife at the same time. I mean, we'd save money on casting as well. With a Bond film, you do know that with anything you write, money is no restraint.

At the same time, Christopher Wood also acknowledged some of the frustrations of working on a Bond picture in which many slightly different conceptions of the Bondian may compete:

> I was very pleased with a sequence I had when we established Bond in the film, which we'd have a scene of the sea . . . On the raft, Bond is lying with the girl, beep, beep, beep, comes a little message. Then in his usual cursory rather boorish way, he waves her farewell leaving her sort of yelping on the raft and just steps aboard his surfboard, picks up the nearest roller, roars forward on a mindbending shot, riding a forty five foot high wave, comes straight down, up the beach, still on the board to where there's a jeep, just slips off the board . . . inside the jeep, flicks up the microphone and gets his orders . . . shoves his foot down on the jeep which raises up at a priapic angle up the side of the sand dune, just roars up

into space and in about thirty seconds I thought we'd establish the persona of Bond . . . Cubby had a better idea . . . when you see Bond's entrance in the movie, it's better . . . which I now accept, but when it was first mooted I was rather sulkily rubbing my foot against the floor and thinking, 'Blast'.

In the event, the pre-credits sequence in *The Spy* involved establishing the loss of British and Russian submarines and the calling, by their respective governments, of Bond and the Russian special agent, triple X, apparently a Bond type figure making love to a beautiful woman but who turns out to be the woman herself. Bond, similarly occupied in a chalet in the Alps, skis off to answer his call only to be attacked by Russian agents whom he avoids and kills in an extended chase finally leaping off an enormous cliff, only to open his parachute which unfolds to reveal the Union Jack. The production team were satisfied that this was an effective 'Bondian' opening to the film, and that the dangerous and costly ski jump was the important factor to build the story around.

The idea of the Bondian also percolates through to those not directly involved in the film production. Saul Cooper, the director of publicity, argued that the only bad publicity for a Bond picture is that which 'destroys the illusion'. 'The illusion', he suggested, 'is the thing that I have learnt from Cubby Broccoli . . . that there are things that are Bondian and things that are not Bondian.' Cooper explained that 'Bondian is our special word . . . everything that involves Bond has to be a little bigger, a little better, to be larger than life, it has to have certain special flair.' In the publicity for the film, the whole notion of the Bondian was pulled into play. Journalists, for example, were invited to a 'Bondian week-end' in which they stayed at an international hotel and were served a banquet of James Bond dishes, culled from the novels. The tanker set was much publicised as the 'biggest set' in Europe. The opening of the set was a publicity event which included not only the bevy of beautiful and scantily clad girls which accompanies most Bond publicity stunts, but also the visit of Harold Wilson and his introduction to Roger

Moore and Barbara Bach, the new Bond girl, dressed in Russian uniform.

While the Open University case-study focused on the background in the British and American film industries for the Bond films and the process of the making of *The Spy Who Loved Me*, it also offered a particular ideological reading of the Bond films and *The Spy*.

> the film is in a sense the perfection of the SPECTRE genre although SPECTRE is never mentioned inasmuch as Stromberg's ransom plan is applied indiscriminately to East and West, playing upon the tensions which subsist beneath detente. Stromberg himself being presented to us as a personification of the irrational forces which permanently threaten to destroy the balance of peaceful co-existence. In this sense, particularly at this precise moment in history, Bond's adventures take on a new significance inasmuch as it is through his endeavours that the ever impending crisis which threatens the world with calamity is averted. The world is led to the brink of nuclear holocaust and back again. It is by thus effecting a purely imaginary resolution of real social contradictions which are themselves misrepresented in the form of the fantastic and the grotesque, that the Bond films attain their ideological effect.[7]

The Spy Who Loved Me was, in effect, read as a fictional working over of contemporary ideologies surrounding international tensions. While the case-study called upon ideas about occupational ideologies and textual analysis, it also implicitly subordinated these to the classical Marxist hierarchy of determinations. Readers of the case-study were led from the financial and economic 'determinants' of the Bond films through the institutional space within which they were made and the occupational ideologies of the film-makers to a reading of *The Spy* as a realist and, in some sense, essentially deceptive text. *The Spy* was conceived of as 'the product of a camera which conceals itself'. Even moments of technological and fantastic excess were seen as part of an ideological project in which the viewer's disbelief is played upon only to reinforce its suspension 'and the false consciousness which that suspension promotes'.[8]

'Conditions of production' versus 'hierarchy of determinations'

There were a number of problems with this approach. The Marxist base/superstructure model has provided an implicit or explicit background for many studies of culture. Raymond Williams has summarised this general proposition of Marxist thinking in the following way:

> The whole of society is governed by certain dispositions of the means of production and when these dispositions – forces and relations in a mode of production as a whole – change through the operation of their own laws and tendencies, then forms of consciousness and forms of intellectual and artistic production (forms which have their place in orthodox Marxist definition as a 'superstructure') change also. Some shift in relatively direct ways, like politics and law, some shift in distant and often indirect ways – the traditional examples are religion, philosophy and aesthetics.[9]

Although few, including Williams himself, would now accept a crude form of the base/superstructure model as an acceptable theoretical framework for the analysis of culture, problems associated with the base/superstructure notion have continued to dog cultural analysis. In the study of film and media organisations, questions of determination frequently remain in the background, but they none the less often implicitly provide the framework for the analysis. As Philip Elliott argued, such studies in America and Britain 'provide the basis for an analysis of the production of media culture under the conditions of democratic capitalism'.[10]

In many film studies, accounts of production processes are either considered in isolation or they are organised around questions of determination posed within the base/superstructure model. Hence Ellis, in his admirable analysis of Ealing Studios, contends that 'to determine the possibilities of any film, the material, technological, aesthetic and ideological determinants in its production have to be examined: only here can it be decided where a film coincides with the dominant ideology and where it diverges from it'. Ellis's listing of the determinants of an Ealing text include 'the entire history of the cinema (its system of production, distribution and exhibition)', 'the specific organization of production' and 'the beliefs of the group controlling production.'[11] The difficulties of attempting to explain films in terms of this type of hierarchy of determinations is often simply that an examination of 'the entire history of the cinema', even 'the specific organization of production' and 'the beliefs of the group controlling production' tends to establish, at best, a series of fragmentary connections between film texts and the views of the owners or controllers of production. Ellis, for instance, suggests that although the concentration of Ealing films on the lower middle class is a result of complex factors, the primary factor is biographical in that the majority of the film-makers were born into middle-class families, many strongly imbued with a lower middle-class liberalism which expressed the class interest of the emergent lower sections of the bourgeoisie. Thus Ealing is seen as the product of a generation which was 'radicalized' by the experience of the Depression and for whom the desire to show 'the people' in films was satisfied by a focus on the characters and situations of the petit bourgeoisie.

The implications of Ellis's analysis seems to be that Ealing films, like all texts or forms of culture, have a number of levels of determination, that they were, in effect, 'overdetermined', but that one of the crucial determining factors was the class origins and views of the group controlling production. The concentration of many Ealing films on lower middle-class characters, shopkeepers, small businessmen and the like is explained in terms of the class position and outlook of those in charge of production. The final variable in Ellis's 'hierarchy of determinations' seems to be 'individuality':

This is Ealing's situation, a group of conventionally educated intellectuals, through a certain liberal radicalism, came to make films about and for 'the people', whom they think of as the lower levels of the petit bourgeoisie. Thus individuals are a vital part of the process, not as finished entities with worldviews and metaphysical pre-occupations, but as social beings.[12]

Yet neither 'individuality', albeit socially formed, nor the class origins of the Ealing film-makers tells us that much about the ideological process of production whereby 'the people' came to be represented as petit bourgeois in the Ealing films.

In this kind of analysis, the inevitable gaps between determining factors and the films tend to be closed through the role assigned to 'individual' activity or, in other circumstances, are left open in accepting an understandable lack of knowledge about the complex interpenetration of different levels of determination because of the absence of any detailed histories of the film industry and the productions of different films. Buscombe's interesting attempt to explore the relationship between Frank Capra's films and the ownership and control of Columbia Pictures Corporation thus sounds a number of warnings about categorising the relationship between films, studios and more general social attitudes, arguing that films 'cannot be explained simply in terms of who owned the studios or in terms only of social attitudes at the time'.[13] Buscombe suggests that the history of the American film industry constitutes a kind of missing link in attempts to make connections between Hollywood films and American society. The assumption in this case is that 'many of the materials needed to forge that link are missing'.[14]

Our case-study on the making of *The Spy Who Loved Me* was similarly preoccupied with the problem of making connections between the film text, more general ideological or societal trends and the occupational ideologies and actions of the Bond production team. Despite the substantial amount of attention given to the views of the film producers, those views were considered in terms of a particular notion of 'occupational ideology', one which places occupational ideologies within a hierarchy of determinations. In their comments on the occupational ideologies of the film-makers,

Stuart Hall and Richard Dyer stressed the limitations and the illusionary quality of the conscious views and actions of the members of the Bond production team.[15] Dyer argued that the whole area of professionalism and commodity production which characterised the Bond team made for a repression of considerations of ideology. Hall perceptively suggested that this involved 'a species of professional unconsciousness', that 'professionalism really means being conscious about certain foreground themes'.[16] While this argument eschews the conspiratorial view that the audience is simply ideologically manipulated by the Bond team, it also suggests that 'you have to recognize that there is a gap between what they (the Bond production team) think they're doing and what they're actually doing'.[17] In combining this view of the occupational ideologies of the film-makers with a version of the base/superstructure model and with an analysis of the ideological meaning of the text of *The Spy Who Loved Me*, the case-study thus suggested that the views of the Bond production team were in some essential ways either irrelevant or misleading for understanding the ideological meaning of *The Spy*.

There are a number of issues raised by this conception of the production of *The Spy Who Loved Me* which, we would argue, also characterises many other studies of film production. The first concerns the effects of the concept of a hierarchy of determinations on the analysis. It is this that allows the views and practices of the film-makers to be seen as not merely inadequate explanations of the determination of film texts but, in some cases, to be discounted altogether. The film-makers' views provide merely ancillary evidence about the determination of film texts, but such views cannot be accepted at face value precisely because other determining forces (technology, ownership etc.) have to be taken into account and ranked in importance within a hierarchy of determinations. The Marxist tradition has included a great many models of 'determination' from those of 'mechanical causality' to those of 'expressive causality', from the billiard ball view of causality to that in which a text is simply rewritten or reinterpreted in terms of some deeper, underlying and more fundamental narrative. *The Spy*, viewed in these terms, is conceived of, on the one hand, as being determined by certain physical and mechanical conditions – the technology and the social relations of film production, for example – and, on the other hand, as expressive of some deeper ideological narratives of a capitalist society, specifically those associated with Cold War mythology, and as more generally implicated in the processes whereby dominant ideologies are maintained. 'When we escape from our daily concerns into the world of Bond,' we argued, 'we escape into an iron cage which offers us no freedom to establish intellectual or creative relations of our own with the world in which we live.'[18] The second important assumption of such an argument is that the ideological meaning of a film can be definitively established and that this ideological meaning is self evidently *not* the meaning with which the film makers themselves would endow the film.

Given these premises, the realm of professional ideology inevitably becomes tinged with notions of 'false consciousness'. Because of these problems, we would argue that it is important to rethink the place of production studies. First, the endeavour to reinsert *The Spy* into its conditions of production should not be seen in terms of the exegesis of determinations derived from the classic Marxist hierarchy of determinations. Secondly, the text of *The Spy* has to be conceptualised as part of a group of texts, including novels, films, advertising and other cultural forms, whose ideological meaning cannot be delivered by a textual reading in a once and for all manner independently of their conditions of production and the history of their productive consumption. To avoid these difficulties we shall be concerned, in this account, with the 'conditions of production' of a James Bond text rather than with its 'determination'. The distinction we have in mind here between the concepts of 'conditions of production' and 'determination' has been most clearly elucidated by Pierre Macherey. Macherey describes conditions of production as the principle of rationality which makes works of fiction accessible to thought rather than as a cause in the empirical sense. 'To know the conditions of a work is not to reduce the process of its production to merely the growth of a seed which contains all its future possibilities from the very beginning,' Macherey argues, 'To know the conditions of a work is to define the real process of its constitution, to show how it is composed from a real diversity of elements which give it substance.'[19]

Macherey's distinctive contribution to literary theory has been to develop a particular conception of the relationship between fiction and ideology, whereby the literary work both organises and in a novel manner 'works over' ideological themes. The direction of Macherey's thinking also operates against the notion of literary works conceived of as 'created' and 'finished' products and towards the analysis of literary texts as they are inscribed in a variety of different institutional and ideological contexts. Studying a particular text does not require elevating it and isolating it from its history of productive consumption, but looking at everything about it, 'everything which has collected on it, become attached to it – like shells on a rock by the seashore forming a whole incrustation'.[20] The production of a literary work, according to Macherey, is a process and a labour which transforms ideologies through formal mechanisms. Such works are then further transformed by literary criticism into a body of works with a particular status and meaning. We would like to extrapolate Macherey's ideas from the area of literary theory and to focus on certain questions of 'intertextuality' which he raises. The term intertextuality is used here to refer to the conjuncturally specific transposition of one or more systems of signs on to another, resulting in a new articulation of the enuciative and denotative positions they produce. In what follows, our interests will centre on the specific transpositions involved in the production of a Bond film. We will also show how the ideological projects of film producers form a part of the 'diversity of elements' which give a film text substance.

First, however, let us take another leaf out of Macherey's book. In his account of Jules Verne, Macherey concentrates on the way in which Verne's work realises a combination of thematic and ideological concerns:

The *act* of the writer is fundamental: he realises a particular crystallization, a restructuration, and even a structuration of the data upon which he works: all that which was no more than a collective foreboding, project, aspiration, *precipitates* abruptly in an image which rapidly becomes familiar, becomes the real itself, becomes the flesh of these projects. Verne's work furnishes a unique example of this process; it endows the ideological with a new form but also, more important, with a visible form.[21]

The work of production of a film is similarly fundamental in reformulating and making visible and watchable both a number of ideological components and a particular articulation of them. Given these provisos, the role of professional ideology and the labour of film production takes on a rather different meaning. It becomes rather less necessary to suggest that the ideological work involved in producing the Bond films takes place largely 'behind the backs' of the Bond production team. Rather, the opposite case could be argued. Film-makers frequently provide rich and detailed material on their use of existing genres and on specific ideological projects. The 'hard work' of making a Bond film is not simply of anecdotal interest, nor yet another example of the role of professional ideologies in the organisation of the mass media. An examination of the process of working on the film actually informs us both about the existing ideologies and textual systems with which the Bond production team were concerned and tells us something about the way in which they were transformed in the making of *The Spy*. It also indicates how there can be contradictions between the ideological project as conceived by the film-makers and the film text as it is read and consumed by audiences.

Adjusting Bond

One of the most obvious aspects of our original case-study was its clear demonstration that the production team of *The Spy Who Loved Me* had clear ideas about the James Bond films generally and about *The Spy* in particular. Some of these ideas were implicitly understood, such as the connotations of the term 'Bondian', while others were much discussed and debated, often assuming clearer definition in the process. The notion that the James Bond films comprised a distinctive genre was taken for granted in these discussions. Clearly, a key element in the making of all the later James Bond films is the existence and popularity of the preceding Bond films. Even Kevin McLory's *Never Say Never Again* followed the pattern established by the early Bond films, although this may have been forced on McLory by his various legal battles over the copyright to *Thunderball*.[22] However, when Broccoli talks about his 'good fortune' in finding the Ian Fleming books, he is quite right to stress that above and beyond 'mere luck' the development of the Bond films was 'all hard work'. As we have suggested in relation to *Goldfinger*, the Bond books were not simply reproduced but were worked over and changed, even in the early Bond films. At the time of the making of *The Spy Who Loved Me* in 1975 and 1976, while the production team were well aware of the heritage of Bond and, indeed, were engaged in a lengthy court case to establish their undivided ownership of it, they were also concerned to 'update' and shift the emphasis of their 'formula' picture.[23] Their concern, equally, to maintain the 'plausibility' or 'realism' of Bond can be seen in the almost obsessive concern with weaponry and 'gadgets'.[24] Nevertheless, they were also involved in clearly formulated ideological projects in relation to at least three areas in which different considerations of inter-textuality played a part: with attempts to relocate James Bond politically; with attempts to engage with ideas about the independence of women and women's liberation; with attempts to construct and maintain a comic strategy around Bond's own sexuality.

The attempt to relocate James Bond politically or, indeed, in some crucial ways to 'depoliticise' him altogether had been of concern to Broccoli and Saltzman from the outset. Cubby Broccoli has said that the Bond films are 'not political' but 'good old fashioned entertainment'. What Broccoli appears to mean by this is that, during periods of détente, he has made efforts to tone down and, in some cases, to eradicate Bond's overt anti-Soviet views. *The Spy* represents the most extreme version of this strategy. Stromberg, the villain, plans a nuclear attack on New York and Moscow, threatening East and West alike indiscriminately. East/West tensions, in this context, are displaced into the sphere of sexuality, and redefined as a matter of the sexual and professional subordination of the East's best agent (Anya, special agent triple X) by the West's best agent (Bond). 'Well, well, well,' remarks Stromberg to Bond, 'a British secret agent in love with a Russian secret agent. Détente indeed.' Stromberg does not even belong to SPECTRE, since Broccoli's right to use this acronym was under dispute at the time in the context of the legal battles over *Thunderball*. Instead, he is represented as a fanatic who rejects the present world as 'corrupt and decadent' and plans to rebuild civilisation in the form of a model city constructed under the sea.

During the making of *The Spy*, the production team actively sought to cultivate an ethos of détente in all stages of film production and presentation. Members of the Russian Embassy were invited to the opening of the tanker set at Pinewood. After much discussion, it was decided that Barbara Bach should wear a Russian uniform and the publicity which surrounded the opening of the set at Pinewood Studios was focused on Barbara Bach, posing with Bond or shaking hands with Harold Wilson. However, the villain's conspiracy lacks not merely any Cold War associations; it lacks any specific political articulations whatsoever. Stromberg intends to 'destroy the world', not to threaten a particular country or just the Western world, but to destroy the whole world, and for no particular reason. Stromberg, in short, is represented as insane. 'It's fun to play madmen,' remarked Kurt Jurgens at the press conference which accompanied the London première of *The Spy*. Owing more to Captain Nemo than to any of Fleming's villains, the threat which Stromberg represents is the use of nuclear power combined with 'irrational' desires for change. At the same time, Stromberg's character takes on the quality of parody in the 'larger than life' excesses of Bond villainy. Stromberg's assistant, whose enormous size and steel teeth constitute the main physical threat to Bond, was conceived of at least in part as a comic take-off of other films. The production team saw the development of the character of 'Jaws' in terms of an elaborate joke about indestructability.

It is worth noting, however, that the desired imagery of détente, most effectively established by means of Anya's sexual subordination to Bond and their joint opposition to Stromberg, is quite specific to *The Spy*. Later films in the series resume a much more anti-Soviet stance. *For Your Eyes Only*, for example, is firmly installed in Thatcher's Britain, with Bond attempting to prevent a top secret nuclear submarine tracking system from falling into Russian hands. Although the key villain is once again a professional who simply wants to make money out of the deal, it is Russian involvement which motivates the plot. Détente has considerably altered character. When Bond destroys the tracking device under the eyes and guns of the head of the KGB, he comments wryly, 'That's détente, comrade. You don't have it and I don't have it.'

The second area in which the Bond production team wished to introduce changes in *The Spy* concerned the image and role of the Bond girl. What was the precise nature of their ideological project? Obviously, they recognised that a crucial and important part of the Bond myth has always centred around sexuality. As we have suggested earlier in relation to the novels, quite a complex form of sexual coding ties together Bond's relationship to M, to the villain and to 'the girl'. Moreover, images of women in the Bond films have always been constructed primarily in terms of male desire and pleasure. When Ursula Andress as Honeychile Rider, clad in a bikini and a knife, walked out of the sea in *Dr No*, the visual image of the Bond girl was resoundingly established. The scenes in which Honey makes her appearance can be read as a textbook illustration of scopophilic pleasure. Bond and his local helper, Quarrel, have arrived on Dr No's island at night. There is a shot of the beach and sea in the sunlit morning, while Honey's voice is heard singing, 'Underneath the mango tree, m'honey'. We see Bond lying sleeping, awoken by Honey's voice, immediately picking up his gun and looking for the source of the voice. The next shot is of Honey striding from the sea, singing, holding her shells and unaware of Bond's gaze. The reaction shot of Bond shows him surprised but appreciative. Honey carries on singing and there is a repetition of the two shots of Bond looking and Honey unaware. Bond then sings a phrase of Honey's song and the next shot of Honey shows her startled and afraid. Bond confidently jumps down and walks towards her, reassuring her as she backs away. The shots are constructed to ensure identification with Bond and pleasure at the sight of Honey. This type of imagery has always been heavily played upon in the Bond films and in the many sub-texts of Bond, the magazine features and the like, in which, nude or otherwise, the new Bond girl has been celebrated on the release of each new Bond film.

The sexual subordination of the 'girl' plays an important part in all the Bond films, albeit that the pattern established by the books was not always *closely* followed. To recapitulate our earlier argument, in the novels Bond's girls always had some initial claim to independence. They were not clinging romantic heroines. But the narrative pattern of the novels establishes the women as in some manner sexually and ideologically 'out of place', too aggressive, frigid or lesbian. In most cases, this 'out of placeness' is also signified by some minor physical disability. The challenge that such girls represent is to a traditional ordering of sexual difference and Bond's sexual subordination of the girl reinserts her back into a patriarchal system. In so doing, he also pulls her into line with his own brand of moral rectitude, loyalty to Queen and country and to the Western world, detaching her from servitude to or an alliance with the villain.

The early Bond films reworked these themes. The sexual ambiguity of the Bond girls was eradicated and, with it, their physical imperfections. The Bond formula, as understood by the production team on *The Spy*, involved a plethora of beautiful women and the repeated demonstration of Bond's mastery over them. The traditional ending of a Bond film sees Bond, having disposed of the villain and spectacularly destroyed his headquarters, making love to the new Bond girl of the film while the credits roll promising his return. The Bond production team were powerfully aware of that tradition and of its past audience drawing power. At the same time, they were well aware of the importance of the women's movement and the implication that Bond was unattractive to women because of his outdated sexism. Hence they saw that while Bond has to fulfil certain sexist expectations revolving around the sexual subjugation of women, it was also important that the girl should be seen to have some contemporary resonance with women audiences. Because of this, the Bond production team reworked the theme of the Bond girl's 'out of placeness'. Anya is not 'out of place' in relation to sexuality, nor even 'out of place' in her attempts to do the same job as Bond, but only in her conviction that she can do it better than Bond.

The heroine of *The Spy Who Loved Me* is thus intended to be a Russian agent who is Bond's professional equal. Barbara Bach was told, and told us, that she was to play a different sort of Bond girl:

> Well, first of all, she's a spy and a serious spy. And she's really not one of Bond's girls, so to speak. She's in the film doing her own bit and she meets up with Bond and it's only almost at the end of the film that there's any kind of attraction between the two of them, other than let's say, professional competition. So it's quite different. Most of the girls in the Bond films have just been merely beautiful girls that, you know, have small parts and come and go. Anya stays from the beginning to the end.

In certain formal terms, the character of Anya was to be given equal status with Bond. They share, for example, the same professional status. Lewis Gilbert, the director, remarked of Anya that 'Womens' Lib would be rather proud of her'. The pre-credits sequence typically involved a joke with audience expectations of a Bond film and *The Spy* is no exception. Between them, the pre-credits sequences prefigure the course of the narrative. As the Bondian catastrophe of missing submarines is unfolded, the governments of Britain and Russia are both seen calling in their secret agents 007 and triple X. In the Russian case, the camera pans across a palatial room, described as a 'People's Rest and Recuperation Centre', to a virile young man making love to a beautiful woman. He is about to leave and she lovingly rests against him asking for just 'five more minutes'. The scene strikes a note familiar from many previous Bond films in which Bond is always recalled from the side or the bed of a girl by M. However, when the silver musical box beside the bed requests that agent triple X report in, it is the girl who responds and identifies herself. Anya is set up as a challenge to Bond but one who is to be subordinated to Bond in the characteristic development of the Bond narrative, fleetingly evoked in the titles sequences when the image of five women, naked except for military caps and guns, fall over like dominoes before the sexual potency of Bond's gaze.

The production team were well aware of the ambiguities attached to the use of this type of heroine and their willingness to exploit a particular notion of the liberation of women was predicated on the assumption that it would, in the final analysis, reinforce the exploits of James Bond. The use of contemporary ideas about women's equality was both conscious and quite cynical. Anya was constructed to be both the Russian and female equivalent to Bond but also to succumb to him in the course of the film. The title song mockingly underlines this point only moments after the character of Anya has been introduced as Carly Simon sings 'Nobody does it better' of Bond. Nor is 'the Bond girl's' subjection to and by Bond secured merely at the level of the plot. Broccoli was not prepared to hire a more experienced actress for the part of Anya. He thought Barbara Bach was suitable for the following reasons:

> She's a very beautiful girl. She's comparatively unknown which I think brings a certain freshness to a Bond film. We have explored getting various well known ladies, high priced ladies to bring in, but in my humble opinion, there's no lady today who contributes that much success if she's high priced or otherwise, unless we like what she does. I don't think there's any actress today that can support a picture box office wise with the possible exception of Barbara Streisand ... But the price doesn't distinguish the girl in our film from the success of a Bond picture. I

mean we've explored a certain lady in Hollywood who commands a 500,000 dollar wage ... and that blew her right out of the box for me because she'd contribute no more than Barbara Bach will.

This casting policy ensures that it is rare for a Bond girl to have a great deal of acting experience or an existing public image which will in any way challenge the Bond/Moore figure. The only Bond girl who Broccoli remembers with distinct respect was Diana Rigg who played Tracey, the girl who Bond marries and is then killed in *On Her Majesty's Secret Service*. This departure from customary casting policy was largely occasioned by Eon Production's nervousness over George Lazenby's replacement of Sean Connery in the role of Bond. The casting of Diana Rigg – an accomplished actress with a star currency of her own from her role in *The Avengers* – was, in effect, a hedge against box office disaster. As a consequence of these considerations, *On Her Majesty's Secret Service* is rather untypical in allowing 'the girl' to function as a centre of dramatic action in her own right rather than merely as 'phallic fodder' for Bond.

The idea of what a Bond girl contributes and what she must contribute was given a particular edge in discussions over publicity for *The Spy*. Barbara Bach had worked both as a fashion model and in some Italian films and was anxious to avoid the 'cheesecake' associations of the usual 'Bond girl' publicity. While members of the production team were, on the one hand, anxious to create a more interesting heroine, they were also, on the other hand, concerned that Barbara Bach should fulfil the traditional expectations of 'the Bond girl'. Saul Cooper, the director of publicity, suggested what he considered to be the crucial characteristics of a Bond girl. 'A Bond girl is part of the whole dream world that Bond creates. She is a woman of fantastic sexual allure and promise, just as Bond is every man's dream of suddenly being able to spring into action.' In the making of *The Spy*, there were some clashes over which view of the Bond girl should prevail as Barbara Bach sought to establish her own publicity organised around the themes of fashion and beauty rather than that of overt sexuality. Inevitably, compromises were made but, as Saul Cooper indicated, usually in the direction of the studio's position:

> You have the traditional Bond girl image, which involves having the girl photographed in a bikini, in a bathing suit. This was something which took a certain amount of hassling with Barbara at the beginning. But it was something that was absolutely required because a Bond girl must, at some point, be seen within the Bond mould.

The Bondian formula, as the production team were well aware, was likely to be strengthened by the creation of a Bond girl whose initial challenge to Bond was more direct and relevant. Barbara Bach's public descriptions of Bond as a 'male chauvinist pig' unknowingly focused the very themes which the Bond team wanted to employ in relation to the Bond formula. Needless to say, the requirements of the formula, and of the studio, prevailed over the wishes of Bach who took her place amongst the series of Bond girls paraded across the pages of *Playboy* just as, in the film, Anya is rescued by Bond and abandons her quest for revenge on Bond for killing her lover in exchange for his sexual attentions.

The third area of adjustment which the production team for *The Spy* sought to effect concerned Bond's own sexuality. Although the sexual subordination of 'the Bond girl' may have been articulated with different themes during different moments of Bond's career as a popular hero, Bond's sexual attraction and phallic power has always been central to the Bond narratives. Again, however, this aspect of the Bond films has been one which has shifted somewhat over the years. Such changes are obviously partly related to specific performances of Bond. Connery's sexual charisma was gently underlined in the early films but never heavily underwritten. With Roger Moore in the main role, Bond came to have a more flippant and self-parodic style. Moreover, in order to make the films less dependent on Connery or any specific actor, Eon Productions came to invest very heavily in other areas of the Bond 'formula' picture, notably in the use of gadgets and spectacular designs. Hence, Bond's physical presence on the screen has increasingly come to be located in his mastery and use of technology. For example, posters of the early films tended to show simply Connery holding a gun, while the later films boast posters in which the technological inventions of the Bondian world almost swamp Bond. Where it was usual for the Bond of the novels to begin his adventures with an interview with M, it is much more necessary to the Bond films that he also sees Q and the heavily played upon jokes of Q's elaborate workshop of gadgets.

The members of the Bond team have always made a conscious effort to avoid what they consider to be overt sexuality and excessive violence, largely because they desire a mass audience and because they perceive that the Bond films are particularly attractive to children. Their concern with visual style and the accomplishment of plausible but impossible technological gadgets is seen as an important, because neutral, area which is none the less crucial to the films' audience appeal. The most detailed planning discussions in the making of *The Spy* concerned the development of sets and gadgets and the use of these in 'action' sequences. At the same time, the Bond team use a recognised technique for comically deflating the spectacular use of technology. Michael Wilson, the assistant to the producer of *The Spy*, pointed out that the one-line jokes for which Bond is famous are part of a well worked out strategy. An exciting action sequence involving some technological excess has to be followed by a joke both to release audience tension over the action and to get over the considerable demands that Bond films make on audiences in terms of the suspension of disbelief by dissipating incredulity into laughter. The visual gag of the Union Jack parachute which follows the ski jump in the pre-credits sequence of *The Spy* follows this pattern and there are innumerable other examples. In a fight with 'Jaws', Bond manages to drop him into a shark pool by the use of an enormous magnet from which Jaws cannot escape because of his steel teeth. As he picks Jaws up, Bond remarks cheerfully, 'How does that grab you?' The new scriptwriter, Christopher Wood, described how he was introduced to this strategy:

I can remember one instance in a place in the script . . .
I'd developed the idea of having a motor-cycle combination –
a sidecar and a motorcycle. The motor-cycle sidecar breaks
away and becomes a rocket which chases Bond when he's
in a car. Now the way I had written it at that stage, Bond
took evasive action and drove off the road; the sidecar
exploded against a wall, blew a big hole in the wall and
that was the end of the sequence. Now somebody in the art
department thought out the idea . . . why shouldn't the
sidecar hit another vehicle or how could you build
something extra into hitting a vehicle, other than just a
blinding flash and bits of explosive material blowing all
over the place, suppose we made that vehicle something
unusual . . . a vehicle that was carrying a load of feather
mattresses so that when you explode the vehicle, voom,
instead of just a big bang, you get a big bang and millions
and millions of feathers.

In the final version of the incident, not only is there an
explosion of feathers but the motorbike rider is also covered
in them before driving over a cliff into the sea. Bond at this
point sardonically remarks, 'All those feathers and he still
can't fly.'

The comic strategy of the production team on *The Spy* was
not simply limited to the area of technology but was also
focused on Bond's sexuality. The comic style of Roger
Moore's Bond, in which Moore clowns for the audience,
contrasts markedly with the Connery style which was to
share a joke about Bond with the audience. The difference
can partly be registered in the different expressions the two
men use to underline jokes: Connery with one eye brow
raised, Moore with both eyebrows raised. Lewis Gilbert, the
director of *The Spy*, tried to persuade Moore that raising two
eyebrows was unsuitable for Bond, too comic and too
reminiscent of Moore's performance in *The Saint*. The script
of *The Spy* also involves some fairly traditional lines of sexual
innuendo, reminiscent more of the *Carry On* films than of the
earlier Bond films. The film ends with Bond and Anya
escaping from Stromberg's headquarters in an escape capsule.
Anya succumbs to Bond's last request to get their wet clothes

off with the willingness of all the other Bond girls before her, while M, Q and the Minister and the Head of the KGB wait anxiously on a nearby ship. 'But James, what will our superiors think?' utters Anya plaintively. Meanwhile, the Minister is anxiously asking, 'Do you think there's any danger of the bends?' and, when the capsule is finally picked up, Bond's reply to the reproving looks of his combined superiors and the question, 'What do you think you are doing Bond?' is, 'Keeping the British end up!' – a line delivered with fully raised eyebrows and an almost coquettish gesture as Bond lets down the blinds in the capsule and returns to kissing Anya.

In these and countless other small particulars, the effect that was consciously aimed for by the production team of *The Spy* was that of a parody of a super hero. The team was well aware of the comic strategy established in the early movies, notably in *Goldfinger*. Indeed, in his part in the scriptwriting, Christopher Wood turned to his own children to attempt to establish what was attractive about Bond and, in response to their replies, reworked the car chase used to great effect in *Goldfinger*. In *The Spy*, Bond drives his Lotus into the sea in his efforts to escape one of Stromberg's helicopters. As his Lotus converts to a submarine, he inspects Stromberg's undersea headquarters and does battle with skin-divers and another small underwater submarine, a battle complete with torpedoes, smokescreens, and depth charges. After the underwater battle, Bond and Anya drive from the waves to the amazed stares and startled interest of holidaymakers on the beach. The switch to comedy is immediately indicated in the reaction shots of the holidaymakers – a curious child pointing, a man drinking beer looking at the emerging Lotus and then suspiciously at the bottle from which he is drinking, a dog fleeing whining. Bond then ostentatiously removes a small fish from the Lotus and drops it through the car window, a very conscious comic rupturing of the spectacular technological excess which has gone before.

Ideology and production processes

Within this chapter, we have tried to indicate fairly briefly some of the ideological processes at work in the making of a Bond film. We don't wish to imply here that all questions of determination are irrelevant to an understanding of the ideological processes involved in film-making. The organisation of the industry, financial constraints, existing conventions and genres and the particular social backgrounds of the people involved in the making of any one film will all necessarily constrain and order the processes of film-making. Nevertheless, we would suggest that the deliberations, calculations and policies which actually inform the making of a film have a direct and discernible bearing on the processes through which ideologies are worked over and transformed into a specific filmic form. These considerations cannot be overriden by invoking the role of the economy as the final, in the sense of ultimate, instance of determination. In each of the areas which we have discussed, that of 'politics', that of rethinking the image of 'the Bond girl' and the pursuit of a comic strategy in relation to Bond, the production team of *The Spy* were involved in consciously shaping their 'formula' picture. It is also the case that what we have termed their 'ideological projects' affected the form of the final text. Such 'ideological projects' were, of course, all dependent on discourses outside film-making and the Bond genre, although they tended to be discussed amongst the film producers simply as 'updating' James Bond. The lack of an appropriate theoretical vocabulary, however, need not be taken as indicating that film-makers are merely the unconscious agents of ideological processes which take place behind their backs.

However, in seeking to reinvest the area of production studies with rather more importance and to treat the views and practices of the film-makers with rather more respect than is customary, we do not intend to argue that only the film-makers have a 'true' knowledge of their films. Texts in their diverse conditions of consumption are not simply the sum of the ideological projects of their producers if only because, as we have shown, audiences read such texts from quite different inter-textual positions.

It could also be argued that films such as *The Spy*, with a real dependence on an existing genre, may come to contain some quite contradictory characteristics. For example, if we return to the question of the sexuality of Bond, we would suggest that the various comic strategies developed by the film-makers have had the unintended consequence of vitiating Bond's sexuality. Although Bond's success with women in the later Bond films continues unabated, the sexual attractiveness of the Bond character is no longer played straight. Bond's sexual adventures have a distinctly comic air. One reason for this is the degree to which Bond's sexuality has become fetished on to machinery, cars, guns, motorcycles, and what have you. In *The Spy*, moments of romance are punctured by gadgetry; Bond is knocked out by Anya's anaesthetic cigarette on a romantic journey down the Nile. When Bond drives his Lotus/submarine into the sea, the action is punctuated by Anya's gasps of admiration shared between him and the vehicle. However, when we laugh at the single 'fish' produced by this exploit, Bond's sexual presence is also thereby diminished – little more than a damp squib – through its identification with and belittlement by technological and spectacular excess. Viewed in this light, as we go on to argue in the next chapter, the pleasures afforded by the Bond films are somewhat more ambiguous and contradictory than most previous accounts have implied.

Chapter 7

Pleasure and the Bond Films

'We don't want to have Bond to dinner or to go golfing with Bond or talk to Bond. We want to be Bond.'—Kingsley Amis[1]

'Bond, like myself, is a male chauvinist pig. All my life I've been trying to get women out of brassieres and pants.'—Roger Moore[2]

'Why do the millions keep flocking to 007's exploits? No offense to Roger Moore, it's not the gadgets, it's the girls.'—Maude Adams[3]

It is frequently suggested in critical accounts of the products of high culture that they are inherently more fascinating not only aesthetically but in their complexity, whereas the products of mass or popular culture are conceived of as essentially *simple*, appealing as it were to a lowest common denominator in human taste. To a large extent, the views of the producers of the Bond films appear to confirm this. The Bond films are easily referred to as 'formula' pictures. This notion of popular fiction, however, poses certain problems in that it ignores the extent to which texts can only be read and understood in terms of their position in different regimes of inter-textuality. This was an issue brought home to us with considerable force when we first began to discuss the Bond novels and films in detail and discovered with some surprise that our own responses, activated as they were by our positions in differently gendered reading formations, could differ very greatly in relation to the same incidents in the same texts. This suggests that popular fiction can, indeed, be expected to activate or sometimes establish different reading formations and that, in this sense, the texts of popular fiction are usually quite complex.

In this chapter, we examine the way in which the Bond films are constructed to allow for different routes of identification through the narrative and to recruit the attention of different spectators. In the first place, we want to point to the operation of production strategies aimed at a mass audience. In the second place, we consider how different viewers in different reading formations may be differently constituted as subjects through the same film, through an interplay between the 'looks' and narrative of the film and reading competences established elsewhere. In particular, we want to consider the question of 'gendered' pleasure in relation to the Bond films. In so doing, we shall comment briefly on the implications of these ideas for those arguments which contend that the whole system of looking, through which Hollywood films work, in terms of the pro-filmic event, the interplay of looks between performers, the look of the camera and the look of the audience, is predicated on a construction of male pleasure.

The pursuit of a 'mass' audience

The production team who made *The Spy Who Loved Me* held a series of assumptions about audiences for the Bond films, which we consider are probably typical of the views of the makers of all the later Bond films. Broccoli, for example, spent some time weighing market and critical response to the films while, at the same time, relying mainly on his trust in what he calls 'a ready made audience out there waiting to see a Bond film':

> Well, after fifteen, sixteen years of making Bond films with the people who helped create them, I think we know between us what the audience want. We've learned over the years. Do they want more gimmicks? Do they want less gimmicks? We've been criticised by certain of our critics that we've gotten too gimmicky and then, next time,

they've said, 'Well, there weren't enough gimmicks in it', so we have to equate whether we've got enough gimmicks or not enough gimmicks.[4]

If Broccoli's views seem to be intuitively commercial, a matter of what people want to pay for and what he can provide, other members of *The Spy*'s production team readily identified different points of attraction for different audiences. We have already referred to some of these in a previous chapter: the scriptwriter's concern, for example, with an audience of children in developing some of the key sequences in *The Spy*, notably the car chase above and below water, and the director of publicity's interest in the creation of a Bond girl of 'fantastic sexual allure' for male audiences. Other members of the publicity team were more concerned to pull in women audiences through advertising on Capital Radio in the morning, using Moore's voice to address the listener directly, with the intention of encouraging housewives to sublimate themselves in the role of the Bond girl.

Moreover, the script of *The Spy Who Loved Me*, on which a number of writers worked, was 'Americanised' in its casual use of American as well as British idiomatic phrases. Christopher Wood, the final scriptwriter, considered some lines to be inappropriate to an English James Bond; lines such as 'how does that grab you?' fell into this category. Nevertheless, Wood accepted the necessity for such lines remaining on the grounds that the film had to appeal to an American audience. The 'formula' of the Bond film overall was implicitly understood as involving an international market;

Well, they're well tailored in the sense that what they understand in places like Japan where the picture is sub-titled — it's not dubbed — they understand action. They understand the symbol of 007, James Bond, and they flock to the theatres to see him because they don't have to stop and think. They watch it all happening on the screen. And, I think that's the basic simple tailoring of a Bond film; action, some interesting gimmicks possibly, beautiful girls, excitement, different locations, bring them closer to new locations – Thailand, Egypt, Nassau – they've seen. All of these new locations, I think help considerably. Plus the fact that we have Roger Moore who in the last film did the biggest foreign business for us of anybody.[5]

While Broccoli's statements appear to tell us that the Bond films are 'simple', a matter of 'basic simple tailoring', it is also clear that the production strategy of the films is based on pulling in some very different audiences. Indeed, it is possible to suggest that the Bond films do not present us with a case of a simple product which appeals to a mass audience but rather with a complex relationship between a series of film texts and a highly differentiated set of audiences.

The novels, as we have already indicated, were both written and initially read within a particular sphere of male reading competence, that organised around the imperialist spy-thriller. We do not, of course, mean to claim that they were never read by women or that they did not, in later periods, have a wide range of readers but just that the pattern of critical response to the Bond novels during the late fifties indicates a group of predominantly male middle-class English readers who either identified strongly with Bond or, alternatively, rejected identification with Bond and the novels with it. Amis takes the former route in arguing that male readers like himself wanted to 'be Bond', although ironically it later transpired that Amis himself wanted to 'be Fleming', writing about Bond rather than being him.[6] The form of identification which Amis characterises as 'wanting to be Bond', implying as it does a whole reading formation, was clearly also a potential form of identification for viewers of the films. However, Amis's own responses to the films indicate some of the differences between the early readers of the novels and the reading formations activated by the films. Amis saw Bond reduced to a joke in the films. Moreover, Amis had clearly always conceived Bond both as more English and more upper class than the Bond/Connery figure of the films. On the question of Bond's accent in impersonating a Scottish baronet, Amis remarks that 'Sean Connery's total wrongness for the part is nowhere better demonstrated than at this point. Mr Connery could put up a show as a Scottish business man all right, but a Scottish baronet never'.[7] In the event, of course, it was George Lazenby rather than Connery who played Bond pretending to be a Scottish baronet, in *On Her Majesty's Secret Service*. However, Bond's visibility in the figure of Connery, his more populist appeal centring on Connery's performance both as a sensualist and as a man amused by the character of the Establishment, meant that 'being' the Bond of the films was very different from 'being' the Bond of the novels.

The constituents of James Bond as a hero changed with the advent of the films and forms of identification with Bond also changed. The films even more effectively than the novels activated a voyeuristic 'free' male sexuality, which was constructed jointly with the host of sub-texts focusing on the appearance of the Bond girl. The films also initially established Bond in terms of Connery's performance in the populist and sensualist mode rather than simply in terms of the élitist and consumerist preoccupations of the novels. When Bond remarks, in *You Only Live Twice* to Moneypenny bent on offering him *Instant Japanese* for his forthcoming trip to Japan, that 'You've forgotten, I took a first in Oriental Languages at Cambridge', the audiences understand and respond to the joke about the excesses of the Bond figure rather than seriously being impressed by Bond's abilities. The comic strategy of the Bond films, although unevenly present, since films such as *From Russia, With Love* and *For Your Eyes Only* clearly follow a more 'straight adventure' pattern than films such as *Goldfinger* and *The Spy Who Loved Me*, tends to establish forms of identification with Bond which incorporate a comic distancing from the hero rather than encouraging a *simple* desire to be Bond.

The comic strategy of the films also operated to recruit different sets of audiences. In terms of different national audiences, the 'sending up' of some aspects of British post-imperialist ideologies combined with the buttressing of others was not only endorsed by British audiences but also allowed the Bond films to work in terms of other national reading formations, feeding in, for example, to American views of the British class system as, on the one hand, an outdated anachronism and, on the other hand, as an amusing eccentricity when used in the service of the United States. Bond can thus be conceived of as, if not an American agent, as an agent who is at the service of American interests. It's not surprising that American presidents from Jack Kennedy to Ronald Reagan have been Bond fans. The pivotal character within the films here is that of Felix Leiter, the CIA agent. As we have already noted, Amis gives a peculiarly British reading of the character of Leiter in the novels:

> The point of Felix Leiter, such a nonentity as a piece of characterisation, is that he, the American, takes orders from Bond the Britisher, and that Bond is constantly doing better than he, showing himself not braver nor more devoted, but smarter, wilier, tougher, more resourceful, the incarnation of little old England with her quiet ways and shoe-string budget wiping the eye of great big global tentacled multi-billion dollar-appropriating America. When in *Live and Let Die*, Leiter has unwittingly led them both into a trap in Leiter's own territory, Bond, though handicapped by a broken finger, punches and kicks and shoots his way out, killing three; Leiter is blackjacked and dumped outside a hospital. Leiter's fight with the Robber ends with Leiter in the shark tank, Bond's with the Robber there. Bond kills Mr Spang; Leiter turns up in time to cheer. Bond frustrates Goldfinger's Fort Knox operation; Leiter arrives with the rescue party wearing his U.S. marines uniform – a nice allusive touch.[8]

In the films, Leiter is still a nonentity as a character, played by different actors in different films, but his role in the narrative is rather different. Leiter functions not as competition (however friendly) for Bond but as a command figure for American power on which Bond's successes in the films frequently rest. In *Goldfinger*, a film that was extremely popular in the United States, receiving a 49 per cent share of the viewing audience on the night that it was first aired on an American network, Leiter sets up an enormous army operation to fool *Goldfinger* and arrives in the nick of time to rescue Bond and the gold from the nuclear detonation. He is in no sense an agent parallel to Bond but rather works as a surrogate M. In *Never Say Never Again*, Leiter, now black and youthful, works in the same way; commenting wryly on Q's experimental pen/gun; emerging from watching Bond in his deadly confrontation with Fatima Bush and legitimising Bond's use of American equipment in the final battle with Largo.

The Bond films were not only aimed at British and American audiences. Just as Felix Leiter links Bond to American government, other 'friends' of Bond work in the same way towards other countries. Tiger Tanaka, for example, in *You Only Live Twice*, acts as a Japanese surrogate M as Head of the Japanese Secret Service. The use of the character is again double-edged. If Bond is the hero and startles the Japanese with his use of a gadget such as little Nellie, a miniature helicopter which arrives in suitcases, Tanaka expresses surprise at the ease with which he pulls Bond in; Bond arrives in his office via a trap-door and metal shute which deposits him unceremoniously in a waiting armchair. Tanaka introduces Bond to Japanese girls, baths and ninja training, making Bond Japanese and arranging his marriage with a Japanese girl and finally, once again, providing the support of the ninjas for Bond's destruction of Blofeld's headquarters. When Connery arrived in Japan in 1966, he was mobbed by fans and the news that the new Bond film was to be set in Japan operated to increase rapidly Bond's already considerable popularity in Japan. If the film-makers consciously sought international audiences for Bond and used both narrative articulations of Bond with other governments and friends and comically inflected the relationships to allow for different readings, they also shrewdly exploited a number of contemporary events and themes. A classic example is the sight of the then recently stolen Goya portrait of the Duke of Wellington in Dr No's headquarters. As we have argued in detail in relation to *The Spy Who Loved Me*, most of the later Bond films rework themes present in other popular fictional forms or in public life in relation to Bond.

Male and female pleasures

It could be argued that, whatever national and political inflections different audiences have read in the Bond films and novels, the common ingredient was that of pleasure in a free male sexuality. As Amis points out in relation to the books, resistance to Bond's advances barely exists. '"I hoped I would one day kiss a man like that," Solitaire says at a very early stage in *Live and Let Die*, "and when I just saw you, I knew it would be you." One gets the general drift.'[9] In all the films from *Dr No* to *Never Say Never Again*, scarcely does an attractive woman appear on the screen but she is eyeing Bond with invitation and relish. Moreover, as we have remarked earlier, the Bond films appear to conform closely to 'the look' incorporated in the forms of Hollywood feature films, in which the viewer can be expected to identify with the hero who is *active* in the narrative, who makes things happen and solves problems, and to share with the hero the desire and accompanying 'looks' at women whose image is *passive*, there to be desired both for the hero and the audience. Mulvey suggests that the scopophilic instinct, that is, the pleasure of looking at another person as an erotic object, combined with ego libido, the process of identification, takes a particular form in the cinema, building the image of women as the passive bearers of the active gaze of men into the cinematic codes of the Hollywood feature film:

> Going far beyond highlighting a woman's to-be-looked-at-ness, cinema builds the way she is to be looked at into the spectacle itself. Playing on the tension between film as controlling the dimension of time (editing, narrative) and film as controlling the dimension of space (changes in distance, editing), cinematic codes create a gaze, a world and an object, thereby producing an illusion cut to the measure of desire.[10]

In Mulvey's analysis of the three looks within the cinema, that of the characters at each other dominates that of the camera as it records what has been placed in front of it and that of the audience as it watches the final product. Even within this structure of looking, however, the unity of the narrative is threatened by the female image which, in its fetishised form, stops the narrative. The recording process and the critical reading of the spectator, Mulvey contends, are 'subordinated to the neurotic needs of the male ego':[11]

> The camera becomes the mechanism for producing an illusion of Renaissance space, flowing movements compatible with the human eye, an ideology of representation that revolves around the perception of the subject; the camera's look is disavowed in order to create a convincing world in which the spectator's surrogate can perform with verisimilitude.[12]

In Mulvey's view, the pleasure of such narrative fiction films is highly dependent on the male look. 'Women', she suggests, 'whose image has continually been stolen and used for this end, cannot view the decline of the traditional film form with anything much more than sentimental regret.'[13] The system that Mulvey describes, therefore, produces definitions of female sexuality as threatening to the male order but the narrative is inevitably closed in favour of male domination. It is in this combination of a threatening female sexuality with final subordination to the male that our pleasure as spectators is to be found.

Mulvey's account of the process of fetishism suggests related forms of pleasure for differently gendered viewers. In the Freudian account of fetishism, the woman's body which lacks a penis implies the threat of castration. In the 'looks' of the cinema, Mulvey argues, the image of woman's body acts in the same way. The problem or threat can be dealt with by an act of displacement in which the absent penis is replaced by another part of the body, or another object. In this case, the fetish object takes on extra value as a phallic substitute. In the cinema, the castration threat embodied in the image of women is handled in two ways; by the flow of the narrative in which the male hero succeeds in his various tasks and/or by fetishising the image of the woman. In both cases, it could be said, the pleasure of the male is the dominant concern. Nevertheless, there are pleasures for women here.

In Freud's view of the castration complex, women are doubly powerless, subject to the power of the phallus and condemned to a position in which they can never attain it. But the process of fetishism both underwrites the images of women with power and endows the spectator with the illusion of a controlling gaze, thereby pulling women spectators as well as men into the pleasures of the film. Women, therefore, could be expected to take pleasure in the Bond films, although of a very much more limited nature than men.

The Bond films were and remain popular with women. IBA statistics and those from Home Box Office in America indicate not only that the Bond films are popular with television and cable viewers, generally receiving between 25 per cent and 30 per cent higher marks for 'viewer satisfaction' than other films, but also that the Bond films are only slightly more popular with men than with women.[14] We have already suggested in an earlier chapter that one possible reason for the popularity of the Bond films with women is that the 'Bond girls' of the films of the early sixties represented a certain 'liberated' sexuality in comparison with other representations of female sexuality in contemporary British and American films, even though organised around a male notion of sexual freedom. However, we wouldn't wish to suggest that all women simply responded to the sexual 'liberation' of the Bond films. Not only do the Bond films differ but their female audiences also may take different pleasures in the films. While our approach to the question has its basis in Mulvey's ideas, we would like to suggest some modifications of Mulvey's views, specifically with regard to women's pleasures in relation to Bond films.

In the first place, Mulvey, in common with the organisation of Hollywood films which she describes, tends to pay little attention to the way in which women viewers or audiences view films outside the parameters of a Freudian castration complex. Moreover, Mulvey's is a monumental critique of all Hollywood films singularly failing to take into account various inter-textual relations, and the different reading formations through which audiences understand film texts. Clearly this is not the place for an extended review of Freud's ideas or of Mulvey's dependence on them, but it is perhaps sufficient to say that the acceptance of psychoanalysis by feminists has always been dependent on some very specific readings of Freud and Lacan, readings which, in the case of Freud, tend to eradicate those parts of the theory in which physiology plays a crucial part,[15] and which, in the case of Lacan, have to ignore the phallic centredness of the theory. If, as we would argue, gendered subjectivity is dependent on the interaction of physiology and the historical and social order, we need to consider how, textually, this may be organised and how it may affect women's readings of and women's pleasures in forms of fiction in which male pleasures may well be dominant.

Mulvey's analysis generally suggests that narrative cinema addresses itself to male spectators, that it is distinguished by an address which, in its organisation of 'looking', presupposes a masculine subjectivity as the only subjectivity available. It would certainly be difficult to avoid the conclusion that the Bond films assume, in narrative and 'looks', a male viewer. Yet in these circumstances how do we explain the pleasures women spectators derive from the Bond films? Kuhn suggests one explanation in arguing that the viewing subject is not constituted as gendered by cinematic address, or 'perhaps that socio-biological gender and gendered subjectivity are not necessarily coterminous so that the specificity of the "masculine" becomes in some ways culturally universalised'.[16] This assumes, of course, that women audiences come to identify with masculine modes of address and provides a rationale for feminist support of films outside 'the masculine structures of voyeurism'.[17] Moreover, this view of women also supports the arguments based on psychoanalysis which place women in a position outside or marginalised in relation to language and the symbolic order.

We would suggest that women come to the Bond films with a gendered subjectivity which is not simply based on a differently ordered oedipal experience in childhood, but is a textually organised subjectivity which gives them different expectations of and responses to a James Bond film than men. We want to consider one form of reading competence, one of the fictional subjectivities which women bring to the Bond films, notably that organised by romance. Before doing so, however, we will discuss two highly relevant but rather differently directed views of pleasure and fiction. In Stephen Heath's fascinating account of 'the sexual fix', he considers fictional descriptions of it in an essay which embraces many other accounts of sexuality. He points to the organising of novelistic fiction around the phallus and 'the big O'; 'making love is the crucial big scene – what in the end it's all about'.[18] Writing about love-making is, according to Heath, a problem of complicity with and support for the sexual fix, 'going over and over the standard pattern'.[19] He quotes a typical example from Jilly Cooper's *Octavia*:

> Then suddenly it happened – like a great glorious whooshing washing machine – it's the only way I can describe it – leaving me shuddering and shuddering with pleasure at the end, like the last gasps of the spin-dryer. And afterwards I cried some more because I was so happy, and he held me in his arms, telling me how much he loved me until I fell asleep.
>
> A few hours later the dawn awoke me. We'd forgotten to draw the curtains. All I could see were huge windows framing the plane trees of Holland Park. I blinked, turned and found Gareth looking at me.
> I must be dreaming.
> I put my hand out to touch his cheek.
> 'Are you real?' I said incredulously.
> He smiled. 'I am if you are.'
> His eyes had turned black, his chest was covered in bruises. 'I think I'm in bed with Henry Cooper,' I said. I never dreamt he'd make such a sensational lover. 'Do you think we could possibly do it again?'
> And we did, and it was even better than the last time and I screamed with delight and joy because I'd been so clever.[20]

This final passage from *Octavia* is compared with a passage from D. H. Lawrence's *Lady Chatterley's Lover* as a more banal and less exalted version of 'the sexual fix' but one which nevertheless repeats, in essence, the main ingredients. Yet if

Heath is undoubtedly right to indicate the similarity in narrative peaks and resolutions in heterosexual love, orgasm and, in the nineteenth-century novel, marriage, it is also the case that he tends to ignore the narrative disruptions and ideological tensions which such orgasms/marriages resolve, thereby ignoring the key to the pleasure in such resolutions which is the particular problems with which men and women identify in fiction and which are fictionally resolved in favour of the sexual fix. *Octavia*, for example, like many a romantic heroine before her from Jane Eyre onwards, is dispossessed, deserted by her parents, inadequately schooled in normal heterosexual relations (her brother is a homosexual), and hence takes the wrong path, herself pursuing male sexual partners and 'unable to experience womanhood', that is, the orgasm given by the male. The hero, like Bond, restores her to the woman's role – but also restores her to the family, and the law of the father. Yet what this not at all untypical format allows is that women who identify with Octavia may experience vicariously some quite contradictory things; the successful pursuit of men by Octavia in her unreformed days, considerable resentment and bitterness towards the 'right' man in her life and, despite these unpromising beginnings, the discovery of happiness, wealth, a family, sexual pleasure and marriage – a magical transformation! In a curious sense, Heath repeats the pattern of the discourses of sexuality which he so effectively outlines, leaving it only in his analysis of 'clever women' whose writing about sexuality reveals desire and pleasure 'beyond the orders, the commandments of identity' but choosing to ignore the ambiguous and contradictory pleasures that 'ordinary' women may obtain from the narratives resolved by the sexual fix.

Existing critiques of Mulvey's work are also characterised by their lack of interest in women's pleasures in popular genres of film-making. The most interesting work in the Mulvey tradition has been the attempt by writers such as Paul Willemen and Stephen Neale to amend and expand Mulvey's ideas to take into account the eroticism of the male figure. Willemen, for example, traces images of men as direct objects of desire back to Freud:

In *Instincts and Their Vicissitudes* Freud wrote that 'At the beginning of its activity, the scopophilic instinct is auto-erotic: it has indeed an object, but that object is the subject's own body'. The identification of the woman as the privileged object of the scopophilic drive is therefore already the product of a displacement. Mulvey doesn't allow sufficient room for the fact that in patriarchy the direct object of scopophilic desire can also be male. If scopophilic pleasure relates primarily to the observation of one's sexual like (as Freud suggests), then the two looks distinguished by Mulvey (fetishism and voyeurism) are in fact varieties of one single mechanism: the repression of homosexuality. The narcissistic identification with an ideal ego in the diegesis would therefore not be a mere mediation in order to get at a desired woman, but the contemplation of the male hero would in itself be a substantial source of gratification for a male viewer – as is demonstrated time and again in the contemporary American cinema's celebration of male couples. In such films, the suggested homosexual gratification appears to be in direct proportion to the degree women are humiliated in/eliminated from the diegesis![21]

Willemen continues the argument in his examination of the films of Anthony Mann, where he points out that spectacle and drama in Mann's films tend to be organised around the look at the male figure and the 'unquiet pleasure' of seeing the male mutilated and restored through violent brutality.[22] Willemen suggests that such films offer pleasures of a repressed homosexual voyeurism in which the figure of the male represents just as much anxiety as the look at the female and provides the erotic focus, which is, however, also the centre of repression and disavowal, marked in the film by mutilation and sadism.

Neale also suggests, following Mulvey's 'Afterthoughts' on *Duel in the Sun*, that the western generally is crucially involved in a form of male narcissism in which images of male narcissistic authority run counter to images of social authority. Here, the hero may reject marriage, social integration and, implicitly, an oedipal resolution to remain an anachronistic outsider in a nostalgic celebration of narcissistic phallic omnipotence. Neale points usefully to the many westerns which deal with a theme of lost or doomed male narcissicism:

> The clearest examples would be Peckinpah's westerns: *Guns in the Afternoon, Major Dundee* (to a lesser extent), *The Wild Bunch* and especially *Pat Garrett and Billy the Kid.* The films are shot through with nostalgia, with an obsession with images and definition of masculinity and masculine codes of behaviour and the threats posed to it by women, Society and the Law. The threat of castration is figured in the wounds and injuries suffered by Joel McCrea in *Guns in the Afternoon,* Charlton Heston in *Major Dundee* and William Holden in *The Wild Bunch.* The famous slow motion violence, bodies splintered and torn apart, can be viewed at one level at least as the image of narcissicism in its moment of disintegration and destruction.[23]

Neale also contends that, rather than voyeurism and fetishism being structured solely round the male look being active and the female look passive, both voyeuristic and fetishistic looks can be directed at males. In war films, westerns and thrillers, there are battles, fights and duels between individual men and groups of men in which male figures on the screen are subject to voyeuristic looking. Elements of fetishistic looking may also be present. Neale uses the example of the highly stylised exchange of looks between hero and villains in Leone films, shot in close-up, which precede most gun battles. He suggests that the shoot out, the final battle between hero and villain, combines both forms of looking, being at one and the same time a moment of spectacle at which the narrative stops and also the culmination of the narrative drive. What differentiates images of men and women in Neale's view is the repression of and displacement of eroticism in the case of men. It is not at all difficult to analyse the Bond films in terms of voyeuristic and fetishistic looks at Bond. We have already suggested in relation to *Goldfinger* that certain scenes, notably the torture sequence in which Bond's body is the focus of all looks, involve erotic characteristics and there are constant spectacular and ritualised fights in the Bond films in which voyeuristic and fetishistic looks are interwoven. The spectacular destruction of the villain's headquarters – frequently housed in a dramatic Ken Adam's set – common to many Bond films is one such moment, the equivalent to the western shoot out. But in the final analysis, we would suggest that for male spectators such eroticism tends to be repressed and/or displaced on to the figure of the girl.

If this seems to be a rather lengthy departure from the question of the pleasures that women may take in the Bond films, it is necessary precisely to establish the direction in which current thinking on film and pleasure takes us: that is, that women's pleasures in films are little discussed except on the assumptions that the spectorial look in the cinema is basically male and that women's pleasures must echo this. What Willemen and Neale do in their analysis of the look at the male is, in effect, to assume a different spectator, one who takes pleasure in erotic images of men, in a sense, the ultimate narcissistic male spectator, and to work through films in which such a spectator could take pleasure, often despite the explicit narrative resolutions of the films. They both, as a result, accurately and usefully point to the way in which 'male homosexuality is constantly present as an undercurrent, as a potentially troubling aspect of many films and genres, but one that is dealt with obliquely, symptomatically, and that has to be repressed'.[24] We want to explore, in a rather similar way, a pattern through which women's pleasures and desires are organised in the Bond films, without assuming a total identification with the male spectatorial look. To do so, we need to assume from the start that identification is rarely a matter of social males identifying with male cinematic heroes and social women identifying with female cinematic images. Ellis suggests something of the mobility and fluidity of identification and desire in the cinema:

Cinematic identification involves two tendencies. First there is that of dreaming and phantasy that involves the multiple and contradictory tendencies within the construction of the individual. Second, there is the experience of narcissistic identification with the image of a human figure perceived as other. Both these processes are invoked in the conditions of entertainment cinema. The spectator does not therefore identify with the hero or heroine; an identification that would, if put in its conventional sense, involve socially constructed males identifying with male heroes and socially constructed females identifying with women heroines. The situation is more complex than this, as identification involves both the recognition of self in the image on the screen, a narcissistic identification, and the identification of self with the various positions that are involved in the fictional narration; those of hero and heroine, villain, bit-part player, active and passive character. It involves the identification of the public, external phantasies of the fiction with personal phantasies. Identification is therefore multiple and fractured, a sense of seeing the constituent parts of the spectator's own psyche paraded before her or him; a sense also of experiencing desire for the perfected images of individuals that are presented over and above their particular phantasy roles.[25]

We would argue that how these shifting forms of identification work is partly organised by existing and socially constructed categories of male and female. No film watcher comes to a film as an empty vessel ready to be filled by the subject positions constructed by the film text. Spectators come with an existing subjectivity and a range of 'reading competences'.

Codes of romance

One way to begin exploring the question of gendered readings and pleasures in the case of the Bond films is to examine the patterns of subjectivity established in 'women's fiction' and the pleasures to be derived from it. This is not to suggest that women's subjectivity can be summarised by a quick reading of a Mills and Boon romance, but simply to note the consistent themes of romantic fiction and to suggest that a reading competence in romantic fiction may lead to rather different forms of identification with the interplay of looks in a Bond film than that experienced by men. We would suggest in the first place that romances are particularly important in structuring women's responses to Bond. Romances, despite a current resurgence of feminist interest in them, constitute a somewhat neglected genre in terms of criticism and analysis if not in terms of publication and reading. Studies of romances which do exist tend to focus on the nineteenth-century classics rather than on the range of contemporary romances. We should make some apology, therefore, for simplifying and categorising briefly what is a complex and ideologically ambiguous form of fiction. Nevertheless, there are, we would suggest, two areas of particular relevance in the genre of romance to the question of women's pleasures in the Bond films. The narratives of many romances are organised initially around female narcissicism (romance is one of the few categories of fiction in which one can normally take for granted that any 'I' telling the story will be female) and the relationship of the heroine to the hero is characterised by some form of phallic castration of the male. Romances, therefore, could be said to rework a female version of the oedipal complex, involving penis/phallus envy. This is not necessarily because of some universal characteristics attached to the female but undoubtedly derives from the particular socio-historic conditions in which such fictions became popular.

The narcissicism of romances is much bound up with the relationship between female identity and appearance, which is not to say that all heroines are beautiful. From Jane Eyre's much described 'plainness' to later Mills and Boon romances ('Caroline wasn't pretty or clever or brilliant'), the heroines of romances are narcissistic in their celebration of femininity rather than beauty and are consistent only in their negotiation of accepted standards of beauty.[26] The figure of the hero intrudes in this feminine world, often in a highly stylised, fetishised way. Amis, as we have noted, posits a similarity between the Bond of the novels and the Byronic hero typical of romances – 'lonely, melancholy, of fine natural physique which has become in some way ravaged, of similarly fine but ravaged countenance, dark and brooding in expression, of cold or cynical veneer, above all *enigmatic*, in possession of a

sinister secret'.[27] Amis argues that Bond operates as a latter-
day Byron, 'going slowly to pieces' and then rather more
rapidly to pieces after the death of his wife in *On Her Majesty's
Secret Service*. By the end of *You Only Live Twice* when Bond,
having destroyed Blofeld, is an amnesiac living in obscurity
on a Japanese island cared for by a diving girl, Amis suggests
that the process is complete:

> Bond has acquired the most important single item in the
> Byronic hero's make up, a secret sorrow over a woman,
> aggravated as it should be, by self-reproach, and framed
> against a pastoral background. The stage is set for some
> contemporary Jane Eyre or Catherine Earnshaw to arrive
> on the island, catch sight of the strange solitary figure in
> the incongruous garb of a humble native fisherman and
> wonder at the mingled authority and despair in the set of
> the rather cruel mouth.[28]

Should Amis's account of the Byronic hero seem somewhat
far fetched and nineteenth century, it's perhaps worth quoting
a few more contemporary examples. The first, from a historical
novel by Georgette Heyer, was published in the late fifties, at
much the same time as the publication of the first Bond
novel:

> Startled she turned her head, and found that she was
> being observed by a tall man mounted on a handsome
> grey horse. He was a stranger, but his voice and habit
> proclaimed his condition, and it did not take her more
> than a very few moments to guess that she must be
> confronting the Wicked Baron. She regarded him with
> candid interest . . . She was unacquainted with any men of
> mode, but although he was dressed like any country
> gentleman a subtle difference hung about his buckskins
> and his coat of dandy grey russet. No provincial tailor had
> fashioned them, and no country beau could have worn
> them with such careless elegance. He was taller than
> Venetia had at first supposed, rather loose limbed, and he
> bore himself with a faint suggestion of swashbuckling
> arrogance. As he advanced upon her, Venetia perceived

that he was dark, his countenance lean and rather swarthy, marked with lines of dissipation. A smile was curling his lips, but Venetia thought that she had never seen eyes so cynically bored.[29]

The second is taken from *Deceit of a Pagan* from the Mills and Boon stable:

She opened the door, her eyes opening wide with shock as they encountered the tall, alien looking man standing arrogantly at Mrs. Marks' side. Her landlady looked quite overwhelmed, and Templar wasn't surprised. The man was looking quite overwhelmed, and Templar wasn't surprised. The man was looking down his haughty nose at both of them, his suit fitting him as if it had been tailored on him. Templar looked at the man again, only to find herself the victim of a contemptuous perusal, his blue grey eyes mentally noting each feature.[30]

And the third comes from Jilly Cooper's *Emily*:

My jaw clanged – for standing in the doorway was one of the most sensationally attractive men I had ever seen. He was tall with broadish shoulders, long black hair, restless dark eyes with a wicked gleam in them. He oozed sexuality. He looked round the room, as cool and haughty as a prince, yet he had an explosive quality – I've come out of the jungle and no one's going to tame me, he seemed to say.[31]

Allowing for a few nuances of style and inflection, these heroes of popular romances do bear some resemblance not only to the Bond of the novels but also to the image of Bond and particularly the Bond/Connery figure of the early films. Bond is consistently shot in the films under the admiring gaze of women, from the adoring gaze of Moneypenny in her quasi-maternal role, to the girl of the credits sequence, bedded by Bond but usually never seen again, to every passing receptionist and nurse, quite apart from his conquest of the villain's girls. In *Goldfinger*, for example, in the opening

few minutes of the film, Bond is looked at and 'desired' by
the dancer of the opening sequence who then betrays him,
openly fawned on by the bikini-clad girl beside the hotel
swimming pool and charms a hotel chamber maid to allow
him to use her keys to open Goldfinger's room, and all this
before he has met the three main girls of the film, Jill
Masterton, Tilly Masterton and Pussy Galore.

There are some keys to a romance scenario in Bond,
however, that go beyond the appearance of Bond. The love
affairs contained in many romances are organised around
some notion of phallic castration. The most extreme form of
fear of the phallus tends to come in the gothic novel where,
typically, the heroine cannot distinguish initially between
hero and villain and whose 'worst fears' about men are
realised by the villain. In Laura Black's *Wildcat*, the heroine's
husband – previously gentle, handsome and charming – is
transformed on her marriage into a drunken sadist, from
whom she cannot escape:

> They stopped me and brought me back . . . They were
> both footmen known to me a little, called James and
> Henry . . . They could not let me go or they would not.
> My husband was entitled by every law, to have me dragged
> back to him. They were obliged to obey him. They did not
> reply to my begging. They did not look at me or at each
> other or at their master, as they dragged me back to my
> master in the bedroom. They had each a hold of one of my
> arms. In struggling, I hurt only my arms.
>
> Soon I would be hurt enough to excite and delight my
> husband.[32]

The fate to which Catriona or 'Pussy' is dragged back is to
be branded by a red hot poker:

> Never in my life had I been in such despair. I was
> completely helpless. Worst of all, worst of all, the branding
> iron would hurt me enough to excite his perverted lust. I
> was sure of it. 'I only like it if I hurt them. The more I
> hurt them, the more I like it.' He would hurt me very
> badly and he would like that very much. There was a red

glitter in his eyes, hotter and more horrible than the red hot steel itself.[33]

The narrative of such gothic romances, however, resolves this fear of sadistic rape, while at the same time playing to erotic fantasies about it, by postulating a double hero, one the embodiment of all that women fear and one a safe haven from that. Catriona runs from her husband and after some trials and tribulations is reunited with the 'real' hero who had previously earned her condemnation for his criticism of Carnmore. The wicked Carnmore is killed by the hero accidentally, because of his relentless pursuit of Catriona.

Rather more typically, romances play with a phallic castration of the hero which can take a number of forms. The wounding, mutilation or blinding of the hero, tends to be a signal for the heroine to fall in love and take over the active male role. The famous line from Jane Eyre is one obvious example. 'Reader, I married him.', she reports of the maimed and blinded Rochester as she prepared to lead Rochester through a life in which he could not manage without her. But the theme is repeated endlessly in other romances. The hero under physical threat inevitably produces a frisson of desire in the heroine:

> My lord was lowered gently on to the cushions and Miss Betty fluttered over to him like a distracted hen . . . Diana looked up as her aunt finished, and studied the pale face lying against the dark cushions. She noted the firm, beautifully curved mouth, the aristocratic nose and delicately pencilled eyebrows, with a little thrill. The duel had set her every nerve tingling: she was filled with admiration for her preserver, and the sight of his sensitive handsome countenance did nothing to dispel that admiration.[34]

> Her heart was thudding violently. Perspiration sprang up on her palms, at the back of her neck, between her breasts. His head lay on the pillowless bed, a swathe of bandages enveloping it.[35]

In taking care of the wounded hero, heroines frequently take over phallic authority over the household, the family, the estate, usually proving that they are more than capable of doing so and occasionally better at doing so than the man. In *Caretaker Wife*, for example, the heroine is a second wife, who takes control of the estate, the household and the children, restoring the estate to solvency, the household to decency and order and the children to health and education before her wounded, armless husband returns from the war.[36]

At the very least, in romances, the heroine is the victim of a moral misjudgement on the part of the hero: she is assumed to be promiscuous, unintelligent, inadequate or mistaken in her views of 'love', 'family life', etc. The hero thereby proves himself to be an inadequate representative of the law without her help. In the mutual apologies exchanged at the end of *Pride and Prejudice*, Darcy apologises for his original views of Elizabeth and the Bennett family and his younger sister notes with surprise that he can be corrected by Elizabeth. Georgette Heyer in her later novels frequently offers a rather witty form of the theme of phallic castration in relation to moral misjudgements, in which the hero is 'silenced' by the heroine, rendered incapable of speech and incapable of articulating the law and the Symbolic Order. In *The Grand Sophy*, Rivenhall, the hero, is constantly shown to be mistaken in his treatment of his family, and in his verbal interchanges with Sophie he never wins the battle of wits:

> 'You will scarcely drive yourself about the town in a curricle,' he said. 'Nor do I consider a high-perch phaeton at all a suitable vehicle for a lady. They are not easy to drive. I should not care to see any of my sisters making the attempt.'
> 'You must remember to tell them so,' said Sophie affably.
> 'Do they mind what you say to them? I never had a brother myself, so I can't know.' There was a slight pause, while Mr. Rivenhall, unaccustomed to sudden attacks, recovered his presence of mind.[37]

When Sophie cries and then reveals that it is her '*only* accomplishment', and that very few persons can do it,

Rivenhall is enraged. '"You, you –" Words failed Mr Rivenhall. "Stop at once!"' When Sophie nurses his little sister, again Rivenhall cannot speak.[38] 'He was staring at her, as though a thought blinding in its novelty had occurred to him. Her gaze remained steady a little questioning. He rose abruptly, half stretched out his hand, but let it fall again, and turning, went quickly out of the room.[39]

In the final analysis, in most romances, the course of true love runs smooth only when there is some curtailment of phallic power and one which requires the involvement and commitment of women. The disturbance with which the narrative begins is the intrusion of the male into a feminine world. Subordination to or partnership with the hero, marked in romances by a kiss, orgasm or marriage (or all three, and not necessarily in that order) is linked to a reduction in the power of the male. We would suggest that romances both assume a feminine reader and construct pleasure around the resentment of the heroine towards the hero and the partial destruction of the hero's power. In one sense, as Amis points out in relation to the novels, James Bond books and films can be understood as an incompleted, a promised but not delivered, romance. Just as in romances, the pleasures of a Bond text for a reader of romances lies in the constant threats to Bond by the villain, in which women are both implicated and waiting on the sidelines to pick up the pieces. The famous shot in *Goldfinger* in which Bond/Connery sees an assailant advancing to kill him in a woman's eyes, has been prefigured in many romances. However, if the Bond films lay out some of the looks and themes of romance, they also order them differently. A spectator who watches the Bond films through a reading competence in romance and identification with a feminine subject constructed by romances is shifted from the tradition of 'long term commitment' and 'the real thing' which marks the romantic affair. In the films too, Bond tends to reach the 'last reel' heroine, unscathed. Only the technological extensions of himself have been destroyed and hit the scrap heap, although he tends to have been comically reduced in stature either by his inability to cope with technology, as with the nuclear device in *Goldfinger*, or by the phallic excesses of his own gadgets. When the serious romance scenario is fully present, as in *On Her Majesty's Secret Service*, in which Bond falls in love and marries, it is abruptly ended with Tracy's tragic death to return Bond to the centre of a promised romance in the next film.

We would suggest that romances provided one part of a pattern of inter-textual relationships for spectators of the Bond films which allowed the exploits of 007 to be greeted by female applause. Images of Bond and some aspects of the Bond narratives lay sufficiently close to contemporary romances as to command some part of the same audiences. However, in so doing, the Bond films push and shift the subjectivity constructed by romances, constantly holding and stopping the drive of a romance narrative from completion and replacing the reduction in phallic power implicit in the male/female partnerships which end romances, with an untroubled sexual relationship, celebrated in the final scenes of the Bond films. The ambiguous ideological implications of the Bond films for women audiences in the early sixties lay in the extent to which they offered an image of women freed from domesticity and allowed sexual desire without either marriage or punishment but only in terms of the compulsions of a 'liberated' male sexuality. Nevertheless, some of the pleasures of the early Bond films undoubtedly lay both in the promised romance of Bond and the shift in subjectivity that the Bondian reworking of romances delivered.

We have looked at romantic fiction in order to suggest that the 'gendered' pleasures of the Bond films may not simply be those of the 'male look', that the popularity of the Bond films with female audiences may involve something more than a commitment to a 'male subjectivity' even though a constructed 'male' subjectivity may be dominant. Moreover, romantic fiction is not the only fictional form seen as belonging to women. Recent studies of television soap operas argue that the viewer of soap opera is constructed within the text as an ideal mother, understanding, tolerant, taking pleasure in observation and expectation rather than action.[40] Charlotte Brunsden suggests that a reading competence in soap opera implies a competence within the ideological and moral frameworks of marriage and family life, apart from familiarity with the plots and characters of any particular series.[41]

Television soap operas have been increasingly popular from the sixties onwards. Are there routes of identification in the Bond films for the 'maternal understanding subject'? The structure of the Bond narratives in which M sends Bond forth to do battle while Moneypenny mediates the relationship inevitably constructs Bond to some extent in a childlike mould. Whilst this was always present in the Bond films, it may have increased in relation to Moore's performance of Bond (despite Moore's age), divided between obvious 'clowning' and a serious deadpan. Moreover, the organisation of the later Bond films, described by the film-makers as 'a series of circus acts', encourages that more 'distant', less involved viewing which is typical of television rather than films. The success of the Bond films on television, whether on the Christmas Day afternoon slot or more regular scheduling, would support this. In these circumstances, the Bond film can be watched as the amusing antics of a child.

We would argue, then, that the gendered pleasures of watching a Bond film are dependent on a variety of inter-textual regimes. Our analysis so far suggests that it is difficult to judge responses to the texts of Bond without taking this into consideration. One of the problems of analysing the relationship between the Bond films and their audiences is the theoretical division between the study of audiences and the study of texts and spectators; that is, between the people who go to see films and the subject positions constructed by texts. Brunsden, for example, in her account of soap opera, distinguishes between the subject positions proposed by texts and the 'social subject' who may or may not take up that position. We have tried to show how the subject positions offered by the Bond films only exist in relation to regimes of inter-textuality, within which 'social subjects' exist and from which they read texts. Yet, rather than reverting to the idea that this is an arbitrary matter of individual subjectivity, we have suggested that it is important to begin to explore gendered reading formations, that is, both gendered audiences of popular fiction and the dominant subject positions produced by such fictions. Obviously, any analysis of subjectivity has to consider a range of representational and non-representational discourses which mould subjectivity in any culture at any particular moment. We will be looking at some of these representational discourses in terms of 'textual shifters' in relation to Bond in the next chapter. Finally, we suggest in relation to Mulvey's thesis that the dominant look in Hollywood films is predicated on male pleasure, that 'the look' is dominant but not all-embracing. The issue of gendered pleasure in relation to the Bond films is, therefore, both more complex and less obviously politically reprehensible than Mulvey suggests.

Chapter 8

Figures of Bond

'I am very much a Domino sort of girl myself. A fun-loving extrovert. Whatever it is I am doing I enjoy doing it – loving, driving, riding, shopping, travelling, even cooking.'

As alluring as all of Fleming's girls are, there is always some masculine trait about them. . . 'Even so', says Claudine, 'they are essentially feminine, the ultimate in modern, emancipated woman.'

'They can live without a man doing everything for them because they are independent. They like to decide their future destinies for themselves. They are highly sexual – but only with men worth their loving. They are free, you see, completely free. I may be married, but I feel I am like this. I am free. I always have been. I always will be.'[1]

So said Claudine Auger, who played Domino Vitali in *Thunderball*, reported in a 1965 fanzine. A decade later, in a *TV Times* feature, she is quoted again on the subject of 'the Bond girl':

I think a woman needs to feel the strength of a man to acknowledge his superiority. The fact that young men today are not strong is basically the fault of women who dress to look like boys. A woman should always keep her feminity. I like the Bond girls because they are free, they make love easily and they are on equal terms when it comes to intelligence. But they are essentially feminine. I married an older man because he knew what life was about. And he married me because I have a feminine

231

body. I would not dare to put on the trousers unless I was going horse-riding or hunting.[2]

Both passages typify the ways in which the figures of actresses and actors have been constructed and made to stand in relation to the Bond films. Functioning as simulacres for either Bond or 'the Bond girl', their lives, views and preferences have been made to mimic the fictional world of Bond in order that that world might appear not entirely fictional. Life is thus modelled on fiction in order that fiction, in appearing to reflect life, might also serve as a model for it. However, the differences between the two passages are equally noteworthy. In the first, the concept of the 'essentially feminine' is articulated to the 'emancipated woman' of the early 1960s whereas, in the second, it functions as a sign of women's necessary subordination to men, limiting the possible scope of women's emancipation in specifying the 'laws of nature' it must respect.

This shift is symptomatic of the general change in the ideological currency of Bond and 'the Bond girl' between the early 1960s and the 1970s as the emphasis moved away from the construction of new and relatively more independent forms of gender identity and sexuality, for women as well as for men, towards the placing of women – already 'too greatly emancipated' – back into a 'properly subalterned' position in relation to men. As we have seen, this was one of the major transformations associated with the Bond films of the 1970s. It is all the more interesting, therefore, that the occasion for the second interview with Claudine Auger was the first television screening of the Bond films produced in the 1960s. In thus being activated for consumption via a different construction of 'the Bond girl', their relations to ideologies of gender and sexuality were, at least tendentially, reordered in being brought into line with the specific network of ideological concerns which the figures of Bond and 'the Bond girl' served to condense and articulate in the 1970s.

This example nicely illustrates our purpose in this chapter, to examine the various 'texts of Bond' which, in contributing to the expanded reproduction of the figure of Bond, have also played their part in remodelling that figure culturally and ideologically. In doing so, we shall relate our discussion to a number of more general concerns.

First, we shall consider the active part such texts play in organising and reorganising the social and ideological relations of popular reading. They function, in effect, similarly to the way in which criticism functions regarding the consumption of texts classified as 'literary' or, more generally, as being of serious cultural value. However, they do so by different means. In the case of valued texts which circulate under the name of an author, Foucault argues, criticism normally organises their reading by constructing the author as the issuing source of their meaning.[3] Popular reading is more typically organised in accordance with different interpretative principles. Here, to put the point in terms of Foucault's formulations, the figure to which a text is made to point and which serves as a support for its meaning is not one which is outside and precedes it (the author), but one which is simultaneously outside and within it (the actor/actress as a cypher for the character portrayed). The result, in the case of the 'texts of Bond', has been the construction of a series of micro-narratives in which the 'real' biographies, views, tastes and preferences of Connery and Moore and the various actresses who have played opposite them have filled out and been filled out by the figures of Bond and 'the Bond girl'. These micro-narratives have thus run alongside and adjacent to the Bond novels and films, complementing them by means of a seeming mimesis whilst in fact actively organising their consumption in particular ways.

While differently organised, however, such texts have effects similar to those produced by the functioning of criticism. In the case of texts classified as 'literary', criticism constitutes a series of bids and counter-bids concerning the inter-textual, ideological and cultural references which are to prevail in animating reading practices in a particular context. It is by the operation of this system of bids and counter-bids that a text is kept alive in history, yet always as other than just 'itself' since, in the process, its relations to history are constantly rewritten. In like manner, the 'texts of Bond' we are concerned with here have functioned as 'textual shifters', drawing the Bond novels and films into the orbit of activity of

the different sets of ideological and cultural concerns that have
been articulated around the figure of Bond at different points in
time.

The implications of these considerations are far-reaching.
A part of our concern in this study has been to study the
Bond novels and films not as completed givens but in the
light of the incessantly mobile reordering of the relations
between them. One consequence of doing so is to call into
question the assumption that the relations between a text
classified as fiction and ideology can be determined, in an
essentialist way and once and for all, purely by an examination
of its internal formal properties. By considering the ways in
which what we have called 'textual shifters' have located the
Bond films and novels within different spheres of ideological
action – or within the same spheres of ideological action, but
placed in different and even contradictory relations to them
at different points in time or within different reading
formations – it will be possible to show that the question of
the 'ideological effects' of the Bond films and novels cannot
be resolved abstractly. Indeed, properly speaking, they have
never had such effects but have rather functioned as pieces of
play within different regions of ideological contestation,
capable of being moved around differently within them.

Furthermore, such considerations also call into question
the view that the distinction between 'literature' – that is, as
Fleming put it, 'literature with a capital L'[4] – and popular
fiction, conceived as an inferior category, can be established
by purely formal means. In the case of Marxist criticism,
these two problems are closely connected since most Marxist
theories of literature have depended on the assumption that
'literature', as a specialising category, can be intrinsically
distinguished from ideology. This view clearly depends on
the assumption that a text's relations to ideology can be
specified once and for all time. It has thus recently become
common to argue, in the wake of the earlier work of Pierre
Macherey and that of Louis Althusser, that the genuinely
literary text is one that inherently ruptures or troubles
dominant ideologies, throwing them into relief so that their
fault-lines become visible.[5] Similar discourses have spilled
over into film criticism where *avant-garde* film practices are

often distinguished from commercial cinema in equally essentialist terms. The corollary of this is the view that popular fiction merely reproduces dominant ideologies and, again, inherently so. Annette Kuhn has taken issue with this line of reasoning, arguing that it takes no account of the ways in which reading its subject to definite forms of social organisation: 'Once the notion of reading as an active and situated practice is adopted, the distinction between films which embody an internal self-criticism and films which are completely ideologically complicit becomes redundant.'[6]

According to such a view, the 'literary effect', or its filmic equivalent, is not an attribute which texts naturally possess. Indeed, it is not property at all but a specific sphere and kind of action that is produced for certain texts by virtue of their being classified as 'literary' and, accordingly, organised for consumption through the application of particular reading norms. The history of the putative literarisation of Fleming's Bond novels – their circulation as 'texts of Fleming' rather than as 'texts of Bond' – thus bears witness to the ways in which 'the same text' may be differently organised for consumption in different regions of textual distribution. In examining the contours of this history, we shall argue that the distinction between the 'literary', as a specialising and privileged category, and the non-literary as the residue of fiction which remains once the 'literary' has been defined, breaks down when conceived as a distinction between different practices of writing. Rather, we shall suggest, the distinction needs to be reformulated in being conceived as relating to the different spheres of cultural operation that are produced for texts by means of the differential distribution of different protocols of reading between them.

Textual shifters

While the ideological preoccupations discernible in the 'textual shifters' bearing most directly on the popular reading of the Bond novels and films have been fairly consistent in scope, their *relative weight* and *specific functioning* have varied considerably. We shall illustrate this by examining the changing function of the ideology of competitive individualism as articulated in relation to the figure of Bond, and by tracing some of the shifts in the representations of sexuality associated with Bond and 'the Bond girl'.

Jerry Palmer has argued that the distinguishing characteristic of the thriller genre consists in its organisation of the relations between the values of amateurism and bureaucratic rigidity and, mediating between the two, those of professionalism in its 'combination of improvisation and programming'.[7] In the case of the Bond novels, Palmer suggests, Bond thus mediates between the values represented by 'the girl' and the villain. 'The girl' (sometimes) represents the values of amateurism in the sense that her actions are ineffective against the organised conspiracy of the villain and likely, moreover, to make life more difficult for the hero: Tilly Masterton's attempt to avenge her sister's death, for example, results in both Bond and Tilly being captured by Goldfinger. At the other extreme, the villain embodies the principle of planning carried to excess: he puts into operation a 'master plan', perfected down to the last detail, leaving no possible room for error or miscalculation. As a consequence, Palmer argues, the villain is 'often incapable of improvizing, and when a contingency that he has failed to foresee arises, he is completely lost'.[8] Bond combines the two virtues and, thereby, dissociates them from their negative aspects. A professional, trained in his occupation, operating within a bureaucracy and, usually, with a back-up team, he none the less retains a capacity to improvise which usually turns the tables decisively in his contest with the villain. It is thus that, in *Goldfinger*, he slashes through the window of the aircraft which Goldfinger has commandeered, with the result that Oddjob is sucked through it, although he 'had had no idea what would happen' when he did it (p. 217). In thus embodying an ideal blend of trained programming and improvisation, Palmer suggests, Bond constitutes an exemplary hero of capitalist competitive individualism constructed in opposition to the rigidities of communist totalitarianism.

It's true, of course, that the opposition between Bond's innovative professionalism and the dead hand of bureaucratic inertia played an important part in the constructions of Bond which predominated in the late 1950s. However, this came to be rather less important, in the early 1960s, than the way in which these qualities were made to stand for a new image of nationhood, fashioning, in Bond, the model for a new 'classless ruling class'. While the earlier, Cold War dimensions of these aspects of Bond's characterisation were not entirely jettisoned, they typically survived only in muted and significantly modified forms. Connery's biography – the son of a Glaswegian van driver who made good, but solely through his own efforts and self-reliance, fighting his way to the top through a series of dead-end jobs and bit parts – was thus endlessly rehearsed, but usually with the effect of constructing these virtues in opposition to the allegedly morally sapping effects of welfare socialism, as part of a diagnostics of national decline, rather than in direct opposition to communist regimes.[9]

Christopher Brooker has commented on the widespread tendency, in the 1960s, to construe the period as a watershed marking a decisive break with the values of Britain's traditional Tory governing élite and those of 'old-fashioned' socialism.[10] Attributing the responsibility for the vicissitudes of Britain's post-war history to the contest between these two anachronistic forms of political and cultural leadership, Brooker argues that the tough, no-nonsense professionalism of a new meritocracy, recognising no loyalties of class or any virtues other than those of ability, was widely regarded as heralding a new way forward for Britain. The key political figures in this respect were Heath and Wilson, the one portrayed as embodying the image of a modernised Toryism and the other, in shedding the shibboleths of socialism, as dragging a reluctant Labour Party into an age dominated by the 'white heat of science and technology'. In thus being grouped together, in spite of their different political philosophies, as exemplifying a critical temper opposed to the dodoism of tradition, Heath and Wilson served as representatives of a new 'spirit of the age'.

More immediately relevant to our concerns here was the operation of this discourse of modernisation in the construction of new types of public heroes and heroines in the media, fashion, advertising and the cinema. Tracing the media's celebration of actors such as Terence Stamp, Michael Caine ('an anti-actor . . . exactly right for 1965 in his triumphant classlessness', according to a contemporary newspaper) and Connery himself, of novelists such as Len Deighton and John Braine and fashion designers like Mary Quant, Brooker contends that the result was to foster an image of a young, talent-based, classless, untraditional, anti-Establishment cultural élite which respected only dedicated professionalism and not birth or privilege. Something of the flavour, and legacy of this period, is captured in John Boorman's introduction to M. F. Callan's *Sean Connery: His Life and Films*:

> There is no bitterness about his [Connery's] deprived childhood. He looks upon it as an enriching experience. He suffered the customary humiliations of the British class system, but today moves up and down classes with tolerance and, above all, without modifying his own behaviour . . . I believe that Connery touches us because he personifies the best qualities that came out of the post-war upheavals, in Britain. The reform of education, the busting of the BBC's monopoly, and so on allowed a lot of new talent to flourish . . . Connery is an archetype of what was best in those times. And that is his power. But like all archetypes, he also represents something timeless. His persona reaches back and touches a tradition in British life. I can best define that by suggesting characters that he could play better than anyone else:

CAPTAIN COOK	TOM FINNEY
THOMAS HARDY	W. G. GRACE
ISAMBARD BRUNEL	KIER HARDIE
	DRAKE[11]

The shift in the signifying currency of the figure of Bond which resulted from its insertion in this discourse of modernisation amounted to little less than an ideological *volte face*. Whilst, initially, Bond had supplied a point of fictional reference in relation to which an imperialist sense of nation and nationhood could be symbolically refurbished, he was now made to point in the opposite direction – towards the future rather than the past. Functioning as a figure of modernisation, he became the very model of the tough, abrasive professionalism that was allegedly destined to lead Britain into the modern, no illusions, no holds-barred post-imperialist age, a hero of rupture rather than one of tradition. Or rather, as Boorman suggests, a hero of rupture *and* tradition, heralding a brighter future by recalling the virtues of a doughtier, more valiant and socially inclusive tradition of Englishness which could be opposed to the cloying and restrictive foibles of the Establishment.

This shift in Bond's ideological currency, while chiefly attributable to the first cycle of Bond films, was not limited to these or to their influence on the ways in which the novels were read. It was also discernible in the classificatory and contextualising practices brought to bear on the 'texts of Bond'. One of the most telling examples of this was provided by the first edition of the *Sunday Times Colour Supplement*, published in 1962. Titled 'A Sharp Look at the Mood of Britain', its purpose was to discern the currents which had allegedly been slumbering within Britain and which, on the brink of awakening, were said to embody a strongly throbbing new sense of national purpose. The 'evidence' for this consisted of six articles on 'people who represent today' – an airline pilot, Jimmy McIlroy of Burnley Football Club, Peter Blake, Alan Little (a sociology lecturer), Sebastian de Ferranti and Mary Quant. Although from different walks of life and backgrounds, these were all portrayed as belonging to the same 'classless class', new leaders, committed to professionalism and efficiency, slicing through tradition like a knife through butter. Alan Little, for example, was described as follows:

> Dr Alan Little is 27 and a sociologist. A milkman's son from Liverpool with a brother at Trinity, Cambridge, he is married to a doctor, earns slightly more than £1,000 a year and lives in a Span house in Beckenham . . . In his way he is typical of something new asserting itself in the life of Britain's Universities . . . Men like him spell the death of the comfortable, feline, cloistered world which dons are supposed to inhabit. At Oxford or Cambridge, the donnish

ideal that still lingers is that of the inspired amateur. By contrast, Little is a tough and highly dedicated professional ... And, during the last few years, men like him have been quietly setting the pattern for a new type of donnish society ... They live in a dispersed, classless society of their own and seem to value the universities for the freedom they have to probe society wherever it is most vulnerable.[12]

The final item in the supplement was a new Bond short story, specially written for the occasion, presenting Bond as a figure ranged alongside the exemplary biographies constructed in the preceding items, a mythic encapsulation and 'capping' of the discourse of modernisation.

It might, of course, be argued that the Cold War construction of Bond's competitive individualism should be regarded as its 'true' or 'essential' meaning, subsequently distorted in being adapted to a new set of ideological concerns. However, this argument can easily be turned on its head. Like Eco, Palmer discusses the Bond novels as variants of the crime thriller represented by Micky Spillane. Looked at through the prism of the imperialist spy-thriller, however, Bond's combination of programming and improvisation could be read differently, viewed primarily as a means of distinguishing him from the amateurism of the earlier heroes within this tradition – as Palmer himself suggests in his later, fuller study. According to such an account, as we argued in Chapter 4, the accent would fall on Bond's programming – on his training schedules, his reliance on technological gadgetry, and so on – rather than on his capacity for improvisation which, in turn, might be regarded as more significant in distinguishing Bond from M rather than from the villain or, alternatively, as no more than a clumsy plot device, an implausible means of enabling the narrative to progress. There is, however, nothing to be gained in representing the relations between these readings such that one is privileged as 'truth' and the other devalued as 'distortion'. The most that can be established is that the novels served as a basis for one set of meanings when hooked into a particular set of ideological and cultural co-ordinates and for another set of readings when uncoupled from those co-ordinates and connected to new ones.

The same is true of the way the figure of Bond has functioned in relation to ideologies of gender and sexuality. The key 'textual shifters' in this respect have consisted in representations of the relations between Bond and 'the Bond girl'. Apart from varying between the early 1960s and the 1970s, these relations have also been differently constructed according to whether the envisaged readership has been male, female or mixed. Throughout all periods, the position of an implied male reader has predominated, and necessarily so, since any discussion which accepts the terms of reference suggested by the phrase 'the Bond girls' is committed to constructing female gender identities and forms of sexuality in relation to the norms of masculinity supplied by the figure of Bond.

The discourse of 'liberation' which governed representations of 'the Bond girls' in the early 1960s would thus be more accurately described as a discourse of female adjustment. A component of the discourse of modernisation, the new set of identities it constructed for women was defined in relation to the requirements of a liberated male sexuality. Representations of 'the Bond girl', in portraying her as the subject of an idependent and free sexuality, served only to make her instantly and always available – but only for men. 'They are women of the nuclear age,' Terence Young argued, 'freer and able to make love when they want to without worrying about it.'[13] From a male point of view, this constituted a strategic and selective 'liberation' of women – free only in the areas (bed) and respects (sexuality) that 'liberated man' required. Moreover, the freedom of 'the Bond girl' was conceived as essentially masculine in form; she was, in fact, Bond's *alter ego*, fashioned in his image. As Luciana Paluzzi, who played Fiona in *Thunderball*, described her part: 'Yes rather like a female Bond in a way. She lives like he does. She's 100 per cent feminine – but able to do things men do.'[14]

The ideal represented by 'the Bond girl' in this period thus consisted of a harmonious blend of tradition, defined in female terms, and modernity, defined in male terms. Although sexually 'liberated', her sexuality, in being represented as merely the female equivalent of a promiscuous male genital sexuality, was devoid of any disturbing threat of otherness. At the same time, she was still 'essentially feminine', still knew 'her place' a place defined in relation to men and to the phallus. Here's Connery again, constructing for himself/Bond the role of Big Prick of the phallic order:

'All feminine women are mobile, adaptable. To be temperamentally mobile is to be like a wheel. The person at the hub is fixed, stable. The person at the end of the spoke goes round the hub. Such a person is mobile, adaptable. One of the first reactions of a mobile person is to cross the legs – men as well as women. If you are attracted to someone, you sit like this' – he leaned forward, knees apart, hands outstretched.[15]

In sum, 'the Bond girl' of the 1960s disconnected female sexuality from traditional female gender identities, preserving these latter virtually intact (although adding to them the requirement of competence in outdoor and physical pursuits) whilst articulating the former to male defined norms of genital sexuality. In essence, her sexuality was the product of a licensed distribution of phallic attributes from men to women. Since the 1970s, this licensed adjustment of traditional norms of female sexuality has given way before an obsessive concern to effect a redistribution of phallic attributes back from women to men. Publicity posters for the Bond films of this period thus typically represented the relations between Bond and 'the Bond girl' in the form of a contest between two rival sources of phallic power and authority.

The poster for *For Your Eyes Only*, read from an anxious male perspective, is a case in point. The foreground is dominated by the buttocks and legs of a girl clad in swimming wear and seen from the rear. She stands with legs astride, the relations between her two feet – clad in high-heeled shoes – and her crotch form a triangle with the crotch forming the apex. Her right hand holds a cross-bow, sprung for action and armed with an arrow, pointing to the ground. Bond is framed within the triangle formed by the girl's legs and crotch. Diminished by the girl's domination of the foreground – his

head is level with her knees – Bond is placed directly below
the girl's crotch, gun in hand with his gaze directed anxiously
not to the viewer or to the girl's face but to her crotch. Outside the triangle formed by the girl's legs, a variety of action
scenes from the film are depicted – a car chase, an underwater
sequence, etc. The 'adventure' elements of the plot are thus
relegated to the margins of the composition, a series of
escapades which have a distinctly Boy's Own flavour
compared with the central challenge which Bond has to
respond to: restoring the symbolic order of the phallus by
'outgunning' the girl whose phallic power threatens to
overwhelm him.

In earlier posters, by contrast, the contest between Bond
and the girl was more usually portrayed as in the process of
being resolved, or as already having been resolved, in Bond's
favour. In the posters for the first cycle of Bond films, the
subordination of women takes the form of a fetishisation of
the body of the hero. Typically, the image of Connery/Bond
predominates, his phallic authority represented by fetishistic
symbols of male power. The girl or girls are usually portrayed
as significantly smaller than Connery/Bond, and adopting
positions of dependency and subservience in relation to him.
The poster for *Thunderball* (1965) portrays Connery/Bond
kneeling in a wet-suit with one knee up and a loaded spear-
gun pointing up vertically from between his thighs. He is
surrounded by four women, kneeling or lying before him, a
sea of swooning and dependent femininity belittled by the
preponderance of his physical presence. The poster for *Live
and Let Die* (1973) strikes a more shrill and anxious note. It
consists of five playing cards bevilled toward the viewer so
that the central one is larger than the rest. The women
portrayed in the frames of each of the two cards on either
side of the central card are thus perspectivally diminished by
the figure of Moore/Bond emerging from the central card,
breaking its frame, with gun to cheek. A piece of flame-
spurting artillery juts from between his thighs with a girl
placed astride it.

Such shifts in time in the signifying currency of Bond and
of 'the girl' are rather less important than the differences
between the ways in which that currency has been manifested,

and contested, in 'textual shifters' aimed at different groups of readers. The cult of Bond has thus been explicitly attacked in women's magazines. *Nova* published a hard-hitting article by Mordecai Richler who attributes Bond's popularity to a regressed formation of male sexuality, locked into the pre-Oedipal phase in its inability to recognise the otherness and autonomy of female sexuality.[16] However, this is the only piece of an explicitly analytical and critical nature that we have come across in women's magazines. More typical was the attempt to puncture the illusionism of the Bond films in a 1979 *Woman's Own* feature on 'Glamour Girls in Bondage'. This consisted mainly of interview material with a series of minor starlets who take the lid off the way the glamour of 'the Bond girls' is carefully contrived and produced, and discuss the personal problems which arise from their surrendering control over their bodies to the studio. The editorial comment mobilises this shared and secret 'inside knowledge' against the gullibility of the male viewer:

> As far as giving shape and form to thousands of male fantasies is concerned, the creators of the James Bond films have got it right . . . The girls in Bondage follow a set formula: it doesn't matter if a girl's blonde or brunette, so long as she displays evenly tanned skin (no knicker elastic marks, please). It's a 'plus' if the script places her on the opposing side, as the tool of the current arch enemy, for then gentleman James can knock her around a little, thus allowing her pneumatic breasts to bob about ever so slightly . . . And Mr Average Man in the cinema will love them all, too. He will never know of the hours spent in Make-up, the specially designed clothing that went into the making of a Bond girl. Nor will he guess at the other problems arising from the transformation. Everything will be perfect in 007's fantasy land – even it isn't in real life.[17]

However, these are exceptions. More typically, features on 'the Bond girls' – whether in the popular press or in magazines aimed at a mixed or a primarily female readership – have been complicit with the general currency of Bond, underwriting its effects rather than opposing them. In some cases, it is true, contradictory tendencies have co-existed, but usually within a definite order of priority. In 1977, for instance, the *Sunday People*, in an article on the production of *The Spy Who Loved Me*, noted that while 'Bond has become the ultimate sex symbol . . . few of his screen heroines share the same feelings about him'. Britt Ekland, who played Mary Goodnight in *The Man with the Golden Gun*, is thus quoted to the effect that she considered Bond 'a total male chauvinistic pig'. All of this, however, is placed within the context of an exemplary tale which, in the case of *The Spy Who Loved Me*, put 'the Bond girl' in her place even before filming had started:

> Barbara Bach, latest of a beautiful line of Bond Birds, feels she is a liberated enough creature of the 1970s not to wear a bra. But when she turned up on the set of the new James Bond epic, *The Spy Who Loved Me*, there was a shock for this russet-haired American beauty.
> 'Go and buy a bra', she was politely but firmly told.[18]

However, even this limited degree of variability is in marked contrast to the part played by the figures of Bond and 'the Bond girl' in the constructions of sexuality in men's magazines. These have exhibited a consistent pattern throughout the various moments of Bond's career, falling into two broad categories. First, articles on the technological gadgetry associated with the Bond films have typically articulated male sexuality to the ability to harness and control the power of machinery. The following commentary on Bond's Aston Martin DBS in *Thunderball*, although taken from a fanzine intended for general circulation, aptly illustrates the ways in which Bondian machinery has thus been 'phallomorphised': 'A twist of the key sets the motor bursting into powerful throbbing life. It is then that you realise that here is a machine that separates the men from the boys.'[19]

However, photo-essays of 'the nudest Miss Bond' variety in men's soft-porn magazines have arguably been more influential. 'You will never,' according to the *Sunday People*, 'ever see an 007 girl in the nude.' The justification for this view was provided by Cubby Broccoli: 'Nudity would destroy Bond's career. His image must be clean cut. We can't risk offending his massive family audience in any way.'[20]

A little while later, Barbara Bach was featured in both semi and total nudity in *Playboy*, photographed in various poses of crouching subordination before Moore/Bond, the inevitable gun in hand. Timed to coincide with the release of *The Spy Who Loved Me*, the feature was clearly a promotional stunt, a requirement of Bach's contract rather than a piece of freelance work. *Playboy* has regularly carried features of this type as has *Penthouse* and, in Britain, magazines like *Mayfair*, *Men Only* and *Rex*.[21] Their function is clear. The film of *For Your Eyes Only* ends as 'the girl', turning to Bond, drops her towel from her shoulders, saying, to Bond: 'For your eyes only.' We look on this scene alternately from behind 'the girl', so that we see Bond looking, and from behind Bond, but with his body shielding that of 'the girl' from our view, so that we may only imagine but do not see what Bond looks at. This is typical of the way the Bond films end, with Bond, in possessing 'the girl', being placed in a position of vision and power withheld from the spectator. The films thus produce a scopophilic drive which is always stopped tantalisingly short of its object. Photo-essays featuring 'the Bond girls' 'as never seen before' realise the scopophilic expectactions engendered by the films in placing the male reader in a position of dominant specularity, inscribing him in the place of Bond in subordinating 'the girl' to his controlling gaze. They complete the work of the narrative in carrying it to a point of visual fulfilment that is impossible within the constraints of the requirements imposed by the family entertainment film.

Nor, according to Michael Denning, is it entirely a coincidence that the first edition of *Playboy* was published in the same year as *Casino Royale* (1953). In his extremely stimulating discussion of the Bond novels, Denning suggests that their role – and that of the Bond phenomenon more generally – in relation to the reformation of sexuality is best understood when they are viewed in relation to the narrative code of the era of mass pornography which *Playboy* inaugurated.[22] Denning argues that the Bond novels construct imperialist and racist ideologies by means of a narrative code of tourism through which the strange and exotic locations of peripheral societies are represented as the object of Bond's Western, metropolitan look. Similarly, he argues that 'the girl' is put into place within a new system of sex and gender relations via the narrative code of pornography in which Bond's 'licence to kill' is less important than his 'licence to look'. Just as the narrative code of tourism represents peripheral societies as objects of spectacle, so the narrative code of pornography codes women as the object of a voyeuristic look; these two systems of looking – the western look and the male look – being privileged in being combined with the secret look of the spy. Denning supports this analysis by drawing attention to the many sequences in the Bond novels in which, much as in the films, 'the girl' is made the object of the reader's look through the relay of Bond's look – the appearance of Honeychile Rider on the beach at Crab Keys, for instance.

The details of this analysis are of less concern to us here than the more general point it illustrates. Denning is less concerned to distil the meaning of the Bond novels than he is to understand the ways in which they operated, within a broader set of inter-textual relations, to promote a genuine shift in sexual practices and a reconstitution of sexuality which continued to subordinate and oppress women, but in ways tailored to the requirements of a mass consumer capitalism. Bond, as bearer of the 'licence to look', becomes the key exemplar of a 'licence to consume' – foreign sights, women, cars, cigarettes and liquor – thus furnishing a model for the reformation of human capacities appropriate to an economic system which requires obedient and diligent consumers as well as willing producers.

In his *Visible Fictions*, John Ellis argues that the function of the various types of film publicity we have considered in this section is to construct a 'narrative image' of the individual film concerned, a promise of a particular type of pleasure which will attract the public to see the film.[23] They may also subtly determine the nature of the film the public sees. Kier Elam has argued that dramatic reviews function in this way:

The review sets up, before the event, a secondary and explicit frame of a 'metalinguistic' kind (i.e. parasitic on the object 'language', the performance) which will determine the decodification to a greater or lesser extent, depending on the credence given by the spectator to the critic's judgement.[24]

Film publicity posters, fanzine articles, interviews with stars, promotional stunts, etc., function in much the same way. It needs to be borne in mind, however, that the forms of publicity brought to bear on films may vary through time and from one context of reception to another and that, thereby, the 'same text' may be differently constituted as a text-to-be-read as a result of its insertion within differently organised social and ideological relations of reading. Moreover, in the case of the Bond films, it's clearly not possible to analyse the functioning of publicity items of this type solely in terms of their relations to the particular films to which they refer. They necessarily spill over the limits of such a one-to-one relationship in being drawn into an association with the full range of texts implicated in the construction and reconstruction of the figure of Bond. They do not just organise expectations in relation to a particular film but reorganise the signifying currency of Bond so as to inflect its ideological and cultural articulations slightly differently.

To put this point more forcibly, this means not merely that the same Bond film may be liable to be read differently in different contexts of reception. Our argument is not that every 'spectator's interpretation of the text is in effect a new construction of it according to the cultural and ideological disposition of the subject'.[25] Rather, it is that what we have called 'textual shifters' function, alongside the other components of a reading formation (systems of inter-textuality, the institutional practices which bear on the formation of reading competencies, etc.), to organise *the relations between texts and readers*. They do not act solely upon the reader to produce different readings of 'the same text' but also act upon the text, shifting its very signifying potential so that it is no longer what it once was because, in terms of its cultural location, it is no longer where it once was. As Jan Mukarovsky puts the point:

[The] work of art itself is not a constant. Every shift in time and space and social surroundings alter the existing artistic tradition through whose prism the work of art is observed, and as a result of such changes that aesthetic object also changes ... And even, for example, when a certain work in two chronologically separate periods is evaluated affirmatively and equally, the aesthetic object being evaluated is a different one in each case, and hence, in some sense is a different work.[26]

Of course, consideration of such 'textual shifters' is not, in itself a sufficient account of 'the role of the reader' or a substitute for it. None the less, their role in structuring the social and ideological relations of reading – producing texts for readers and readers for texts – is of considerable importance. Much previous debate on the question of reading has deadlocked on the opposition between the view of the text as dictating its readings and the view that readers are able to mobilise cultural resources which enable them to read against the grain of the text or to negotiate its meanings in particular ways. Our purpose has been to displace the terms of this dispute by suggesting that neither approach takes sufficient account of the cultural and ideological forces which organise and reorganise the network of inter-textual relations within which texts are inserted as texts-to-be-read in certain ways by reading subjects organised to read in certain ways. The relations between texts and readers, we have suggested, are always profoundly mediated by the discursive and inter-textual determinations which, operating on both, structure the domain of their encounter so as to produce, always in specific and variable forms, texts and readers as the mutual supports of one another.

The functioning of discourses of culture provides an especially vivid example of the ways in which such determinations operate, whilst also raising some more general questions concerning the effects of the forms of classification under which textual phenomena are put into circulation.

Bond and culture

A common ingredient in many formulations of the relations between high and popular culture is the supposition that the former is made up of texts which require a specific cultural competence in order to be fully understood, whereas the latter is comprised of texts which, requiring no such competence, are accessible to everyone. Recent criticisms of this view have argued against its essentialising tendency, suggesting that the distinction between high and popular culture is primarily a representational one – a distinction between texts which are *represented* as requiring such a specific competence and those which are *not* so represented, rather than one between texts which *do* or *do not* require such a competence in some intrinsic or essential way. This directs attention to the effects of the classificatory and institutional practices through which the relations between texts are organised and represented, especially in being differentially valorised.

Pierre Bourdieu and J. C. Passeron, for example, suggest that texts which are so classified and valorised function as tokens of exchange within a 'game of culture', which serves as a means of both transmitting privilege from generation to generation and legitimating the resulting perpetuation of class differences in representing it as the consequence of unequally distributed natural aptitudes. In rewarding those who exhibit the special competence which such texts are represented as requiring, the education system operates in collusion with broader mechanisms of class reproduction to the degree that these organise the conditions of access to such special competence. The education system thus passes off the trick of appearing to reward and measure intelligence and ability whereas, in valorising a specific set of cultural competences above others, it merely exchanges qualifications with those who, by virtue of their class background, have acquired the appropriate tokens of culture to enter into the educational/exchange relationship. The valorisation of texts thus serves as a means of valorising persons – establishing their economic currency by cultural means – and, thereby, of separating them for, and justifying, their largely preordained economic destinies.

Given that the stress here is placed on the competences which particular texts are *represented* as requiring, it is clear that, in principle, any text may, if appropriately classified, function as a part of such a system of exchanges. Indeed, Bourdieu and Passeron argue that, in the case of Parisian university students, knowledgeability of *all* forms of culture, including those classified as popular, serves as a means of distinguishing students of bourgeois origin from those of working-class or even petit-bourgeois origin, although less within the official university culture than within the unofficial student milieu. 'In every area of culture in which it is measured,' they write, '– be it the theatre, music, painting, jazz, or the cinema – students have richer and more extensive knowledge the higher their social origin.'[27] It is thus not only in relation to texts officially classified and valorised as high culture that relations of cultural superiority/inferiority may be produced and reproduced. Relations of a similar kind may also be produced in relation to texts classified as popular which, although generally available to be read in a 'naive' way, may, via the application of particular reading norms, be constituted to be read as both requiring and testifying to a superior cultural competence. This, in turn, suggests that the forms of cultural stratification that may be produced in relation to textual phenomena are more complex and varied, less cut and dried, than is usually supposed.

Although it is primarily as popular texts that the 'texts of Bond' have been classified, produced and circulated, they have also, as we have seen, been differently constituted within particular contexts of reception. This has been particularly true of Fleming's novels which, on occasion, have been organised to be read along culturally stratified lines. The attempt to produce a 'knowing reader' – largely undertaken in the pages of the *Spectator*, the *London Magazine*, and the like – thus constituted an attempt to organise reading in such a way that pleasure could be aestheticised and the possession of 'cultural capital' be confirmed in the superior vantage point afforded in relation to merely 'vulgar readings', which failed to see beneath the surface level violence, sexuality and snobbery of the novels to appreciate their redeeming literary qualities. Whilst this putative literarisation of the Bond novels has been an admittedly marginal component in the history of the Bond phenomenon, it is none the less of considerable interest in the light it throws on the contrasting ways in which texts may be classified and on the effects of their classification.

The key issues here centre on the ways in which the figure of Fleming has been constructed and made to stand in relation to the Bond novels written by Fleming. In the 'textual shifters' bearing most directly on the organisation of popular reading, the figure of Fleming has been constructed in the same way as those of Connery and Moore: that is, as a 'real life' site for the expanded reproduction of the figure of Bond. One of the most telling examples of this is provided by an article in *For Bond Lovers Only*. Allegedly an eye-witness account of a meeting between Ian Fleming and Len Deighton, these writers are represented as entirely the *alter egos* of the fictional heroes they respectively produced. Witness the following exchange, initiated by Fleming:

'Ever been to Tokyo?'
'Yes,' said Deighton.
'Fly?'
'BOAC,' said Deighton.
'Pleasant?'
'I was a steward,' said Deighton.
Again that circling, first-round silence. 'I have a rotten feeling,' Deighton said moodily, 'that my car's going to be towed away.'
'What do you drive, old boy?' asked Fleming, perhaps sensing a common bond in cars.
'A beaten-up Volkswagen, actually,' said Deighton, adding brightly, 'but I've installed a telephone. Yours?'
'I've just got one of those new Studebaker Avantes. Nought to 60 in 4.5 seconds. 175 miles an hour with 4 passengers up. Supercharged, of course. I must say I adore it,' said Fleming.[28]

This contrasts markedly with the ways in which the figure of Fleming has been constructed within the discourses of critics of varying tendencies. Relating a conversation with a young relative who, entertaining literary ambitions, described himself as an author, Fleming recalled that he replied: 'Well, I describe myself as a Writer. There are authors and artists and then again there are writers and painters.'[29] Critical representations of Fleming have tended to concur. Whilst relating the Bond novels to Fleming as their extra-textual origin and the source of their meaning, the ways in which such relations have been constructed have differed from those in evidence in critical discourses where the author function is more fully developed. Perhaps the most important of the functions which Foucault attributes to the category of the author is that of supplying a means of neutralising the apparent contradictions within a set of texts:

> Governing this function is the belief that there must be – at a particular level of an author's thought, of his conscious or unconscious desire – a point where contradictions are resolved, where the incompatible elements can be shown to relate to one another and to cohere around a fundamental and originating source.[30]

It has been this demand for a unity and consistency of meaning that has been most conspicuously lacking in critical discussions of the Bond novels, resulting in a different articulation of the relations between life and work than those which prevail when it is present. In the latter case, criticism seeks to tie life, work and meaning into an indissoluble unity – the whole life, the whole work and a whole meaning. Most critical discussions of the Bond novels, by contrast, have sought to connect life and work only associatively, via homology at the level of their respective parts – the similarities between Fleming's views, tastes and preferences and those of Bond, for example – rather than seeking to knit the two together as unities. There's another difference, too. We have argued elsewhere that criticism, in order to value a text, must also value the life of its author, 'that a text that is valuable for life should also be seen to be the product of a valuable life'.[31] Where a set of texts grouped under the name of a writer are denied the status, unity and consistency of an authorial *oeuvre*, this principle may operate in reverse. In such cases, as sign and justification of their mutual lack of value, life may be related to the work by the 'bad side' only. The most noted example of this construction of Fleming is the discussion of the Bond novels in David Holbrook's *The Masks of Hate*.[32] Deploring the Bond novels as dehumanising – as 'gilded faeces' – Holbrook interprets what he regards as their most unattractive aspects as the product of a series of supposed psychological disorders or personality deficiencies on the part of Fleming.

In short, critical reactions to Fleming's Bond novels have fallen mainly within two broad categories. They have either taken the form of a warning against reading, seeking to produce a 'non-reader' in stressing the inferior moral or artistic qualities of the novels, or, in reacting against this tendency, and somewhat defensively, they have sought to produce a 'knowing reader', placed above harm in being recruited as the subject of a 'superior reading' in which the novels function as tokens of exchange in a game of cultural connoisseurship between writer and reader.

However, there have also been attempts to effect a full-blooded literarisation of the Bond novels; to construe them not merely as permissibly readable but as worthwhile reading. This has involved attributing to Fleming the full range of functions Foucault assigns to an author in the case of culturally valorised texts. Moreover, the means by which this putative literarisation of the Bond novels has been attempted are indistinguishable from those involved in the case of texts which have been successfully literarised. Ian Hunter has argued that the constitution of a text as literary is effected by the application of a specific set of rules of reading which function 'not to reveal a hidden meaning but rather to alter the public deployment of a text and to transmit definite criteria of textual recognition in the form of a practice of commentary'.[33] 'Literariness', thus construed, is not a property which texts have but a particular status and mode of cultural action that is produced for them by means of the classificatory and reading practices brought to bear on them.

In an article concerned with similar issues, David Saunders has shown how 'the same text' may be classified in different ways in different regions of a society's legal and ideological apparatuses. He further shows how the constitution of a text as 'literature' may require that literary principles of classification and rules of reading establish their pertinence by displacing the influence of contesting ones. He thus examines the contending rules of evidence brought into play in the prosecution of Penguin Books, under the Obscene Publications Act, 1959, for its publication of D. H. Lawrence's *Lady Chatterley's Lover*. An obscene publication or literature? The very fact of the trial is testimony to the fact that, at the time, the text was ambiguously installed between these two categories, its 'place' unsettled. Penguin's successful defence and the resultant classification of the text as 'literary', Saunders argues, was due to the fact that legal pertinence was accorded to literary rules of reading invoking criteria of artistic merit and authorial intention even though these had no legal force within the rules of evidence provided for by the Obscene Publications Act. It is worth noting that, according to Saunders, the testimony of the 'expert witnesses' called by the defense (Raymond Williams and Richard Hoggart, for instance) rescued Lawrence for literature by means of four procedures for the placement of texts in the class of literary works:

> the representation of an authorial intention; the representation of an authorial corpus or *oeuvre* in which the text was placed; the performance of allegorical readings, represented as grounded in expert knowledge of an authorial intention; and the representation of a literary tradition in which the text was placed.[34]

These are exactly the procedures which Anne Boyd deploys in *The Devil with James Bond*. Approaching the Bond novels from an existential-cum-Christian perspective, she argues that they constitute 'a deliberate analysis of the relationship between the "demonic" and individual responsibility' and sees, in Bond, 'one of the seven greatest legendary champions of Christendom', a defender of 'justice and humanity'.[35]

Construing Bond as a modern-day St George sent to do battle with the dragon (the villain), Boyd interprets the contest between Bond and the villain as an allegory of man's struggle against the seven deadly sins, and particularly against the sin of sloth or *accidie*, the capital sin in its 'refusal of life and joy'.[36] In short, she constitutes the novels as a medium for the transmission of a set of significant moral and cultural values from Fleming, as author, to the reader. She does so by means of a particular application of the four protocols of reading outlined above:

1. Boyd's comparison of Bond with St George is based on analogically derived principles of plot analysis. The Bond novels are likened to the story of St George because their plot elements are similar: in both cases, the hero rescues a damsel in distress and rids the world of a monster (the dragon/the villain) which threatens it with destruction. Furthermore, a number of explicit references to the story of St George suggest, Boyd argues, that Fleming intended the reader to compare the two. In *You Only Live Twice*, for example, the mission Tiger Tanaka entrusts to Bond is to 'enter this Castle of Death and slay the Dragon within' (p. 78).

2. Boyd justifies reading the Bond novels allegorically by marshalling textual evidence to support her contention that the villains stand for the 'dragons of inner life', a series of inner temptations externalised in the contest between Bond and the villain. Goldfinger thus embodies the sin of avarice, Blofeld – in seeking the dignity of noble ancestry – those of snobbery and vanity, Emilio Largo – who made a 'fetish of inertia' – that of sloth, and so on. Boyd further argues that a constant theme runs through all the novels, connecting them into a coherent cycle within which there is developed a coherent philosophy. This consists in Bond's ongoing inner struggle against the sin of sloth as he fights off the 'dog-days', the slough of despondency into which he slips during his periodic bouts of inactivity between missions, to engage, once again, in life affirming activity.

3. The broader discursive strategies which organise Boyd's reading are supplied by the frameworks of inter-textual reference within which she locates the Bond novels. These operate along both 'vertical' and 'horizontal' axes. Vertically,

she places the Bond novels within a classical tradition, comparing them to the works of Bunyan, Wordsworth, Ruskin and Spenser whilst likening Bond himself to a series of earlier mythological heroes – Perseus, Hercules, David, even Christ. Horizontally, she compares the Bond novels to contemporary spy-thrillers, a genre which she theorises – and is by no means alone in doing so – as a fictive means for exploring the identity problems of the individual in mass society. The key to this reading of the spy-thriller is provided by Boyd's interpretation of the 'blackout sequence' in which the secret agent loses consciousness only to recover revitalised, a renewed subject of action fully committed to seeing his mission through to the end no matter what the cost. Boyd construes this 'blackout sequence' as a rite of transition in which the hero crosses an existential threshold, passing through death (the death of his inertia, passivity and lassitude) into new life, a life lived at the limits. In this, she argues, it represents an analogue for the 'culture shock' experienced by modern man as a result of the 'cosmic insult' of the Copernican revolution, the 'psychological insult' of Freud and the 'cultural insult' of Marx, Tönnies, Durkheim and Simmel. All these, in depicting man as determined, are alleged to have created a modern man 'who has been rendered senseless, lost his image of himself and of his God; and who is now reawakening, trying to reorient himself spatially, temporally, and morally'.[37] The spy-thriller represents this moment of reawakening and produces, in its hero, a model for it. The secret agent, having experienced the 'culture shock' of modern times and come out of it to maintain a sense of identity, integrity and purpose, points towards 'a positive image of man who is able to act creatively and responsibly in a world come of age'.[38] Bond, in consistently triumphing over the 'dog-days', is simply the most life-affirming secret agent of them all.

4. Finally, Boyd seeks an authorial warrant for her reading in the intentions of Fleming. She deploys three strategies in doing so. First, she cites remarks attributed to Fleming which suggest a degree of coincidence between her reading and Fleming's conscious purpose. For example: 'But Bond is really a latter-day St. George. He does kill wicked dragons

after all.'[39] Or, as Fleming once said of Bond: 'He's like Bunyan's Pilgrim, he has to get through the Slough of Despond before he gets to the prize that is really worth having.'[40] Secondly, Boyd excerpts from Fleming's journalistic writings passages which suggest that the concerns she attributes to the novels were a continuing preoccupation of Fleming's. Fleming's foreword to *The Seven Deadly Sins* – a collection of essays instigated by Fleming – is used in this way. Reviewing the seven ancient deadly sins, Fleming writes that 'only sloth in its extreme form of *accidie*, which is a form of spiritual suicide and a refusal of joy ... has my wholehearted condemnation' – a passage which is made to stand behind Bond's views in *From Russia, With Love*: 'Just as, in at least one religion, *accidie* is the first of the cardinal sins, so boredom, and particularly the incredible circumstance of waking up bored, was the only vice Bond utterly condemned' (p. 78).

Perhaps most distinctively, Boyd deals with those statements attributed to Fleming which would seem to gainsay not only the ethical purposes she attributes to him but any serious purpose whatsoever – 'I write for warm-blooded hetero-sexuals in railway trains, aeroplanes and beds', for example – in construing these as smokescreens; part of a conscious attempt by Fleming to conceal his moral didacticism so that his purpose, in being hidden, might work all the more effectively with a mass readership.

None of this, of course, is to endorse Boyd's reading. But it is a *possible* reading and, moreover, one produced by quite conventional means. Indeed, Boyd presents her analysis as an attempt to rescue the Bond novels from the history of their previous misunderstanding in uncovering their true but previously hidden meaning. One may argue that Boyd fails to observe certain critical procedures, just as one may query her interpretation of the spy-thriller genre, cite contradictory evidence from the Bond novels and Fleming's other writings, and so on. To do so would be invoke another set of rules for reading and, within those rules, to produce the Bond novels as objects for analysis in a different way. In effect, it would be to make a counterbid for the discursive organisation of the text–reader encounter by attempting to yoke reading on to a different set of inter-textual, ideological and cultural co-ordinates. However, there would be no point within such an analysis at which the discursive and inter-textual wrappings placed around the Bond novels might be peeled away to permit any claims to be made on the basis of a supposedly unfettered access to those novels 'in themselves'.

More to the point, the influence of Boyd's reading cannot be gainsaid by referring it to another set of reading norms in relation to which it is found wanting. It's difficult, now, to determine either the extent or type of influence exerted by Boyd's study. Clearly, it has been relatively marginal. On the other hand, considering that it has been published in three separate editions, it seems likely to have played some role in enabling the Bond novels to be used as 'pre-texts' for the development of moralising or theologically inclined pedagogies. Her views were thus widely circulated in Catholic educational circles in Australia in being summarised and further elaborated by a Father Malone in the *Compass Theological Review*. There is, indeed, a wide and considerably developed body of Catholic writing which has articulated virtually the entire galaxy of popular and super-heroes to the Christian cause.[41] Whatever its precise impact, Boyd's reading and the uses to which it has been put constitute determinations which would have to be taken into account within any approach which aimed to 'net' the total range of cultural and ideological traffic that has been conducted around the 'texts of Bond' in the light of the history of their rereadings and rewritings.

Nor is it only the Bond novels that have led a double life in being installed simultaneously in 'popular' and 'literary' reading formations. The same has been true of the films, although probably to a lesser extent and in ways that cannot be so readily chronicled. In their study of *Doctor Who*, John Tulloch and Manuel Alvarado show how the Tom Baker episodes of the series tended to divide the audience. Baker's camp style tended to alienate committed fans whilst, together with other modifications to the series format, it proved popular with audiences whose education equipped them with the competence to read the Baker episodes as a parodic send-up of the science fiction genre or, in some quarters, as a

modernist critique of realism. In this case, such readings
were provided for in the process of production through the
deployment of a series of allusions – to classical mythology
and other science fiction texts – as part of an attempt to
create a double-layered text which would recruit a new,
sophisticated audience without losing the series' regular
viewers. The history of the cinema likewise affords many
examples of films achieving cult status without this having
been in any way planned for in the process of production:
Casablanca, for example.[42] This has not yet happened with the
Bond films, although they did recruit a cult following from
students on campuses across Europe and North America
when they were first released in the 1960s. A cult audience
was also recruited when the National Film Theatre ran a
season of Bond films in 1980. Of all the films shown, George
Lazenby's performance as Bond in *On Her Majesty's Secret
Service*, the least successful Bond film in commercial terms,
was the only one to be singled out for special appreciation: it
received a standing ovation as the audience applauded itself
for having 'seen' what the mass audience had 'missed'.

Texts in history

We have indicated, at various points in this study, that a
part of our interest in 'the Bond phenomenon' consists in the
degree to which its analysis requires that methods be used
which differ from and call into question the more usual ways
in which texts are grouped into sets in being constituted as
objects of analysis. A 'limit case', its value is that of
highlighting a series of problems concerning the purposes of
textual analysis and the means by which they should be
pursued. We have thus, in approaching the various individual
'texts of Bond', stressed the degree to which these have
always been variably produced – not as 'the same text' but
as different 'texts-to-be-read' – as a result of their insertion
within different regimes of inter-textuality. Further, we have
suggested that it is not possible to abstract any of the
individual texts of Bond from the mobile and changing
systems of inter-textual relationships through which their

reading has been organised in order to constitute a space in which such texts might be stabilised as possible objects of knowledge 'in themselves'.

This is to query the way in which the relations between texts and their readings are normally conceived. Virtually without exception, all approaches to this question have assumed that the intra-textual and the extra-textual determinations of reading can be specified separately.[43] Moreover, they have assumed that the former can be specified *first* – that is, that the processes through which a text organises its reading can be specified independently of the variable extra-textual determinations which may bear in upon it. This entails that these latter determinations are construed as secondary phenomena which cannot touch or modify a text's essential properties. This is true even of the encoding/decoding model, perhaps the most socially oriented approach to the question of reading. We have already touched on the limitations of this approach in Chapter 3. At root, however, they are traceable to their dependency on a set of founding assumptions derived from Saussurean linguistics. The study of reading, within the encoding/decoding model, stands in relation to the study of texts much as, within Saussure's dichotomous division of the study of language, the study of *parole* stands in relation to the study of *langue*. The view that the 'fixed codes' of a text should be analysed *first*, both before consideration of the reading practices of different subjects and as a means of establishing *what it is* that is variantly decoded by such subjects, effects an ordering of the relations between the objective and the subjective, the necessary and the contingent, across the relations between texts and readers that is analogous to their distribution across the relations between *langue* and *parole*. To the text, as to readers, there belong all those systematic properties – the 'fixed codes' – which inform its objective structure. The study of reading, by contrast, like that of *parole*, is concerned with the subjective and contingent determinations which, so to speak, flow into the text (but without affecting its fixed properties) through the practice of the reader.

Clearly, this model holds good only so long as the linguistic paradigm on which it is based is not itself called into question. According to Michel Pêcheux, however, the *langue/parole* couplet has constituted a major impediment to the development of an adequately social approach to the analysis of the mechanisms whereby meaning is produced within and in relation to language. Echoing Volosinov's earlier criticisms of Saussure,[44] Pêcheux contends that it is not possible to constitute *langue* as a system of rules governing the meaning of individual linguistic elements by virtue of the relationships of difference, similarity and substitutability it establishes between them. The unity of *langue*, he argues, is only tendential, incompletely achieved, in the sense that it is always riven by different, socially determined discursive formations – that is, different principles of organising the relationships of difference, similarity and substitutability which govern the meaning of individual linguistic elements – which serve as the basis for the initiation of different discursive processes within and in relation to language. Meaning, he says, exists and is produced only within such discursive formations. There is no place outside or behind them, no neutral linguistic domain such as that proposed by the concept of *langue*, within which meaning can be said to be operative. 'A meaning effect,' as Pêcheux puts it, 'does not pre-exist the discursive formation in which it is constituted.'[45]

In like manner, we have suggested, texts are productive of meaning only within particular and determinate reading formations – a concept we have ventured as a means of specifying the inter-textual and discursive conditions which mould and configure the text–reader encounter. This is not, we should stress, so much a question of reducing text to context as an attempt to rethink the concept of context such that, ultimately, neither text nor context are conceivable as entities separable from one another. Terry Eagleton has argued against such a construction of the relations between a text and the context of its production in arguing that analysis must show how a text bears within it the impress of its conditions of production rather than such conditions being conceived as 'the sociological outworks of the text'.[46] The same demand has not been made of the relations between texts and the contexts of their reception. According to most formulations, such contexts are conceived as social; that is, as sets of extra-discursive and inter-textual determinations to which a text is related as an external backdrop or set of reading conditions. The concept of reading formation, by contrast, is an attempt to think contexts of reception as sets of discursive and inter-textual determinations which, in operating on both texts and readers, mediate the relations between them and provide the mechanisms through which they can productively interact.

As such, these determinations bear in upon a text not just externally, from the outside in, but internally, shaping it – in the historically concrete forms in which it is available as a text-to-be-read – from the inside out. According to such a view, there is no fixed boundary between the extra-textual and the intra-textual which prevents the former from pressing in upon the latter and reorganising it. The intra-textual, in effect, is always the product of a definite set of inter-textual relations. Clearly, this is to undermine conventional conceptions of texts, readers and contexts as separable elements, fixed in their relations to one another, in suggesting that they are variable functions within a discursively ordered set of relations. Different reading formations, that is to say, produce their own texts, their own readers and their own contexts, not to mention, to complete the list, their own authors.

In short, any appeal to the authority of 'the text itself' should be recognised for what it is: a rhetorical device used to support a particular intervention within what Frederic Jameson calls the 'Homeric battlefield' of interpretation.[47] Such appeals are inherently paradoxical in their functioning in that the claim to have uncovered the true but previously hidden meaning of 'the text itself' invariably forms a part of a political bid to reorganise reading by pinning it down to a new set of inter-textual, ideological and cultural co-ordinates. While the political and ideological use–value of such claims may be considerable, they are, from a theoretical point of view, of zero, indeed minus value. They do not enable any work to be undertaken that could not otherwise be undertaken, and they constitute a serious impediment to work that urgently needs to be done.

We place particular stress on this last point. It is not our purpose to query the concept of 'the text itself' in the interests of a fashionable 'anything goes, everything is permissible' relativism tacked on to the coat-tails of Derrida's project of deconstruction.[48] Our contention is not that all possible knowledges of 'the text' are of equal value but that 'the text', as such, is an impossible object of knowledge. Nor, by this, do we intend a neo-Kantian position according to which 'the text' is posited as an unknowable *ding an sich*. Our argument is not that 'the text itself' is somehow 'there' (wherever that might be) but unknowable, but that there is no 'there' in which its existence might be posited other than the varying reading formations through which its actual history is modulated, and that, therefore, to seek to produce a knowledge of it is to chase a chimera. In all of this, we are not denying the objective material existence of *texts*, as if these were products of our imaginations. However, as we have been at pains to point out in the case of the 'texts of Bond', texts are different even when they appear to be the same – different in their material forms and in the way their external relations to other texts and practices are ordered. Rather, our argument is directed against the notion, most succinctly expressed by F. R. Leavis, that there is, lodged somewhere behind the diverse forms in which texts are materially produced, the social relations in which they are inscribed and the interpretative horizons in which they are embedded, a shadowy, ideal text which is the source of a true meaning.[49]

It is this view of 'the text itself', massively influential within Marxist criticism too, which must be jettisoned in the interests of developing a consistently historical and materialist approach to the study of the processes whereby meanings are produced in relation to textual phenomena. It is necessary, in order to analyse the functioning of texts in the historically varying forms of their social use and inscription, to refuse the specious concreteness of the text as given, 'the text on one's desk', whose seductive facticity is rather like that of the commodity. Marx, introducing his critique of commodity fetishism, argued that:

A commodity appears, at first sight, a very trivial thing, and easily understood. It's analysis shows that it is, in reality, a very queer thing, abounding in metaphysical subtleties and theological niceties. So far as it is a value in use, there is nothing mysterious about it ... But, so soon as it steps forward as a commodity, it is changed into something transcendent.[50]

Much the same is true of texts. So long as a text is conceived as a 'text in use', there is nothing mysterious about it. We are dealing here with a set of material notations taking an objectively verifiable form and circulating within social and cultural relations of a determinable kind. As soon as an attempt is made to go beyond such 'texts in use' to locate 'the text itself' that is ideally present in all such uses, then, indeed, 'the text' becomes a transcendent entity abounding in metaphysical subtleties and theological niceties. And for much the same reason as a commodity:

A commodity is therefore a mysterious thing, simply because in it the social character of men's labour appears to them as an objective character stamped upon the product of that labour; because the relations of the producers to the sum total of their own labour is presented to them as a social relation, existing not between themselves, but between the product of their labour.[51]

By analogy, 'the text itself' is a mysterious thing because, in it, the social character of its resignification – of its incessant rewritings and reinscriptions in history – assumes the form of an objective character stamped on the product of that labour. Ultimately, to subscribe to such a view of the text is to be taken in by the history – the whole ensemble of material, social and ideological relations – which, in conditioning the given form of the text, simultaneously occludes itself.

None of this, of course, is to oppose the practice of arguing for certain readings and against others. To the contrary, this is necessarily the sharp end of any politically concerned critical practice. However, the inherently relational nature of

such practices should be recognised. To argue for certain
readings and against others is to attempt to clear a space
within which the former can become active; it is to mount a
bid to shift the horizons of inter-textuality within which the
texts concerned are read and, thereby, to modify their
signifying function. It is, in short, an attempt to *make texts
mean* some things and not others by organising texts, readers
and contexts into a particular configuration. Of course, it
may be necessary to represent such readings as textually
'more adequate' than the contending readings whose social
power they seek to displace. It is also necessary that such
readings should *be* more adequate – but more adequate in
relation to the text as a historically constituted object rather
than as a metaphysical essence. Real difficulties arise,
however, when 'the text' which is mobilised as a rhetorical
device at the level of criticism is granted, theoretically, an
ontological–epistemological value such that it is allowed to
arbitrate between readings, qualifying some and disqualifying
others.

Most obviously, this would entail an idealist and historicist
approach to the history of reading. It would be idealist in the
sense that it would have to posit, as the standpoint from
which to broach the history of reading, a position which
was represented as standing outside, above and beyond
that history in rescuing the text from its previous
misunderstandings, restoring to it the neglected, forgotten or
hitherto unseen – but none the less essential – properties
brought to light only by criticism's most recent endeavours.
Such a history of reading could account for earlier readings
only by correcting them, situating them as one-sided,
inadequate or incomplete when measured against the criteria
for reading (achieved or anticipated) provided by a valid
knowledge of 'the text itself'. It would also be teleological, as
Jameson is bold enough to make explicit in his *The Political
Unconscious*, in the sense that each reading would thus have to
be assigned its place in relation to an anticipated 'final
reading' to be reached when, once the 'text of History' has
been completed, the meaning of each text within it will finally
become transparent. The idealism of such an approach is
apparent. The text whose readings are thus understood as

comprising a history of (relative) incomprehension is that text which achieves a full and adequate relationship to itself only when the 'text of History' has been fully realised. It is an ideal text which assumes a social and material form which is fully adequate to itself only at the end of History pending which it exists only as a shadowy presence, an ideal form lodged behind the diverse social, material and ideological relations which regulate the real history of its reading.

Nor, finally, to complete our list of possible objections, do our criticisms imply that all readings have the same cultural weight or that any old reading can come along, parachute itself into the arena of readings and secure a space for itself. Many approaches in reception theory and reader–response criticism have seemed vulnerable to the charge of endorsing an anything-goes voluntarism. The defence against this has usually been worked through in terms of the problem of determinacy: that is, of identifying some determinate properties within the text which do act as an unmediated given, a check on the interpretative process which precludes readings from being either totally random or infinitely varied. The problem is real although, in our view, its resolution requires that attention be paid to texts as and within social relations rather than to 'the text' as an isolated structure. Texts *are* encountered as a resisting force; they *do* have to be taken into account as a constraining factor which has to be reckoned with. But this is to speak of *texts* and not 'the text', of material entities which carry the history of their rereadings and rewritings with them, transmitted – rarely without discontinuities, but also rarely without continuities – from one context of reception to another through the reading formations and institutional apparatuses which organise and reorganise the social and ideological relations of reading. It is for these historical, rather than for essentialist reasons that, in practice, apart from moments of profound rupture which significantly revolutionise the horizon of reading possibilities, the readings of a text cluster around a limited set of options.

Limited, but not closed: paradoxically, while Marxist criticism has, at least implicitly, always acknowledged this in one area of its practice, it has simultaneously denied it in others. We have in mind here the contrasting orientations it has exhibited in relation, on the one hand, to texts classified as 'literary' or as 'high culture', and, on the other, to texts classified as 'popular' or, more perjoratively, as 'mass' or 'pulp' fiction. With regard to the former, Marxist criticism has always functioned as an active, transformative practice – making texts mean differently in and for the present by rewriting their relations to history. In this – since, in doing so, it has had to argue against bourgeois constructions and appropriations of the 'great tradition' – it has thus implicitly recognised the 'movability' of texts; that is, the fact that they may be plucked from the organisation of reading expectations produced by one set of inter-discursive and inter-textual relations and installed in another such set of relations with different political consequences. This contrasts markedly with the essentially passive orientation that most Marxist critics have adopted in relation to popular texts, usually regarded as mere vehicles for the transmission of dominant ideology and as being somehow inert, impossible to mobilise in any way. As a consequence, analysis of such texts has largely taken the form of attempts to expose their effects or lay bare their mechanisms so as to reveal their repressive operations, as if these were given and fixed independently of the way in which the reading of such texts may be differently organised in different reading formations. The upshot of this has been that Marxist criticism has been unable to intervene in this area of reading except negatively, by means of a series of warnings – either 'Don't read this stuff', or 'Danger. Reading this stuff may damage your ideological well-being'. Not only are such gestures Canute-like given the prevailing distribution of reading habits; they block off in advance the development of critical strategies which may engage with popular reading without hectoring the reader as a subject whose tastes need to be reformed.

It is for these reasons, whilst far from wishing to reclaim the 'texts of Bond' as 'progressive' or, indeed, to literarise them, that we have been concerned to stress the *historical variability* of the cultural and ideological business that has been conducted around, through and by means of those texts. Nor has this traffic been all one way. To suppose that it has is a consequence of limiting attention to the spaces and possibilities for reading produced within culturally dominant reading formations. The explanation for Bond's popularity consists not only in the range of cultural and ideological concerns that have been condensed and articulated in relation to the figure of Bond but also in the ambivalent and sometimes contradictory ways in which the relations between these have been organised within different reading formations.

Chapter 9

Never Again?

'M says without you in the service he fears for the security of the civilized world.'—Small Fawcett from the swimming pool to Bond in *Never Say Never Again*.

At the end of the Bond films produced by Broccoli and Saltzman the title, 'The End' appears on the screen with an additional sentence: 'But James Bond will be back in . . .' In this chapter we want to discuss why James Bond could depart from and return to the sphere of popular fiction so effectively and over such a long period and 'speak' to many different reading formations. In order to do so, we want to reconsider the nature of 'popular heroes' and popular fictional genres in relation to more general and widespread ideologies. We have stressed from the beginning of this book that we do not consider that popular fiction can be seen as a simple conveyor belt of ideologies from dominant to subordinate social groups, nor can it be seen as a spontaneous expression of the views of subordinate social groups. At the same time, we have attempted to suggest various ways in which the James Bond texts are implicated in more general ideologies in a complex and ambiguous variety of ways. We want to review those suggestions at this point and examine the role of popular heroes such as Bond and popular genres such as the Bond films and novels in relation to the ideological formations present in British society during the periods of Bond's popularity.

A star, according to John Ellis, is 'a performer in a particular medium whose figure enters into subsidiary forms of circulation and then feeds back into future performances'.[1]

In the case of cinema, he argues, star images tend to be incomplete and incoherent. They are composed of snatches and fragments, miscellaneous chunks of 'real life' and different and sometimes contradictory narrative identities which do not add up to a coherent or rounded whole. Thus the star image functions as an invitation to cinema, it promises that the film's performance will present the completeness of the star and reveal the mystery of the star's essential being which the various bits and pieces out of which the star image is assembled can only hint at. At the same time, Ellis suggests that 'the star image echoes, repeats and develops a funadamental aspect of cinema itself'; it mimics and helps to support 'the photo-effect which is fundamental to cinema as a regime of representation'.[2] By 'photo-effect', Ellis is referring to the inherent paradox of the cinematic image, namely that a film presents an absence that is present. It presents an illusion of the real but the real that is re-presented in the form of the figures on the screen is always absent, belonging to another time and place. According to Ellis, the star image serves as a reminder of the photo effect. Compounded of various textual representations the star image incorporates a portrayal of the star as an ordinary person and portrayal of the star as extraordinary. The star is therefore at one and the same time like us and beyond our experience, a characteristic analogous to the 'present yet absent' quality of the photo effect.

The television personality, Ellis suggests, is constructed in relation to different principles. First, the image of the television personality tends to be restricted to his or her particular role in the medium – Pat Phoenix has no television identity apart from her role as Elsie Tanner in *Coronation Street*, for example. Secondly, the elaboration of the image of television personalities, as in features in the *TV Times*, tends to stress qualities of ordinariness and familiarity, to focus on the ways in which such personalities are like the readers, in being members of families, having weight problems etc., rather than elevating them to another plane of emotional intensity or luxurious consumerism. The images of television personalities are thus different from the images of stars which oscillate between the ordinary and the extraordinary.[3]

Popular heroes such as James Bond clearly hold something in common with film stars, and rather less so with television personalities. Bond is not ordinary in the sense of a television personality. At times the figure of Bond does involve a mixture of the extraordinary and the ordinary, the spectacular and the prosaic, as Ellis characterises star images. Bond's taste in food and wine, much dwelt upon in the novels, is organised precisely in terms of a combination of the ordinary and extraordinary. In *From Russia, With Love*, Bond's breakfast preferences are lovingly listed:

Breakfast was Bond's favourite meal of the day. When he was stationed in London it was always the same. It consisted of very strong coffee, from De Bryx in New Oxford Street, brewed in an American Chemex, of which he drank two large cups black with sugar. The single egg in the dark blue eggcup with a gold ring around the top, was boiled for three and a third minutes.

It was a very fresh, speckled brown egg from French Marans hens owned by some friend of May in the country. (Bond disliked white eggs and, faddish as he was in many small things, it amused him to maintain that there was such a thing as the perfect boiled egg.) Then there were two thick slices of wholewheat toast, a large pat of deep yellow jersey butter and three squat glass jars containing Tiptree 'Little Scarlet' strawberry jam; Cooper's Vintage Oxford Marmalade and Norwegian Heather Honey from Fortnum's (pp. 80–1).

In more exotic surroundings he eats very differently: 'The yoghort, in a blue china bowl, was deep yellow and with the consistency of thick cream. The green figs ready peeled, were bursting with ripeness and the Turkish coffee was jet black and with the burned taste which showed it had been freshly ground' (p. 99). As Amis points out, Bond's tastes and drinking problems are never initially very far removed from the ordinary and that is one key to the reader's identification with Bond in the novels.[4] In the films and in other subsidiary forms of circulation for the figure of Bond, by contrast,

Bond's extraordinary and spectacular qualities tend to be stressed.

In the films, it is certainly the case, as we have suggested earlier, that the figure of Bond has been partly constructed in terms of the performances of Sean Connery and Roger Moore. However, the relationship between the figures of Connery and Moore and that of Bond seems to work in a different direction from that which obtains between a fully developed star image and the character which the star plays in a specific film. In the case of John Wayne movies, Wayne's star image overlays and resonates with the character Wayne plays in any one film; the character becomes a part of the 'John Wayne' identity rather than John Wayne becoming a fragment of the identity of the character portrayed. In the case of Connery and Moore, as we have seen, their lives have been 'Bondianised' rather than the reverse: they have become parts of the composite signifier 'James Bond' rather than Bond being a fragment of the star images of Connery and Moore. In both cases the identity of Bond has proved dominant, in that the star images of the actors who have played the part are relatively undeveloped except in terms of their incarnations of Bond. The public space in which such images might have been developed successfully has already been usurped by the figure of Bond. When Connery won at the tables in an Italian casino, the newspapers thus ran the story under the headline 'Bond Breaks the Bank' or, again, when he presented a donation to found Israel's branch of the Variety Club International, the *Daily Mail* reported 'Bond hands over £103,000 for Israel'.[5]

In some senses, this may also explain the very different success enjoyed by the two men in playing Bond. Connery was greeted on the release of *Never Say Never Again* with press comments such as 'This is the better Bond and by a wide margin' and 'This is Connery's seventh 007, and you can't beat the one and only!'[6] Connery has experienced this pre-eminent identification with Bond partly because he was the first actor to play the part at the then 'moment' of Bond, but also because the images of Connery which abound in magazine and newspaper features stress his *likeness* to Bond, whereas Moore's character and private life have been seen to 'fill' only inadequately the Bond parameters. The operation of this system of identifications was partly summarised in an episode of *Minder* when a character said that he 'preferred Sean Connery before he became Roger Moore'.

Something of the metaphysical subleties which characterise the precise nature of Bond's being were nicely illustrated by the publicity posters which, when Moore first replaced Connery in the screen role of Bond, announced 'Roger Moore is James Bond'. Read in its context, this assertion of an unmediated identity between two non-identities (Roger Moore and James Bond) was a disavowal of the opposing statement which it worked against and whose terms it sought to uncouple: namely 'Sean Connery is James Bond'. Yet at the same time, this disavowal ('Sean Connery isn't James Bond, Roger Moore is') cancels out the equation of the two non-identities which the film-makers were attempting to establish. The denial that Sean Connery is James Bond, since it requires the construction of Bond as a figure who can survive the process of reincarnation, entails that Roger Moore is not and cannot fully become James Bond either. In being detached from an earlier incarnation (that of Connery) in order to be reincarnated in Moore, the figure of Bond was thus 'floated' as an identity complete in and of itself. Only James Bond can be James Bond. A mythic figure who transcends his own variable incarnations, Bond is always identified with himself but is never quite the same – an ever mobile signifier. As Fleming suggested, 'It is other people who have put their own overcoats on him and built him into what they admire.'[7] We have tried to show that Bond has been fleshed out in different ways, subject to different ideological inscriptions and material incarnations at different moments in the history of 'the Bond phenomenon'.

Thus, as a popular hero, the figure of Bond forms part of a system for the patterning of the cinema-goer's expectations and desires that is relatively distinct from the star system. Audiences don't go to see a Bond film simply for the sake of the quality of Connery's or Moore's performance or for the sake of the finally completed realisation of their otherwise fragmented star images; they don't go to see their favourite star playing another character. Indeed, many viewers don't go to see Connery play Bond or to see Moore play Bond (since they tend to be played by Bond rather than vice versa) but to see James Bond. Ellis argues that in most cases, the narrative fictions of individual films always exceed the star's image, serving as a check on it, inhibiting its complete unfolding, 'except at that single point where the fiction is suspended in favour of the pure performance: the "fetishistic moment" '.[8] Such moments, in which the star image is conspicuously foregrounded as the star plays him or herself, have their equivalents in the Bond films, but they are moments centred on Bond rather than Connery, Moore or Lazenby. Hence, the opening shot of the Saltzman and Broccoli film productions in which Bond is seen through a lens and turns and shoots at the camera is a moment in which Bond is established in a relationship of unmediated identity with himself, independent of the various performers. At such moments, the audience is placed at the holding centre of the 'Bond phenomenon'. There are other moments such as these in the films as, for example, when Bond introduces himself, normally to the girl, with the words 'My name is Bond, James Bond'. Narrative and performance are 'flooded' at such moments by the demonstration of the 'pure beingness' of Bond.

The conditions of production of the Bond films have had an important bearing on these specific qualities of Bond. As we noted in Chapter 2, the Bond films are virtually unique in constituting a thematically linked corpus of texts produced, with the exceptions of *Casino Royale* and *Never Say Never Again*, by the same production company. We have also seen, in Chapter 6, that the ideology of 'Bondian' has played a major role in co-ordinating all phases and departments of production in the making of James Bond films. It is this that has accounted for the high degree of unity which has characterised Bond's persona throughout the different stages of his career; his mobility and adaptability as a signifier have been bounded within quite specific limits, determined by both the marketing strategies of Eon Productions and the discrete set of intersecting ideologies within which he has operated. *Doctor Who* affords an instructive contrast. Tulloch and Alvarado note the respects in which the persona of the Doctor has been successively revised:

> Since the first traumatic regeneration, the Doctor's lead has been changed three more times. Each Doctor has been the site of intersection of different codes and each one has been encouraged to foreground the rhetoric of 'difference' – the Edwardian grandfather, the clown with recorder and baggy pants, the dandy, the 'student' bohemian with long trailing scarf, the vulnerable action-hero – although fundamentally working for similarity and continuity to establish programme identity, orderliness and stability.[9]

In this account, however, such similarity and continuity is achieved by *Doctor Who* as a television institution – ' the star of the series', Tulloch and Alvarado argue, 'is the series'[10] – rather than by the identity of Doctor Who. There are two main reasons for this. The first is that, as a character, the Doctor is an empty site – the Who is intended as a question (Doctor Who?) rather than as a given name. This has meant that it has been possible to redefine the Doctor's character almost entirely, subordinating it to the constructed persona of the lead actor rather than vice versa, with each regeneration. It has also meant that the generic and ideological articulations of the series have been able to be shifted quite massively – encompassing, at various times, science fiction, gothic and historical romance. In thus being conceived as an empty space which may be filled with different contents there are, in principle, no limits to the longevity of the Doctor, whereas for Bond the total ideological and cultural remodelling which such longevity requires is ruled out because his identity is more positively filled. As a second factor, however, the Doctor's greater malleability as a character is partly attributable to the effects of the conditions in which the series has been produced. In contrast to the strongly unified production team which has been responsible for most of the Bond films, *Doctor Who* has been the responsibility of different producers all of whom – in terms of casting policy, the writers they have commissioned, set design, etc. – have sought to put their distinctive signature on the programme.

Yet neither the conditions of existence nor the effects of Bond's functioning as a popular hero are limited to the cinema. The nature of 'the Bond phenomenon' and its consequences have ultimately to be reckoned in terms of the public space which the figure of Bond has occupied. In *The Rape of Clarissa*, Terry Eagleton argues that the characters created by the eighteenth-century novelist, Samuel Richardson – characters such as Clarissa and Pamela – transcended the originating textual conditions of their production in ways akin to the characters of *Coronation Street* and *The Archers* and, indeed, even Superman. Commenting on the degree to which these characters were taken up, used and developed in other contexts (plays, operas, sermons, moral tracts), Eagleton argues that they became 'public mythologies, co-ordinates of a mighty moral debate, symbolic spaces within which dialogues may be conducted ... lynchpins of an entire ideological formation'.[11] In this respect, he argues, analysis should focus less on what such fictions mirror than on what they *do*:

> For Richardson's novels are not mere images of conflicts fought out on another terrain, representations of a history which happens elsewhere; they are themselves a material part of those struggles, pitched standards around which battle is joined, instruments which help to constitute social interests rather than lenses which reflect them.[12]

The argument is, perhaps, a little overstated: Clarissa and Superman make queer bedfellows in any company, and Clarissa and Bond even more so. None the less, the shift of emphasis away from studying fictions as representations of historical processes to examining the part they play within such processes, as a part of them rather than as their abstracted reflections, is of decisive significance. According to this formulation, fictional forms are not to be studied as the epiphenomenal reflections or representations of real social relations but as active ingredients in the constitution of social relations, playing a part – not as abstracted fictions, but alongside the other ideological phenomena with which they are imbricated – in determining the direction in which those relations unfold and develop.

We have tried to approach the fictional forms in which
Bond has appeared as the central character, not as
hypostatised entities to be studied 'in themselves' or as
mediated reflections of social and ideological processes whose
more fundamental determinations are located elsewhere, but
as integrally a part of those processes, pieces of play within a
wide range of cultural and ideological transactions through
which human subjectivities have been produced and moulded.
To bend Eagleton's terminology a little, we might say that
Bond has functioned as 'the lynchpin of an entire textual
formation', drawing a range of texts into a network of
interactive relationships through which they have played a
part alongside rather than separate from other practices, as
points of key cultural reference around which a series of
ideological adjustments and readjustments have been
proposed and, in part, effected. As a figure implicated in the
ideological production of images of nation and nationhood,
sexuality and gender and of the relations between East and
West, Bond has constituted a nodal signifier, active in the
relations between a series of ideologies, a point at which they
have been criss-crossed and compacted into a unified
formation in assuming a tangible, identifiable form.

We have argued so far that fictional forms are not simply
representative of social relations but are a part of them. Yet
we have not done so in order to avoid considering what kinds
of relations do pertain between fictions and other ideological
formations, to suggest that the popular hero is *independent* of
the ideologies through which he is produced and read. We
have attempted to analyse in some detail specific forms of
these relationships at different moments in the history of the
Bond phenomena and to suggest that the figure of the
popular hero operates in a particularly complex and
ambiguous manner in those social relations. One important
way of conceiving social relations and ideologies in Britain
during the period of Bond's popularity is through the concept
of hegemony. The term hegemony is normally used to refer
to a position in which a social class not only plays a decisive
part in the economic relations of a society but also exerts
moral and intellectual leadership over other classes. In such
a case, the subordinate and allied classes consent to the rule

of the dominant classes and the whole process of constantly forming and reproducing that consent is vital to such a society.

This view suggests that, rather than there being a dominant ideology which serves the interest of the dominant classes and is to a certain extent imposed upon other classes, the area of ideology involves much more negotiation between dominant and subordinate values. These processes of negotiation, however, are organised around the winning of consent to the leadership of a particular group. Moreover, in a given mode of hegemony, popular consent is secured around an articulating principle which provides the terms of reference for other ideologies. A 'crisis in hegemony' involves a major disruption in these processes which achieve consent:

> A crisis of hegemony marks a moment of profound rupture in the political and economic life of a society, an accumulation of contradictions. If, in moments of hegemony everything works spontaneously so as to sustain and enforce a particular form of class domination while rendering the basis of that social authority invisible through the mechanisms of the production of consent, the moments when the equilibrium of consent is disturbed ... are moments when the whole basis of political leadership and cultural authority becomes exposed and contested.[13]

Hence, in *Policing the Crisis*, the authors argue that the post-war years have seen a movement from a consensual to a more coercive management of class relations, from a period of expansive hegemony in the 1950s organised around the politics of affluence to a crisis in which the politics of 'law and order' came to provide the articulating principle. Taking mugging as their starting point, the authors point to its orchestration by the media, political spokesmen, courts and police, as a key part in the development of a discourse of 'law and order' which in the 1970s produced consent to more coercive and repressive political strategies on the part of the state. In this situation, quite discrete and local events (incidents of industrial militancy, troublesome youth cultures, student protest movements and mugging) were pulled together as part of a crisis in 'law and order'. The early 1960s, in this view of the post-war period, was the time of the erosion of 1950s style hegemony, based on affluence and individualism, and the not entirely successful attempt to build a new basis for consent by both the Conservative and Labour parties in terms of corporatism and the national interest.

Popular fiction and popular culture generally constitutes an important terrain through which the relations between rulers and ruled are negotiated, separate from and not a reflection of other equally crucial areas. In particular, popular fictions perform in our society to establish or shift subject identities in relation to other ideological formations with the active consent of their readers. For example, popular fictional genres tend to rise to a position of cultural pre-eminence in terms of both production and reading because they re-work current ideological tensions to effect, in their specific narrative forms, either a repetition of existing subject identities or a shift of such subject identities. It is clearly no accident that during the 1970s, when Hall *et al.* argue that the dominant articulating principle of hegemony was a discourse of 'law and order', the most popular television dramatic form was the police crime series, a form in which both reservations about and identification with the law could be put into play in terms of the subject positions produced by the genre.

The Bond films operated in a similar fashion in the early 1960s. Drawing together and working upon a series of ideological tensions in relation to the nation, gender and the Cold War, they operated both to shift and stabilise subject identities at a time when existing ideological constructions had been placed in doubt and jeopardy, when, if you like, the articulating principles of hegemony were in disarray and alternatives had not been successfully established. However, the establishment of Bond as a popular hero meant that Bond could be 'floated' from this textual and ideological base and implicated in later social relations. He was given a 'law and order' inflection in a number of the 1970s films (*Diamonds are Forever*, *Live and Let Die*), pushed into an increasingly comic mode and then reactivated in relation to the re-emerging Cold War of the 1980s and the flickering reawakening of British post-imperialist ambitions. We would thus argue that, viewed as a whole, the significance of the Bond phenomenon should be assessed in terms of the degree to which it has contributed to the reformation of a series of dominant ideologies. In supplying, in Bond and 'the Bond girl', the condensed ingredients of fantasy in relation to which subjects might be moved or move themselves, they have formed part of the whole process whereby the adjustment and readjustment of those ideologies has taken place, enabling a shift from an archaic to a modernised myth of nationhood, a reworking of images of female sexuality in line with the requirements of a 'liberated' male sexuality, a movement from Cold War to détente and back again. But such adjustments have only been effected by creating spaces in which popular values and ideologies have been allowed to operate so as to dismantle outmoded dominant ideologies. When Blofeld taunts Bond in the film of *Diamonds are Forever* – 'Surely you haven't come to negotiate, Mr Bond. Your pitiful little island hasn't even been threatened' – or when, in the film of *You Only Live Twice*, Bond, cutting the shoulder straps of Helga Brandt's dress, complains 'Oh, the things I do for England', we can understand why audiences laugh and why, at least in some respects, the Bond films can be experienced as a liberating send-up of redundant ideological categories.

These arguments have a more general pertinence. We would suggest – although only tentatively, as an issue worthy of further exploration rather than as one we could attempt to substantiate in detail here – that periods of generic change and innovation in popular fiction often coincide with those in which the ideological articulations through which hegemony was previously secured are no longer working to produce popular consent. In such moments, popular fictional forms may often prove more mobile and adaptable than more 'organic', deeply implanted and institutionally solidified political ideologies which, owing to the longer term nature of the work they have to do, are not so conjuncturally pliable. The emergence of popular heroes, such as Bond and Sherlock Holmes, often born in moments of crisis, may – and again, this is no more than a hypothesis – play a particularly significant role in acting as a sounding board in relation to which generic readjustments in the fictional field may be articulated. In periods of established hegemony, popular fictional forms are linked to other ideological practices – in education and the media – in complex relations of mutual support and dependency. In periods of crisis, popular fiction seems to enter into the public arena rather more formidably, carrying and spreading the seeds of a new hegemony, filling the gaps in other practices in producing consent. Figures like Bond and Holmes (although not Dr Who, who has not entered the public arena in the same way) may thus serve a crucial role in reorganising the configuration of the ideological field.

It is in view of these considerations in particular, we would argue, that popular fictional forms should be analysed not as relatively autonomous reflections of ideology, no matter how highly mediated, but as a specific region of the ideological field to be assessed in terms of the services it performs in relation to other regions of that field, acting as a catalyst enabling other ideological forms to be rearticulated in a new configuration. Its particular sensitivity in this regard may be attributable to the fact that, through the market, it is more closely in touch with popular sentiment, quicker to register when specific ideological combinations are losing their 'pulling power' and able to act as a testing ground for new ideological combinations. Popular fiction thus acts, in effect, as a touchstone for the entire field of ideological representations, sounding out where, ideologically speaking, 'the people' have moved to and piloting the ideological adjustments which, by dismantling the previous prevailing hegemony so as to make real concessions to changed popular taste and sentiments, will be able to stitch 'the people' back into a newly constituted place within a restructed hegemony.

It is in this respect that Bond's functioning as a popular hero has been marked by a degree of ambivalence; he has supplied a site around which popular values and sentiments have been articulated to reformed dominant ideologies rather than the latter simply being imposed in a pure and undiluted form. It is for this reason that we consider that a politics of simple opposition to the Bond phenomenon is inappropriate. To simply reject Bond is to ignore the problems that the pleasures of Bond pose. We have tried to analyse the elements from which the figure of Bond has been constructed so that, in reading the 'texts of Bond', some of those elements may be bent back against themselves and Bond emerge as a site around which very different values may be articulated. Popular heroes are public property, not in the sense that anyone can produce a Bond film, but in the sense that their images can be reworked, inflected in different directions and to different ends. Certainly such figures occupy too important a position within the terrain on which popular consciousness is shaped and defined, to be simply abandoned.

It is, of course, impossible to know for how much longer Bond will remain a significantly popular figure. Nor is it possible to specify in advance the directions in which the signifying currency of Bond may be modified to enable it to respond to, elaborate and partly construct, changing ideological and cultural tendencies. For the immediate future, however, three possibilities seem clear. First, if *Octopussy* is anything to go by, Bond seems destined to become a Cold War hero once more. Secondly, as the conditions of production of Bond become more clearly and unequivocally American, Bond is likely to be increasingly Americanised. John Gardner's *For Special Services* is a clear sign of this. At the end of his mission, Bond receives a revolver as a token of especial appreciation of his services – but from the President of the United States rather than from M. He also receives a gift of a daughter from Felix Leiter. The writing is on the wall: henceforward Bond will function as the delegate of the American phallus; the double gift of gun and girl marks the completion of Bond's trans-Atlantic passage, his final dependency on America in supplying both the means and the object of his continued phallic activity. Thirdly, if *Never Say Never Again* is to be taken as a model, Bond may be used to reward 'supportive women' and to punish and kill those whose sexualism and aggression is seen as threatening.

For our own part, we have proposed an alternative scenario for Bond's future development, a kind of identity kit from which a Bond for the left might be assembled:

An ideal Bond for the 1980s would try to unionize espionage

workers, *campaign for gay rights in the Secret Service, encourage Miss Moneypenny to leave M and set up an abortion clinic, leak all he knows to END, exchange his supercharged Bentley for a bike and switch from Martini to beer – shaken, not stirred, if he must. If he could also attach a limpet mine to the royal yacht, secretly arrange for the peaceful transfer of the Malvinas to Argentina and deliver Thatcher bound hand, foot and especially mouth to Arthur Scargill at a secret destination somewhere near Barnsley, that would be handy too.[14]

To which we would add:

A Bond of the 1980s should become disillusioned with the opportunistic politics of his government, abandon killing and spying and take up the defence of other 'freedoms' in Britain; joining the peace movement would seem particularly appropriate. He should find a woman or women who could instruct him in the intellectual niceties, which have so far escaped him, share with them the occasional bottle of Tattinger and Foie Groie along with the housework and childcare, and, whilst cultivating his ardent affection for sexual pleasures, perhaps widen his scope a little.

No more than utopian musing, of course; on the other hand, the meaning of a signifier, its relationship to an ultimate signified, is never finally determined until the lonely hour of the last instance which never comes.

Postscript: A Licence to Kill

A View to a Kill, the thirteenth Bond film, was released in 1985. So was *Mad Max Beyond Thunderdome*, the third of the Mad Max movies. There can be little doubt as to which was the more significant event of the two. The release of *Mad Max Beyond Thunderdome* was something of a media occasion. Accompanied by a television special (narrated by Tina Turner) showing various aspects of the film's production, the publicity for *Mad Max Beyond Thunderdome* both contributed to and benefited considerably from the more general promotion of the star currencies of Tina Turner and Mel Gibson over the same period. Tina Turner's world-wide concert tour; her appearance with Mick Jagger in the Live Aid telethon for Ethiopia; Mel Gibson's role as Christian in *Mutiny on the Bounty* and his construction as Hollywood's most recent and hottest discovery; the general American interest in 'things Australian' stimulated by the success of the Paul Hogan tourist advertisements – this network of associations served to mark the release of *Mad Max Beyond Thunderdome* as a cultural moment, a distinctive and integral component in the media constructed cultural landscape of 1985. The release of *A View to a Kill*, by contrast, was an altogether more routine affair. In the absence of anything like the Connery/Moore rivalry which had renewed a flagging public interest in the Bond phenomenon when *Never Say Never Again* and *Octopussy* were released, the Bond publicity machinery – although as well-oiled as usual – had to work hard to generate public interest in *A View to a Kill*. Nor was this too surprising. Apart from the exploitation of the film's most obvious novelty factor (Grace Jones), the central message of the pre-release publicity was: business as usual.

While the comparison is obviously a convenient one, it's also more than that. Considered more closely, it interestingly foregrounds the differences between successive stages in the careers of popular heroes. *Mad Max Beyond Thunderdome* clearly marks a moment of qualitative significance in the career of Mad Max: the moment of his transition from a cult figure with a relatively small circulation to a generalised popular hero suitably tailored to meet the requirements of an international market defined primarily in terms of family audiences. It is, if you like, the *Goldfinger* of the Mad Max forumla; that is, the moment of its institutionalisation, of its transformation into ritual. *A View to a Kill*, by contrast, is merely another moment in the history of a long-standing institution and one in which the weight of the past, while providing the chief cultural asset which the film mobilises, also makes itself felt as something of a burden. On the one hand, the familiar Bond formula is what the film trades on, promising the pleasures of repetition with minimal variation; on the other hand, that formula proves an impediment in the respect that the variations it permits are so minimal as to limit the film's ability to capture new audiences on the wing. Either that or, where more significant innovations are introduced, the resulting uncertainties and lack of a clear overall direction are likely to leave traditional Bond fans feeling dissatisfied.

Indeed, while clearly attempting to reconcile the requirement for innovation with the preservation of tradition, the film conspicuously fails to achieve a satisfactory balance between these contradictory tendencies. A concern with tradition is most evident in the film's stunt sequences which, almost without exception, function as extended quotations from earlier Bond films. The opening ski scene in which Bond flees from his would-be KGB assassins recalls the opening of *The Spy Who Loved Me*, and does so by means of parody as Bond, switching from skis to an improvised surf-board, escapes his pursuers to the accompaniment of the Beach Boys singing *California Girls*. Similarly, the chase sequence through the crowded streets of Paris as Bond tries to keep track of May Day's hang-glider descent from the Eiffel Tower is reminiscent of the *Moonraker* sequence in which Bond drives a motorised gondola through the streets of Venice. A similar self-referential structure is evident in the system of cultural associations which the film deploys. For the most part these associations are historical in order, referring either to earlier Bond films or to cultural forms contemporaneous with them and sometimes to both simultaneously. The cameo part played by Patrick McNee, alias John Steed of *The Avengers*, thus serves to recall the pairing of Sean Connery and Honor Blackman in *Goldfinger* while also playing a crucial role in redefining the currency of Bond's Englishness. From the point of view of the plot, the casting of McNee is quite incidental. His function as Sir Godfrey Tibbet, a prominent figure in government circles, is to assist Bond's cover during his first encounter with the villain by playing chauffeur to Bond's James Saint-John Smythe. Culturally, however, this pairing works to associate Bond with the quirky, eccentric and aristocratic style of English hero represented by John Steed, an association which is reinforced by the reference to Dr Who via Q's invention of 'a highly sophisticated surveillance machine' which turns out to be little more than an up-market version of K-9. It also works to suggest the impotence of this style of heroism as Tibbet is unceremoniously despatched by May Day (Grace Jones).

The plot, by contrast, shows signs of considerable effort having been made to adjust and renovate the Bond formula in order to accommodate new cultural and ideological concerns. The result, however, is that, while breaking with the traditional Bond formula in certain respects, the film tends more to display and foreground its own fracturing of that formula than it does to replace it with a new one with any longer-term developmental prospects. Although all of the individual ingredients are present – the contests between Bond and the villain and Bond and 'the girl', the discourses of Cold War and détente, a play on the Englishness of the hero – the mode of their combination is acutely uncertain. They fail to gel into a coherent whole with the result that the film is caught awkwardly between a traditional formula which it does not entirely jettison and a new one which it does not fully develop.

This tension is most evident in the film's relations to the SMERSH and SPECTRE variants of the formula. Placing its bets both ways, it uncomfortably straddles the two with the consequence that the plot becomes confused and its ideological articulations fuzzy as it zig-zags between the discourse of Cold War and that of détente and, ultimately, distances itself from both of them. Initially, the plot has a Cold War aspect and, in a clear concession to the ideological climate of Reaganism, a triumphalist one. The threat seemingly represented by the Soviet Union is merely that it might catch up technologically with the west. In the pre-credits sequence, Bond retrieves a micro-chip that was en route to delivery to the KGB. Developed by British scientists, the chip is vital to the defence systems of the west in its immunity to the 'magnetic pulse damage' that would otherwise render all computers inoperable in the event of a nuclear attack. In this respect, the film locates itself firmly in the era of the Star Wars programme and exudes an unperturbable confidence in America's supremacy over Russia. Only industrial espionage can close the gap between the two. Bond's mission, accordingly, is to discover and eradicate the source of the leak through which the secret micro-chip came so perilously close to falling into the possession of the KGB.

It is true of a number of earlier Bond films – *The Spy Who Loved Me*, for example – that what initially appears to be a Soviet threat to the west subsequently turns out to be the result of a SPECTRE conspiracy which, in threatening both Russia and (usually) America, prompts east and west to join their espionage forces in order to avert a global disaster. While *A View to a Kill* follows a similar trajectory, this aspect of the plot is subordinated to another and, for the Bond films, quite distinctive transition that is most clearly manifested in the character of the villain and the nature of his conspiracy. Indeed, Zorin, the villain in question, is the point at which the traditional Bond formula is most visibly unsettled. Conforming to neither the SMERSH nor the SPECTRE models of the villain, he combines aspects of both – although somewhat awkwardly – as well as introducing new elements into the lexicon of Bond villainy.

Trained by the KGB and set up in the west as a wealthy industrialist, the industrial empire Zorin runs serves as a front for his espionage activities on behalf of Russia while also serving as a base from which he develops his own freelance conspiracy. Upbraided by his KGB superiors for having acted without orders in attempting to dispose of Bond on the occasion of their first encounter, Zorin attributes the KGB's failure to secure Britain's secret micro-chip to the bureaucratic incompetence of his superiors and announces his resignation from the KGB: 'I no longer consider myself a KGB agent.' In so doing, he manifests qualities of independence and disobedience which tend to undermine the usual basis of the opposition between Bond and the villain inasmuch as the latter traditionally embodies the quality of bureaucratic planning carried to excess whereas Bond symbolises the virtue of unprogrammed improvisation. While Bond displays this latter quality – most notably when he escapes the watery grave that has been planned for him by taking in air from the tyres of the submerged Rolls-Royce in which he and the dead Sir Godfrey Tibbet have been placed – so does Zorin. In the midst of orchestrating impromptu arrangements for Bond's death in San Francisco's City Hall, Zorin announces that his genius consists in his capacity for 'intuitive improvisation'.

It is, however, the nature of Zorin's conspiracy which most unhinges the traditional Bond formula. Having manufactured and accumulated a massive stockpile of micro-chips, Zorin's ambition is to head a syndicate that will dominate the world's micro-electronics market by eliminating its main rival: California's Silicone Valley which Zorin plans to flood by means of an explosion strategically placed to activate the region's major geological fault-lines. While this conspiracy incorporates aspects of the SPECTRE formula, two crucial ingredients are lacking. The first concerns the motivation of the conspiracy. Although there are exceptions – Stromberg in *The Spy Who Loved Me*, for example – the villain is usually motivated by a compound of avarice and a utopian altruism. The financial rewards of the conspiracy are sought not as an end in themselves but, to take the case of *Moonraker*, as a means of cultivating a perfectible humanity when the world has been cleansed of the presently existing, but imperfect and corrupted representatives of the species. Zorin's motivation, by contrast, is entirely devoid of any ethical rationalisation, no matter how warped or perverted. As a power-hungry industrialist and a psychotic, Zorin has only two ends in view. To express these in terms of the somewhat laboured play that is made with the film's title, his conspiracy is motivated with a view to making a financial killing and 'with a view to a kill' – that is, to the pleasure of witnessing the infliction of pain, suffering and death by observing the destruction of Silicone Valley from an airship. Secondly, the conspiracy is localised in its import. Far from threatening a global catastrophe, it portends merely the end of America's dominance of the high-tech economy and, as a consequence, lacks the broader political and ideological articulations of either the SMERSH or the SPECTRE formulae.

In thus constricting the scope of the villain's conspiracy so that it is directed solely against the interests of American capital, *A View to a Kill* realises the trans-Atlantic passage of the Bond plot more thoroughgoingly than any of the earlier films. The discourse of détente, while present, survives as little more than a vestigial appendix to the main plot dynamics, its main function being to underscore the triumphalist view that America need no longer take the Soviet Union seriously. For reasons that remain opaque until toward the end of the film, the KGB assigns one of its own agents – Pola Ivanova, whom Bond routinely beds and outwits – to investigate Zorin's activities and, if possible, thwart his conspiracy. This coincidence of interests between east and west, between the Soviet military and American capital, is accounted for when the head of the KGB, announcing that 'Comrade Bond' is to be awarded the Order of Lenin for his services to the Soviet state, explains this unprecedented gesture by wryly insinuating that Russian research would have been severely hampered by the destruction of Silicone Valley. The removal of the erratic individualism represented by Zorin allows 'normal relations' to be restored between the Soviet Union and the Unite States – normality, in this instance, consisting in Russia's lagging behind and being dependent on American advancement if it is to close the gap between the two. The preservation of the American high-tech industry offers the Soviet Union a cheap and easy way (industrial espionage) of securing its own continued – but always tardy – technological development.

However, while witnessing a radical Americanisation of the

plot, *A View to a Kill* also marks a limit to the trans-Atlantic passage of the hero. Bond's Englishness, conspicuously foregrounded throughout the film, serves as both a butt of parody and a sign of limitation. The covers Bond adopts – James Saint-John Smythe, an amateur sportsman; James Stock of the London Financial Times – establish his associations as those of the traditional English gentleman hero, a style of heroism which is appraised as largely redundant. Bond's Englishness cuts no ice. Nor does his reputation. When Bond finally breaks his cover to reveal his true identity – 'Well, actually, I'm James Bond,' he tells a San Francisco cop, anticipating instant recognition and full cooperation as a consequence – the only response is a gruff 'Yeah. Well I'm Dick Tracy and you're still under arrest.' Nor finally, and more critically, is Bond particularly effective. He is consistently bested by May Day (and it's worth noting that it is May Day who sinks the Rolls-Royce containing Bond and Tibbet/Steed, packing them off like a couple of old has-beens) just as it is May Day who is ultimately decisive in averting Zorin's conspiracy. Bond's skill and improvisation prove, in the end, to be insufficient. The day is saved not by an English male hero but by an American black woman as May Day, putting her extraordinary strength in Bond's service, lowers him into the pit containing the explosive device that is to trigger off the flooding of Silicone Valley, hoists him out again and, sacrificing her life in the process, ensures that the device is removed to a place where its detonation will be harmless. Bond's task remains merely to tidy up the pieces.

It is tempting to see in this a progressive departure from the traditional Bond formula, a celebration of black womanhood, particularly when viewed in the light of the related breaks with tradition which characterise the relations between Bond and women in the film. These have principally to do with the fact that the narrative function of 'the girl' is split between May Day and Stacey Sutton both of whom, albeit in different ways, have fallen under the domination of the villain: May Day sexually, and Stacey through Zorin's take-over of her dead father's oil company whose pumping stations play a vital role in his conspiracy. This, in its turn, introduces a new aspect into the coding of the villain – who is usually neuter or sexually deviant

– while also considerably complicating the narrative function of
May Day: as well as sharing the function of 'the girl' with
Stacey, she is also, so to speak, Zorin's chief henchman, a Pussy
Galore and Oddjob all rolled into one. What is most decisive,
however, is the fact that Bond's sexual charisma plays no part
in seducing either May Day or Stacey away from the service of
the villain. Stacey, while destined to become Bond's sexual
partner at the end of the film and while indebted to Bond for
saving her from Zorin's hit-squad, determines to oppose Zorin
prior to her rescue by Bond and for her own reasons. Similarly,
in opposing herself to Zorin, May Day is motivated entirely by
her determination for vengeance when confronted with the
evidence of Zorin's preparedness to abandon her to a certain
death. The assistance she renders Bond is not accompanied by
any ideological shift or support for the American cause, nor is it
prepared for her sexual subordination to the hero.

Indeed, it is Bond who submits to the sexual domination of
May Day. This aspect of the film is quite conspicuously
accentuated in following closely on May Day's sexual
submission to Zorin. In the course of instructing Zorin in
karate, May Day is thrown and pinioned to the floor where,
after a struggle, she yields her smouldering consent to Zorin's
domination and, by implication, to his sexuality also. Shortly
after, she refuses and successfully resists Bond's attempt to
place her in a similar position. Returning, from a clandestine
sortie, to Zorin's chateau Bond finds that his room is being
searched. To produce an alibi for his absence, he slips into May
Day's room and then into her bed, cheerfully reminding her,
when she subsequently appears, that she had earlier promised
to 'look after him personally'. Without deigning to reply, May
Day disrobes and slips into bed beside him. When Bond leans
over to her, however, she roughly thrusts him aside and – with
his pliable acquiescence – places herself on top of him leaving
the viewer with little doubt as to who is going to do the
lovemaking to whom.

In brief, Bond's sexuality, like his Englishness, is little more
than a damp squid. When Zorin inquires, the next morning,
whether he slept well, Bond replies, somewhat limply: 'A little
restless, but I got off eventually.' While allowed his conquests –
with Pola Ivanova, for example – these are mostly chummy

affairs and, in any case, are quite incidental to the main dynamics of the plot. So far as these are concerned, Bond's sexuality is entirely without consequence.

Yet it would be precipitate to conclude that any major changes in ideological direction follow from these modifications to the traditional plot elements. For all that she serves to expose the sexual and practical insufficiencies of the English hero, the ultimate significance of the character May Day is that – as black woman – she blow herself up. Moreover, as we witness this from the vantage-point of Zorin's airship, this is the only kill that the film finally delivers a view of. Yet it is one that is prepared for from the outset. In the credits sequence, which function as a synecdoche for this cental ideological aspect of the film, the spectator is offered 'a view to a kill' – to the killing of women, especially black women, who are represented, in their nakedness, as targets for Bond's tracer-bullets or as objects transfixed in the gaze of a sniper's telescopic lens. The associations this sequence establishes are transferred to May Day via the way in which she is first introduced into the film as we see her through the controlling vision of Bond's binoculars and are made to reverberate again when, from the controlling vision of Zorin's perspective, we witness her self-destruction.

In these respects, in spite of its liberated facade, the film is deeply misogynist. Although Bond's own license to kill has been curtailed, a Bond film is still a license for the killing of women. It is also, and in spite of an equivalent facade, profoundly racist. As the product of experiments in genetic engineering undertaken by Hans Glab (alias Doktor Morton), a Nazi physician subsequently captured by the Russians, Zorin – in both physique and character – embodies the myth of Aryan supremacy. While Zorin's death and the frustration of his conspiracy – inevitable requirements of the formula – free the film from the taint of anti-semitism, they also, given Bond's failures in these areas, remove the only source of challenge to May Day's apparent sexual and racial superiority. Her self-destruction as not merely the embodiment of unsubjugated woman but as the only black person in the film is, therefore, no mere contingency. Rather, it is the point at which the underlying ideological tensions which most powerfully motivate the narrative are resolved. The threat to the dominance of white American male culture is removed not by a representative of that culture, and certainly not by a somewhat foppish English spy, but by the self-destruction of the forces ranged against it. May Day's death, to put it bluntly, expresses the pious hope that both the women's and black liberation movements might take themselves off somewhere into the California desert and blow themselves up.

Our utopian musings at the end of the last chapter, then, remain just that: utopian musings. While *A View to a Kill* attests to a further attenuation in the ideological currency of Bond and, we would guess, a consequent narrowing in the scope of his appeal, his personal qualities are not appreciably enhanced in the process. For all that, although the early indicators suggest the film is unlikely to prove the usual Bond blockbuster, it will, no doubt, make a reasonable profit. It will do so, however, less because of the cultural and ideological resonances of the hero or because of the Bond formula than because it is, simply, a Bond film. James Bond, well past the twilight of his career, is now, more than anything else, a trademark which, having established a certain degree of brand loyalty among certain sections of the cinema-going public, remains a viable investment in the film industry. However, it is debatable how long this will continue to be the case. Quite apart from the creaks and strains produced by the adjustments to the Bond formula and the fact that Bond's potency as a cultural icon is clearly diminishing, the Bond property itself does not offer unlimited possibilities. *A View to a Kill* clearly proved a difficult title for the scriptwriters to negotiate. By our reckoning, only a handful of Fleming's original Bond titles (the rights to which are owned by Eon Productions) are left, and few of these – *Risico* and *The Hildebrand Rarity*, for example – look promising.

Yet, viewed from the broader perspective of the Bond phenomenon as a whole, it would be a mistake to read too much into the success or failure of any one particular film. After all, several of the Bond films made in the 1970s were limited in their audience appeal and some – *The Man with the Golden Gun*, for example – were downright quirky. Equally, the Bond publicity machinery continues to do its work, keeping the Bond phenomenon simmering on the back-boiler of public interest.

At least one more Bond film is planned and, at the time of writing, there is considerable media speculation as to whether Roger Moore will continue in the role of Bond and, if not, who the next James Bond will be. Whether this will prove sufficient to re-install Bond in the position he occupied in the 1960s and 1970s, or whether it will merely mark another step in the fading away of a popular hero, remains to be seen. Whichever the case, though, it will be some time yet before obituary notices are called for.

Notes and References

Introduction

1. Cited in M. F. Callan, *Sean Connery: His Life and Films*, W. H. Allen, London, 1983, p. 149.
2. J. Tulloch and M. Alvarado, *Doctor Who: The Unfolding Text*, Macmillan, London, 1983.

1 The Bond Phenomenon

1. Cited in J. Pearson, *The Life of Ian Fleming*, Jonathan Cape, London, 1966, p. 300.
2. *007, James Bond in Focus*, Glidrose Production Ltd and Marvyn Bruce Associates Ltd, London, 1964. (Not paginated.)
3. See S. Flack, 'Broccoli's Bond Bonanza', *TV Times*, 22 February 1977.
4. See *Cinema TV Today*, no. 9991, 29 July 1972.
5. See, for a discussion of the functioning of Robinson Crusoe in these respects, I. Watt '*Robinson Crusoe* as a Myth', in E. and T. Burns (eds), *Sociology of Literature and Drama*, Penguin, Harmondsworth, 1973.
6. See A. E. Murch, *The Development of the Detective Novel*, Greenwood Press, Westport, Conn., 1958, pp. 167, 175.
7. Cited in J. Pearson, *The Life of Ian Fleming*, p. 304.
8. See A. Bear, 'Intellectuals and 007: High Comedy and Total Stimulation', *Dissent*, Winter, 1966.
9. K. Amis, *The James Bond Dossier*, Jonathan Cape, London, 1965, pp. 14, 38.
10. See J. Tulloch and M. Alvarado, *Doctor Who: The Unfolding Text*, p. 58.
11. D. Cannadine, 'James Bond and the Decline of England', *Encounter*, 53(3), November 1979, p. 46.

2 The Moments of Bond

1. I. Fleming, 'How to Write a Thriller', *Books and Bookmen*, May 1963, p. 14.

2. Cited in J. Pearson, *The Life of Ian Fleming*, Jonathan Cape, London, 1966, p. 299.

3. It subsequently did rather better when published by the American Popular Library under the title *Too Hot to Handle*.

4. See P. Johnson, 'Sex, Snobbery and Sadism', *New Statesman*, 5 April 1958.

5. See B. Bergonzi, 'The Case of Mr Fleming', *The Twentieth Century*, March 1958.

6. I. Cameron, *The Spectator*, 12 October 1962.

7. Cited in L. Murray and R. Eglin, 'The Gilt-edged Bond', *Business Observer*, 16 January 1972.

8. For a summary and illustrations of Bond's various strip-cartoon incarnations, see *The Illustrated James Bond 007*, James Bond 007 Fan Club, New York, 1981.

9. See, for details, L. Tornabuoni, 'A Popular Phenomenon', in O. Del Buono and U. Eco (eds), *The Bond Affair*, Macdonald, London, 1966.

10. Cited in *The Hollywood Reporter*, 31 December 1971.

11. See D. Moriot, 'James Bond and America in the Sixties: An Investigation of the Formula Film in Popular Culture', *Journal of the University Film Association*, xxviii(3), Summer, 1976.

12. According to Lacan, the arbitrary relationship of signifier to signified – the fact that the relationship of signifier to signified is engendered only via the relationship of one signifier to another – opens up the possibility of an infinite sliding of meaning in which the signifier glides over the signified, slipping into adjacent signifiers, rather than becoming attached to it. Lacan argues that this is avoided by the functioning of certain privileged signifiers – *points de capiton* – which button down the system of language around certain crucial co-ordinating signifiers. These furnish fixed anchoring points of meaning in relation to which the potentially infinite circulation of meaning within language can be stopped and the meaning of each signifier 'button-holed' by pinning it down – not to its signified, but by referring it to the central co-ordinating signifier through which its relationship to other signifiers, and hence to its signified, is organised. According to Lacan, the Symbolic Father and the concept of the phallus function, within the context of the castration complex, as such *points de capiton*; points of anchorage in relation to which sexed identities are constructed, subject positions within language assumed and signifiers clasped to their signifieds through the relations of similarity and difference which mark their position in relation to such *points de capiton*. (For further elaboration of this concept, see A. Wilden, 'Lacan and the Discourse of the Other', in J. Lacan, *The Language of the Self: The Function of Language in Psychoanalysis*, Delta Books, New York, 1968, pp. 237–49, 270–84). Although the analogy is not intended as a strict one, Bond's functioning as a *point de capiton* within British popular culture is closely related to the way in which the figure of Bond has been phallicly coded.

13. See J. Tulloch and M. Alvarado, *Doctor Who: The Unfolding Text*, Macmillan, London, 1983, p. 99.

14. Bruce Merry has thus noted the widespread use of references to Bond in contemporary spy-thrillers, usually as a means of advancing their claims to realism by dissociating themselves from Bondian fantasy. References to Bond function in this way in Frederick Forsythe's *The Day of the Jackal*, Len Deighton's *Funeral in Berlin* and Desmond Bagley's *Running Blind* and *The Freedom Trap*. Merry also notes the way in which M supplies the implied point of reference in relation to which the control figure is constructed in the novels of Deighton and Le Carré. See B. Merry, *Anatomy of the Spy Thriller*, Gill & Macmillan, Dublin, 1977, pp. 64–5, 135–9, 142–3, 159–60. Mention should also be made of the exceedingly wide range of Bond parodies, Examples from the cinema in the mid 1960s include *Our Man Flint* (1966), starring James Coburn, Woody Allen's *Casino Royale* (1967) and *The Intelligence Men* (1966) starring Morecambe and Wise. For details of literary parodies, see section 24, 'Not Quite Like James Bond', of I. Campbell, *Ian Fleming: A Catalogue of a Collection*, Liverpool, 1978.

15. S. Rubin, *The James Bond Films*, Arlington House, Norwalk, Connecticut, 1981, p. 187.

3 Reading Bond

1. See J. Pearson, *James Bond: The Authorized Biography of 007*, Sidgwick & Jackson, London, 1973.

2. For earlier discussions of these problems, see T. Bennett, 'Texts and Social Process: The Case of James Bond', *Screen Education*, no. 41, Spring/Winter, 1982, and T. Bennett, 'James Bond: Theorizing a Popular Hero', *Southern Review*, XV(2), 1983.

3. M. Foucault, 'What is an Author?', *Screen*, XX(1), Spring, 1979, p. 22.

4. Ibid., p. 19.

5. See D. Cannadine, 'James Bond and the Decline of England', *Encounter*, 53(3), 1979.

6. See A. S. Boyd, *The Devil with James Bond*, Greenwood Press, Westport, Conn., 1975. (Originally published by the John Knox Press, Richmond, Virginia, 1967.)

7. R. Dyer, 'Stars as Signs', in T. Bennett, S. Boyd-Bowman, C. Mercer and J. Woollacott (eds), *Popular Television and Film*, BFI, London, 1981, p. 266. For similar observations regarding the way in which the text of *Doctor Who* has been crossed by a whole variety of star images and performance codes, see Tulloch and Alvarado, *Doctor Who: The Unfolding Text*, Macmillan, London, 1983, p. 299.

8. O. F. Snelling, *Double O Seven, James Bond: A Report*, Neville Spearman Holland Press, London, 1964.

9. Cited in M. F. Callan, *Sean Connery: His Life and Times*, W. H. Allen, London, 1983.

10. Cited in A. Walker, *Hollywood England: The British Film Industry in the Sixties*, Michael Joseph, London, p. 187.

11. K. Amis, *The James Bond Dossier*, Jonathan Cape, London, 1965, p. 36.

12. Cited in K. Passingham, 'James Bond', *TV Times*, 15 October 1975.
13. W. Iser, *The Act of Reading: A Theory of Aesthetic Response*, Routledge & Kegan Paul, London, 1978, p. 138.
14. *Playboy*, November 1965, p. 78.
15. Ibid., p. 76.
16. Ibid., p. 81.
17. See, for an example of this approach, W. Iser, *The Act of Reading*.
18. See D. Morley, *The 'Nationwide' Audience*, BFI, London, 1980.
19. For a discussion of the ways in which the 'frame' separating the literary from the extra-literary may shift, see J. Frow, 'The Literary Frame', *Journal of Aesthetic Education*, 16(2), 1982.
20. See, for expositions and critical discussions of the encoding/decoding model, S. Hall 'Encoding/Decoding' and D. Morley 'Texts, Readers, Subjects', both in S. Hall, D. Hobson, A Lowe and P. Willis (eds), *Culture, Media, Language*, Hutchinson, London, 1980.
21. R. Holub, *Reception Theory: A Critical Introduction*, Methuen, London, 1983, p. 99.
22. For a fuller discussion and exemplification of the concept of 'reading formation', see T. Bennett, 'Texts, Readers, Reading Formations', *The Bulletin of the Midwest Modern Language Association*, 16(1), Spring, 1983. Reprinted in *Literature and History*, vol. 9, no. 2, Autumn, 1983.
23. It is in this, its material social supports, that the concept of 'reading formation' differs from the concept of 'horizon of expectations' associated with the work of H. R. Jauss. For Jauss, 'horizon of expectations' refers to the subjective associations which inform the reading practices of any individual reader. The concept of reading formation, by contrast, specifies a set of objective determinations which mould and structure the terrain of the text–reader encounter.
24. See U. Eco, *The Role of the Reader: Explorations in the Semiotics of Texts*, Hutchinson, London, 1981, pp. 140–1.
25. See E. D. Hirsch Jr, *Validity in Interpretation*, Yale University Press, New Haven, 1967.
26. See U. Eco, 'Narrative Structures in Fleming', in *The Role of the Reader* (originally published in O. Del Buono and U. Eco, *The Bond Affair*, Macdonald, London, 1961).
27. In his approach to 'closed texts', Eco relies on the distinction proposed by the Russian Formalists between the concepts of *fabula* (story) and *sjuzet* (plot or discourse). *Fabula* is 'the basic story stuff, the logic of actions or the syntax of characters, the time oriented course of events', whereas *sjuzet* or plot is 'the story as actually told, along with deviations, digressions, flashbacks, and the whole of the verbal devices' (p. 27). While the distinction is a useful one, the particular terminology used to express it departs from more familiar usages of the concept of plot.
28. V. Propp, *Morphology of the Folk Tale*, University of Texas Press, Houston, 1968, p. 23.
29. T. de Lauretis, *Alice Doesn't: Feminism, Semiotics, Cinema*, Macmillan, London, 1984, p. 176.

30. See J. G. Cawelti, *Adventure, Mystery and Romance: Formula Stories as Art and Popular Culture,* University of Chicago Press, 1976, pp. 40–3.
31. S. Neale, *Genre,* British Film Institute, London, 1980, p. 48.
32. D. Porter, *The Pursuit of Crime: Art and Ideology in Detective Fiction,* Yale University Press, New Haven and London, 1981, p. 5.
33. *New York Times,* 30 May 1963.
34. See M. Denning, *Cover Stories: Narrative and Ideology in the British Spy Thriller,* Routledge & Kegan Paul, forthcoming.
35. See, for an account of the origins of this genre, D. A. Stafford, 'Spies and Gentlemen: The Birth of the British Spy Novel, 1853–1914', *Victorian Studies,* Summer, 1981.
36. See E. S. Turner, *Boys will be Boys,* Penguin, Harmondsworth, 1976.
37. See K. Warpole, *Dockers and Detectives. Popular Reading: Popular Writing,* New Left Books, London, 1983.
38. See M. Denning, *Cover Stories,* chapter 2 for a discussion of the significance of this aspect of the novels of Buchan and NcNeile.
39. C. McNeile, *Bull-Dog Drummond,* Hodder and Stoughton, London, n.d., p. 25.
40. Fleming goes on, after this passage, to develop an elaborate and flirtatious series of references to Bull-Dog Drummond. McNeile, commenting on Drummond's heroic leadership in the Great War, adds: 'Which is why there are in England today quite a number of civilians who acknowledge only two rulers – the King and Hugh Drummond' (*Bull-Dog Drummond,* p. 15). Fleming alludes to this in the position he accords Bond within the hierarchy of loyalty and deference constituted in the system of relationships the novel posits between God, King, Churchill, M and lastly Bond. See chapter 4, pp. 106–7.
41. See Merry, *Anatomy of the Spy Thriller,* Gill & Macmillan, Dublin, 1977, p. 4.
42. See D. Lammers, 'Nevil Shute and the Decline of the "Imperial Idea" in Literature', *Journal of British Studies,* 1977.
43. See D. Ormerod and D. Ward, 'The Bond Game', *The London Magazine,* May 1965, p. 42.
44. Amis has Colonel Sun reflect on the intimacy of the union which torture effects between the torturer and his victim by means of a quotation from de Sade's *Justine,* develops his plot by means of a series of overt references to the myth of the Cretan Minotaur, and playfully debunks his own critical comparison of Bond to the Byronic hero.
45. B. Merry, *Anatomy of the Spy Thriller,* pp. 162–3.
46. R. Tomashevskii, 'Literature and biography', in L. Matejka and K. Pomorska (eds), *Readings in Russian Poetics,* MIT Press, Cambridge, Mass., 1971, p. 47.
47. I. Fleming, 'How to Write a Thriller', *Books and Bookmen,* May 1963, pp. 14–15.
48. Sands' article is contained in S. Lane (ed.), *For Bond Lovers Only,* Panther, London, 1965, p. 115. It is allegedly the report of a conversation between Sands and Simenon. Since many of the comments attributed to Fleming, supposedly in the context of a conversation with

Simenon, seem to be lifted from Fleming's other writings on the subject of thriller writing, its authenticity is very much to be doubted.

49. Apart from Pearson's biography of Fleming and his 'fictional biography' of Bond, this construction of Fleming can be found in the following: R. Gant, *Ian Fleming: The Man with the Golden Pen*, Mayflower/Dell, New York, 1966; I. Bryce, *You Only Live Once: Memories of Ian Fleming*; O. F. Snelling, *Double O Seven, James Bond: A Report*, and the various articles and notes on Fleming in S. Lane (ed.), *For Bond Lovers*, and *James Bond in Thunderball*, Sackville Publications, London, 1965.

50. F. Jameson, 'On Raymond Chandler', *Southern Review*, vol. 6, no. 3, 1970, p. 135.

4 Bonded Ideologies

1. Cited in R. Gant, *Ian Fleming: The Man with the Golden Pen*, p. 99.
2. I. Fleming, 'How to Write a Thriller', *Books and Bookmen*, May 1963, p. 14.
3. S. Neale, *Genre*, BFI, London, 1980, p. 20.
4. Penguin edition, p. 25.
5. M. Denning, *Cover Stories: Narrative and Ideology in the British Spy Thriller*, Routledge & Kegan Paul, forthcoming.
6. K. Amis, *The James Bond Dossier*, Jonathan Cape, London, 1965, p. 86.
7. Ibid., p. 89.
8. D. Cannadine, 'James Bond and the Decline of England', *Encounter*, 53(3), 1979, p. 48.
9. R. Usborne, *Clubland Heroes: A Nostalgic Study of Some Recurrent Characteristics in the Romantic Fiction of Dornford Yates, John Buchan and Sapper*, Constable, London, 1953, p. 155.
10. Ibid., p. 134.
11. J. Cawelti, *Adventure, Mystery and Romance*, University of Chicago Press, 1976, p. 40.
12. R. Usborne, *Clubland Heroes*, p. 101.
13. Penguin edition, p. 53.
14. S. Heath, *The Sexual Fix*, Macmillan, London, 1982, pp. 96–7.
15. T. Eagleton, *Literary Theory: An Introduction*, Blackwell, Oxford, 1983, p. 179.
16. This is especially true of D. Ormerod and D. Ward, 'The Bond Game', *The London Magazine*, May 1965, which we draw on substantially in what follows.
17. R. Trahair, 'A Contribution to the Psychoanalytical Study of the Modern Hero: The Case of James Bond', *La Trobe Sociology Papers*, La Trobe University, 1976.
18. Instances of this approach are David Holbrook's discussion of Fleming in *The Masks of Hate* and, in some respects, Pearson's biography of Fleming.
19. To avoid misunderstanding, but without getting involved in a complicated debate, we do not mean to imply that the phallus is

naturally or universally the privileged signifier of sexual difference in relation to which sexed identities are formed but merely that, in patriarchal societies, it tends to be so and frequently assumes this role within cultural artefacts produced within such societies.

20. J. Lacan, *The Language of the Self: The Function of Language in Psychoanalysis*, Delta Publishing Co., New York, 1968, p. 271.

5 The Transformations of James Bond

1. P. Johnson in *The New Statesman*, 5 April 1958.
2. K. Amis, *The James Bond Dossier*, Cape, London, p. 144.
3. Quoted in 'The Bond Phenomenon', *Newsweek*, 19 April 1965, p. 95.
4. Cited in R. R. Dow, 'Bond Films: Exploits of a Culture Hero', in *Screen Education*, September/October 1964, p. 110.
5. G. B. Zorzoli, 'Technology in the World of James Bond', in O. Del Bueno and U. Eco (eds), *The Bond Affair*, Macdonald, London, 1966, p. 127.
6. R. R. Dow, 'Bond Films: Exploits of a Culture Hero', in *Screen Education*, September/October, 1964, p. 115.
7. P. Houston, '007', in *Sight and Sound*, Winter, 1964/65, p. 14.
8. Cubby Broccoli from an interview carried out in relation to the Open University case-study on *The Making of the Spy Who Loved Me*.
9. K. Amis, *The James Bond Dossier*, Jonathan Cape, London, 1965, p. 111.
10. U. Eco, 'The narrative structure in Fleming', in O. Del Bueno and U. Eco (eds), *The Bond Affair*, p. 11.
11. L. Mulvey, 'Visual Pleasure and Narrative Cinema', in T. Bennett, S. Boyd-Bowman, C. Mercer and J. Woolacott (eds), *Popular Television and Film*, BFI, London, 1981, p. 209.
12. K. Amis, *The James Bond Dossier*, p. 20.
13. Cited in '007's Oriental Eyefuls', *Playboy*, June 1967, p. 87.
14. P. Mayersberg, *Hollywood, The Haunted House*, Penguin, Harmondsworth, 1969, p. 69.
15. M. F. Callan, *Sean Connery: His Life and Films*, W. H. Allen, London, 1983, p. 8.
16. P. Cook, 'Star Signs', *Screen*, vol. 20, no. 3/4, Winter 1979/80.
17. Cited in L. Lilli, 'James Bond and Criticism', with a number of other comments on Bond's sexuality, racism and other qualities in O. Del Bueno and U. Eco (eds), *The Bond Affair*.
18. Quoted in 'Sean Connery: He Is James Bond and He Isn't', in the *New York Post*, 4 October 1983, p. 23.
19. Cited in M. F. Callan, *Sean Connery: His Life and Films*, p. 144.
20. J. Brosnan, *James Bond in the Cinema*, Tantivy Press, London, 1972, p. 55.
21. P. Houston, '007', in *Sight and Sound*, Winter, 1964/65, p. 16.
22. Quoted in L. Lilli, 'James Bond and Criticism', p. 163.
23. Cited in A. Walker, *Hollywood England*, p. 196.

24. J. Brosnan, *James Bond in the Cinema*, p. 11.
25. P. Houston, '007', p. 15.
26. S. Aspinall, 'Women, Realism and Reality in British Films', in J. Curran and V. Porter (eds), *British Cinema History*, 1983, p. 272.
27. Ibid.
28. Ibid., p. 276.
29. C. Barr, *Ealing Studios*, Cameron and Taylor, London, 1977, p. 17.
30. J. Hill, 'Working Class Realism and Sexual Reaction: Some Theses on the British "New Wave"', p. 310.
31. Ibid., p. 308.
32. Ibid.
33. Ibid.
34. Ibid., p. 308.
35. R. Dyer, *Marilyn Monroe: Star Dossier One*. BFI, London, 1980.
36. Ibid., p. 31.
37. Ibid., p. 32.
38. Ibid., p. 32.

6 The Bond Films: 'Determination' and 'Production'

1. Interview with Cubby Broccoli, undertaken by the authors for the Open University case-study on *The Making of The Spy Who Loved Me*, 1977. All quotations in this chapter, unless otherwise stated, are taken from the transcripts of interviews conducted in the course of this study.
2. T. Bennett *et al.*, *The Making of The Spy Who Loved Me*, The Open University Press, Milton Keynes, 1977.
3. L. Ross, 'Picture', in *Reporting*, Mayflower Books, London, 1964.
4. H. Powdermaker, *Hollywood the Dream Factory*, Universal Library, Boston, 1950.
5. There are many examples of auteur studies such as Robin Wood's account of *Howard Hawks*, Secker & Warburg, London, 1968. More recently, Donald Spoto's *The Dark Side of Genius*, Little, Brown, Boston and Toronto, 1983, intensively traces Hitchcock's psychological development and suggests that this is the basis of the main shifts in his films.
6. See *The Days of Hope* debate reproduced in T. Bennett, S. Boyd-Bowman, C. Mercer and J. Woollacott (eds), *Popular Television and Film*, BFI, London, 1981.
7. T. Bennett *et al.*, *The Making of The Spy Who Loved Me*, p. 29.
8. Ibid., p. 31.
9. R. Williams, 'Marxism, Structuralism and Literary Analysis', *New Left Review*, no. 129, 1981, p. 55.
10. P. Elliot, 'Media, Organizations and Occupations: An Overview', in J. Curran, M. Gurevitch and J. Woollacott (eds), *Mass Communication and Society*, Edward Arnold, London, 1977.
11. J. Ellis, 'Made in Ealing', *Screen*, vol. 16, no. 1, 1975, pp. 80–1.

12. Ibid., pp. 80–1.
13. E. Buscombe, 'Notes on Columbia Pictures Corporation, 1924–41', *Screen*, vol. 16, no. 3, 1975, p. 82.
14. Ibid.
15. Radio Programmes 14 and 15 from the Open University case-study on *The Making of The Spy Who Loved Me*.
16. Stuart Hall in Radio Programme 15 from the Open University case-study on *The Making of The Spy Who Loved Me*.
17. Ibid.
18. T. Bennett *et al.*, *The Making of The Spy Who Loved Me*, p. 29.
19. P. Macherey, *A Theory of Literary Production*, Routledge & Kegan Paul, London, 1978, p. 49.
20. P. Macherey, interview in *Red Letters*, no. 5, Summer, 1977, p. 17.
21. P. Macherey, *A Theory of Literary Production*, p. 232.
22. The legal manoeuvrings over *Thunderball* have a long history. At the end of the first court case between Ian Fleming and Kevin McLory in 1963, it was decided that *Thunderball* would remain a published Ian Fleming novel, but that all future copies of the book were to include a reference stating that it was based on an original screen treatment created by Jack Whittingham, Kevin McLory and Ian Fleming. More importantly, McLory won the film and television rights to *Thunderball*. He then made a deal with Saltzman and Broccoli to co-produce *Thunderball*. Since then Mclory has spent some time in legal battles to make his own Bond film based on *Thunderball*. He finally succeeded in producing *Never Say Never Again* released in 1984. During the period of the making of *The Spy Who Loved Me*, Eon Productions was involved in a court case with McLory over ownership of the plot and themes of *Thunderball*. The script of *The Spy* was altered in relation to this.
23. Michael Wilson, the assistant to the producer and many other members of the production team, referred to *The Spy* as a formula picture, but one in which certain changes could be made while certain aspects of character and narrative had to remain the same.
24. Broccoli and the production team, which he had gathered around him, spent an enormous amount of time and energy in considerations of weaponry and gadgets. As they saw it, Bond's weapons had to be, at one and the same time, plausible and fantastic, at the edge of but within the boundaries of credibility. Broccoli was convinced that this was what distinguished the Bond films from other similar spy-thrillers.

7 Pleasure and the Bond Films

1. K. Amis, *The James Bond Dossier*, Jonathan Cape, London, 1965, p. 38.
2. Cited in 'Bond's Beauties', *People Weekly*, 18 July 1983, p. 38.
3. Ibid., p. 38.
4. Interview with Broccoli, in relation to the Open University case-study.
5. Ibid.

6. Amis wrote a James Bond novel, *Colonel Sun*, first published 1968, Jonathan Cape, London, under the pseudonym Robert Markham.
7. K. Amis, *The James Bond Dossier*, Jonathan Cape, London, 1965, p. 39.
8. Ibid., pp. 89–90.
9. Ibid., p. 45.
10. L. Mulvey, 'Visual Pleasure and Narrative Cinema', in T. Bennett, S. Boyd-Bowman, C. Mercer and J. Wollacott, (eds), *Popular Television and Film*, BFI, London, 1981, p. 214.
11. Ibid., p. 214.
12. Ibid., p. 214.
13. Ibid., p. 215.
14. Cited in P. Gurin, *The James Bond Trivia Quiz Book*, Priam Books, Arbour House, New York, p. 220.
15. See J. Mitchell's *Psychoanalysis and Feminism*, Penguin, Harmondsworth, 1974 or for a summary of some of the relevant literature S. Burniston, F. Mort and C. Weedon, 'Psychoanalysis and the Cultural Acquisition of Sexuality and Subjectivity', in *Women Take Issue* from the Woman's Study Group, Centre for Contemporary Cultural Studies, Hutchinson, London, 1978.
16. A. Kuhn, *Women's Pictures: Feminism and Cinema*, Routledge & Kegan Paul, 1982, p. 64.
17. Ibid., p. 65.
18. S. Heath, *The Sexual Fix*, Macmillan, London, 1982, p. 126.
19. Ibid., p. 126.
20. J. Cooper, *Octavia*, 1977, quoted in Heath.
21. P. Willemen, 'Voyeurism, the Look and Dwoskin'. *After Image* no. 6, June 1976.
22. P. Willemen, 'Anthony Mann: Looking at the Male', *Framework*, 15/16/17, Summer, 1981.
23. S. Neale, 'Masculinity as Spectacle', *Screen*, vol. 24, no. 6, November/December, 1983, p. 10.
24. Ibid., p. 15.
25. J. Ellis, *Visible Fictions*, Routledge & Kegan Paul, London, 1982, p. 43.
26. B. Neale, *Caroline's Waterloo*, Mills and Boon, London, p. 1.
27. K. Amis, *The James Bond Dossier*, p. 36.
28. Ibid., p. 42.
29. G. Heyer, *Venetia*, Pan Books, London, pp. 31–2, 1971, first published in 1958.
30. C. Mortimer, *Deceit of a Pagan*, Mills & Boon, London, 1980, p. 19.
31. J. Cooper, *Emily*, Corgi Books, London, 1976, p. 11.
32. L. Black, *Wild Cat*, Pan Books, London, 1982, first published in 1979, p. 90.
33. Ibid., p. 92.
34. G. Heyer, *The Black Moth*, Pan Books, London, 1965, first published in 1929, p. 115.
35. C. Lamb, *Storm Centre*, Mills & Boon, London, 1980, p. 20.
36. B. Whitehead, *The Caretaker Wife*, Pan Books in association with Heinemann, 1977.

37. G. Heyer, *The Grand Sophy*, Pan Books, London, 1960, first published in 1950, p. 60.
38. Ibid., p. 224.
39. Ibid., p. 238.
40. T. Modelski, *Loving with a Vengeance: Mass Produced Fantasies for Women*, 1982, The Shoe String Press, Hamden, Conn.
41. C. Brunsden, 'Crossroads: Notes on Soap Opera', *Screen*, vol. 22, no. 4, (1981).

8 Figures of Bond

1. 'The Bond Girls', in *James Bond in Thunderball* (not paginated).
2. K. Passingham, 'The Gorgeous Girls of James Bond', *TV Times*, 23 October 1975, p. 27.
3. See our discussion of Foucault in Chapter 3, pp. 46–7.
4. I. Fleming, 'How to write a Thriller', *Books and Bookmen*, May 1963, p. 14.
5. See P. Macherey, *A Theory of Literary Production*, and L. Althusser, 'A Letter on Art', in *Lenin and Philosophy, and Other Essays*, New Left Books, London, 1971.
6. A. Kuhn, *Women's Pictures: Feminism and Cinema*, Routledge & Kegan Paul, London, 1982, p. 92.
7. J. Palmer, 'Thrillers: The Deviant Behind the Consensus', in I. Taylor and J. Taylor (eds), *Politics and Deviance*, Penguin, Harmondsworth, 1973, p. 142. See also, for a more extended analysis along similar lines, J. Palmer, *Thrillers: Genesis and Structure of a Popular Genre*, Edward Arnold, London, 1979.
8. Ibid., p. 140.
9. See, for example, Connery's *Playboy* interview discussed in Chapter 3 and D. Lewin, 'Sean Connery – the Screen's James Bond', in *James Bond in Thunderball*.
10. See C. Brooker, *The Neophiliacs: A Study in the Revolution in English life in the Fifties and Sixties*, Collins, London, 1969.
11. See M. F. Callan, *Sean Connery: His Life and Films*, W. H. Allen, London, pp. 1–2.
12. *Sunday Times Colour Supplement*, no. 1, 4 February, 1962, p. 18.
13. Cited in 'What happened to the Bond girls?' *Telegraph Sunday Magazine*, 17 September 1978, p. 10.
14. *James Bond in Thunderball* (not paginated).
15. 'Sean Connery takes apart the Blood, Guts and Girls Man', in S. Lane (ed.), *For Bond Lovers Only*, p. 30.
16. See M. Richler, 'Ian Fleming: A Voice for Little England', *Nova*, January 1970.
17. *Woman's Own*, 30 June 1979.
18. *Sunday People*, 26 June 1977.
19. *James Bond in Thunderball* (not paginated).
20. *Sunday People*, 26 June 1977.

21. The following are examples of features of this type: 'James Bond's Girls', *Playboy*, November 1965; 'The Girls of Casino Royale', *Playboy*, February 1967; '007's Oriental Eyefuls', *Playboy*, June 1967; '8 Bond Beauties', *Playboy*, July 1979; 'Stella, Bond's Black Beauty', *Mayfair*, vol. 9, no. 5; 'Uncovered: James Bond's Lotus-Flower Girl', *Mayfair*, vol. 8, no. 7; and 'The Bond Girls – Vintage '73', *Rex*, no. 9.

22. See M. Denning, *Cover Stories: Narrative and Ideology in British Spy Thrillers*, chapter 4, Routledge & Kegan Paul, forthcoming.

23. See J. Ellis, *Visible Fictions. Cinema: Television: Video*, Routledge & Kegan Paul, London, 1982, chapter 2.

24. K. Elam, *The Semiotics of Theatre and Drama*, Methuen, London, 1980, p. 94.

25. Ibid., p. 95.

26. J. Mukarovsky, *Aesthetic Function, Norm and Value as Social Facts*, University of Michigan Press, Ann Arbor, 1970.

27. See P. Bourdieu and J. C. Passeron, *The Inheritors: French Students and Their Relation to Culture*, University of Chicago Press, Chicago and London, 1979, p. 17.

28. P. Evans, 'Rendezvous with the Man from the Ipcress File', in S. Lane (ed.), *For Bond Lovers Only*, p. 40.

29. I. Fleming, 'How to Write a Thriller', *Books and Bookmen*, May 1963, p. 14.

30. M. Foucault, 'What is an Author?', *Screen*, xx(1), Spring, 1979, p. 22.

31. T. Bennett, 'Marxism and Popular Fiction', *Literature and History*, vol. 7(2), Autumn, 1981, p. 160.

32. See D. Holbrook, *The Masks of Hate: The Problem of False Solutions in the Culture of an Acquisitive Society*, Pergamon Press, Oxford, 1972.

33. I. Hunter, 'The Concept of Context and the Problem of Reading', *Southern Review*, vol. 15, no. 1, March 1982, p. 87.

34. D. Saunders, 'The Trial of *Lady Chatterley's Lover*: Limiting Cases and Literary Canons', *Southern Review*, vol. 15, no. 2, July 1982, p. 165.

35. A. S. Boyd, *The Devil with James Bond*, Greenwood Press, Westport, pp. 24–7.

36. Ibid., p. 87.

37. Ibid., p. 67.

38. Ibid., p. 71.

39. Ibid., p. 50.

40. Cited in R. Gant, *Ian Fleming: The Man with the Golden Pen*, p. 127.

41. See, for a brief review of this literature, A. Gill, 'The Messiah 007', in the Australian *National Times*, 30 March to 5 April 1980.

42. See C. McArthur, 'Reconstructing *Casablanca*', unpublished paper.

43. However, one possible exception – although, ultimately, his work does not lead in the same direction as ours – is H. R. Jauss. See his 'Literary History as a Challenge to Literary Theory', *New Literary History*, vol. 2, no. 1, 1970.

44. See V. Volosinov, *Marxism and the Philosophy of Language*, Seminar Press, New York, 1973.

45. M. Pêcheux, *Language, Semantics and Ideology*, Macmillan, London, 1982, p. 187.

46. T. Eagleton, *Criticism and Ideology: A Study in Marxist Literary Theory*, New Left Books, London, 1976, p. 48.

47. See F. Jameson, *The Political Unconscious*, Methuen, London, 1981, p. 13.

48. As is implied by Terry Eagleton. See his *Walter Benjamin, or Towards a Revolutionary Criticism*, Verso Editions and New Left Books, London, 1981, p. 122. For a discussion of the respects in which our approach to reading departs from and is critical of the project of deconstruction, see T. Bennett, 'Texts in History: The Determination of Readings and Their Texts', in D. Attridge, G. Bennington and R. Young (eds), *Post-Structuralism and the Question of History*, Cambridge University Press, forthcoming and T. Bennett, 'The Text in Question', *Southern Review*, July, 1984. (This latter piece forms part of a symposium on 'The "Text in Itself"' with contributions from Terry Eagleton, Noel King, Ian Hunter, Peter Hulme, Catherine Belsey and John Frow.)

49. See, for one of his more revealing discussions of the status of 'the text' within literary criticism, F. R. Leavis, 'The Responsible Critic or the Function of Criticism at any Time', *Scrutiny*, Spring, 1953.

50. K. Marx, *Capital*, vol. I, Lawrence and Wishart, London, 1970, p. 71.

51. Ibid., p. 72.

9 Never Again?

1. J. Ellis, 'Star/Industry/Image', *Star Signs*, BFI, London, 1982, p. 1.

2. Ibid., p. 3.

3. See, for a critical discussion of the limitations associated with Ellis's approach to television personalities, J. Tulloch and M. Alvarado, *Doctor Who: The Unfolding Text*, Macmillan, London, 1983, pp. 194–6.

4. K. Amis, *The James Bond Dossier*, Jonathan Cape, London, 1965, p. 18. 'Mr. Fleming is careful to make Bond's achievements and abilities seem moderate: moderate on the heroic secret-agent scale naturally' (pp. 14–15). Amis points to the attractions of the secret agent fantasy as using the ordinary as cover to conceal the extraordinary.

5. See M. F. Callan, *Sean Connery: His Life and Films*, W. H. Allen, London, 1983, p. 152.

6. Judith Crist, WOR TV, quoted in publicity for *Never Say Never Again* in *The New York Times*, Friday, 14 October 1983.

7. Cited in 'Sean Connery: He Is James Bond and He Isn't', *New York Post*, 4 October 1983.

8. J. Ellis, 'Star/Industry/Image', p. 7.

9. J. Tulloch and M. Alvarado, *Doctor Who: The Unfolding Text*, p. 63.

10. Ibid., p. 303.

11. T. Eagleton, *The Rape of Clarissa*, Basil Blackwell, Oxford, 1982, p. 5.

12. Ibid., p. 4.

13. S. Hall, C. Critcher, T. Jefferson, J. Clarke, and B. Roberts, *Policing*

the Crisis: Mugging, the State and Law and Order*, Macmillan, 1978, p. 217.
14. T. Bennett, 'James Bond in the 1980s', *Marxism Today*, vol. 27, no. 6, June 1983, p. 39.

Index

References to the Postscript are not included in this Index